HG   Fry, Earl H.
4910
.F8   Financial invasion
            of the U.S.A

DATE			

FINANCIAL INVASION OF THE U.S.A.

A Threat to American Society?

EARL H. FRY

State University of New York at Plattsburgh

McGRAW-HILL BOOK COMPANY

New York St. Louis San Francisco Auckland Bogotá
Düsseldorf Johannesburg London Madrid
Mexico Montreal New Delhi Panama
Paris São Paulo Singapore Sydney
Tokyo Toronto

To Elaine, Chris, Lisa, and Anna

Library of Congress Cataloging in Publication Data

Fry, Earl H
  Financial invasion of the U.S.A.

  Includes bibliographical references and index.
  1. Investments, Foreign—United States. I. Title.
HG4910.F8   332.6'73'0973   79-13168
ISBN 0-07-022591-5

The editors for this book were Kiril Sokoloff and Esther Gelatt,
the designer was Naomi Auerbach, and the production supervisor
was Teresa F. Leaden. It was set in Baskerville
by University Graphics, Inc.
Printed and bound by R. R. Donnelley & Sons Company.

Contents

Preface

More than a decade ago, French publisher Jean-Jacques Servan-Schreiber wrote a book entitled *The American Challenge* which presented a highly provocative thesis. In effect, Servan-Schreiber warned that American-based multinationals were inundating the European marketplace at an alarming rate and would soon dominate economic decision making unless the quiescent Western European business community was willing to close ranks and accept the challenge from abroad.

Today the tables have been somewhat turned with the United States emerging as the most attractive haven in the world for foreign investment money. Many of the mammoth European and Japanese multinationals have recently established major facilities in the United States and are employing technological techniques which are often superior to those of their American competitors. In addition, billions of dollars of overseas money has entered the country for the purchase of commercial, farm, and timber properties and for investment in key U.S. banking and financial institutions.

The author's interest in the foreign investment issue stems from his years of research into the scope and nature of international linkages in an increasingly complex and interdependent world. The author lived in Western Europe during the period when Servan-Schreiber's thesis was hotly debated. Provocative and polemical discussions similar to what occurred in Europe in the latter part of the 1960s are now taking place in the United States as the level of foreign investment activity in the U.S.A. escalates dramatically. For example, after the main portion of this text had been sent to press, the Iowa legislature enacted a law which absolutely prohibits foreigners from purchasing farmland in that state. Some of the impetus for this legislation apparently came from the widespread concern that OPEC investors were grabbing up huge chunks of Iowa's fertile soil, in spite of federal government claims to the contrary. A popular bumper sticker seems to have aptly summarized the feelings of many citizens of that Midwestern state: "Dear Arab, grain is my oil."

As overseas money continues to pour into the U. S. A., many Americans may be tempted to follow the Iowa example and react harshly to foreign investment in general. Such overt resentment, of course, could have a dramatic impact on the evolution of America's international trade and investment linkages. Thus, it is the purpose of this book to examine the various dimensions of foreign investment in the United States and to discuss the impact which such investment might have on American society as a whole. Ideally, the book will shed some much-needed light on this controversial topic and will help ensure that future debates on foreign investment are based more on objectivity and less on innuendo.

The author wishes to thank the staffs of the Library of Congress and the Boalt Law Library at the University of California for helping to facilitate his research endeavors. He would also like to express his gratitude to numerous officials in the public and private sectors and to foreign representatives who have provided valuable leads and insights for this study. Kiril Sokoloff and the able McGraw-Hill staff have also offered very sage advice in the preparation of the final manuscript. Most important, the author wishes to thank his wife and children for their persistent support, love, and boundless patience.

Earl H. Fry

ONE

Foreign Investment in the United States: The Setting

The Surge in Foreign Investment Activity

Extensive Japanese holdings in the Hawaiian tourist industry, British Petroleum's majority interest in the rich oil reserves of Alaska's Prudhoe Bay, a West German consortium's joint agreement with Playboy Enterprises to build an Atlantic City casino, an Italian family's purchase of one of the largest farming units in the Midwest, the Deutsche Bank's offer to acquire New York City's World Trade Center, the acquisition by citizens of the Middle East of dozens of Beverly Hills' most palatial estates, an Iranian's bid to assume control of the Los Angeles Rams football team, a Belgian Baron's takeover of a Wall Street brokerage house, and alleged Russian overtures to buy into a California bank group are all illustrations of recent foreign investment activity in the United States.

The examples given in the opening paragraph contain the ingredients from which provocative headlines are easily concocted. Indeed, foreign investment in the United States has lately been the subject of a *Newsweek* cover story, a "60 Minutes" exposé, a Jack Anderson probe, and an Art Buchwald satire. Yet are these media grabbers simply distortions of the general foreign investment trend or are they actually a harbinger of things to come in the United States? Is America in the process of being

1

inundated with a surge of corporate takeovers from abroad, and do overseas investors have what seems to be an insatiable appetite for U.S. farmland and other natural resources?

Official U.S. government statistics clearly indicate that direct investment in the U.S. corporate sector by nonresident aliens has accelerated dramatically in recent years, doubling over the past 60 months (see Figure 1-1).

FIGURE 1-1
Foreign Direct Investment in the United States, 1954–1977

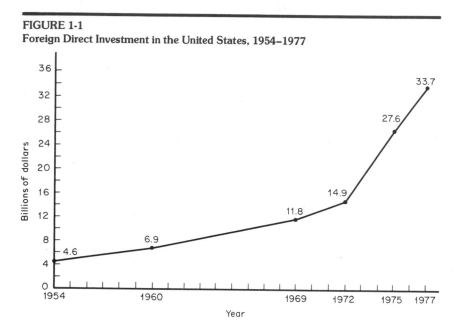

Foreign investors have now penetrated most sectors of the American economy and more than 5,000 foreign-controlled businesses are now operating in the United States.[1] Government agencies have also predicted that this investment from abroad will continue to surge upward.[2] More precisely, Arthur D. Little, Inc., has estimated that foreign direct investment, which represents a controlling interest in U.S.-based firms, will grow by an average of 8.5 to 13 percent over the next decade. If this prognostication turns out to be correct, foreign direct investment in the United States will total more than 50 billion dollars by the early 1980s, and this figure does not include the billions of dollars which will be pumped into portfolio investments, treasury bond purchases, and many types of real estate transactions. In a speech before the National Press Club, Chairman G. William Miller of the Federal Reserve Board expressed great concern about the lack of U.S. control over the 500 billion dollars of American money which is currently held abroad, swelled by the huge U.S. trade deficits in recent years. Miller contended that this is "the most serious threat to us in terms of currency actions" and conceded that "we don't yet have any solutions."[3] What would happen, for example, if massive Organization of Petroleum Exporting Countries (OPEC) reserves, estimated at 60 billion dollars or more, suddenly began to flow into the United States in the form of direct investments? Is it within the realm of possibility that foreign investment activity as a whole might eventually disrupt the U.S. economy and make the U.S. marketplace more vulnerable to international economic and political conditions?

Americans are generally well aware that Mercedes-Benz, Toyota, Volkswagen, Sony, and Shell Oil have foreign origins. On the other hand, many do not know that some of the products which they may use on an everyday basis are also controlled by foreign interests (see Table 1-1). For example, no one was more pleased with the much-publicized success of the Denver Broncos' vaunted "Orange Crush" defense than the Canadian company which makes the soft drink bearing that name. The average American junk-food addict could gorge on Libby fruits and vegetables, Keebler cookies, Stouffer cakes, Nestlé's chocolates, and Good Humor or Baskin-Robbins' ice cream, all the while using products which are now owned by overseas interests. To relieve the ensuing stomachache, this average American might turn to the old reliable Alka-Seltzer, but even the "plop, plop, fizz, fizz" is now enunciated with a heavy German accent after being purchased by a giant conglomerate from the North Rhine-Westphalia region. For reading material, this American might pick up the *New York Post, The Village Voice, Parents' Magazine, Esquire, New West, New York,* or a Bantam paperback, all of which are now foreign-owned. In addition, Clorox, Borax, Bic pens and lighters, Kiwi polish, Pepsodent toothpaste, Kool cigarettes, French's mustard, Coats and Clark thread, SOS soap pads, Gimbels, Saks Fifth Avenue, A & P and Grand Union supermarkets, Magnavox, and Capitol Records are among the more established American favorites which currently have strong foreign linkages.

Foreign investors have also been increasingly active in the U.S. computer industry and other high technology sectors. In particular, a great deal of overseas money has recently flowed into California's famed "Silicon Valley" which is located along the peninsula south of San Francisco. Foreign money sources are cognizant of America's clear-cut lead in many technological spheres and they naturally want a piece of the action. Gaylord Nelson, Chairman of the Senate Committee on Small Business, has publicly warned that foreigners are now acquiring small U.S. high technology firms at such a fast rate that a continuation of this trend might well lead to a technology drain from the United States to overseas nations.[4]

In the past few years, foreigners have also set their sights on the acquisition of huge parcels of American real estate. The San Francisco-based Amrex Corporation estimates that up to 20 percent of all farmland cur-

TABLE 1-1 The Dozen Largest Foreign Investments in the U.S. Industrial Sphere, 10 Percent or More Ownership, 1979

Foreign investor	Country	U.S. company	Percent owned	Industry	Revenues, $ millions
1. Royal Dutch/Shell Group	Netherlands U.K.	Shell Oil Asiatic Petroleum	69 100	Oil Oil	12,359
2. Anglo American of South Africa	S. Africa	Engelhard Minerals & Chemicals Inspiration Consolidated Copper Terra Chemicals International	29 73 51	Industrial materials Copper Chemicals	10,457
3. Tengelmann Group	Germany	Great A & P Tea	42	Supermarkets	7,500
4. British Petroleum	U.K.	Standard Oil (Ohio) BP Pipelines	52 100	Oil Alaskan pipeline	5,578
5. Friedrich Flick Group	Germany	W. R. Grace U.S.Filter	28 35	Chemicals, consumer activities Pollution control, chemicals	4,851
6. B.A.T. Industries	U.K.	Brown & Williamson Ind. BATUS	100 100	Tobacco, retail Paper, cosmetics	3,500
7. Solvay	Belgium	Allied Chemical Soltex Polymer Hedwin	5 100 100	Chemicals Chemicals Plastics	3,418
8. Cavenham	U.K.	Grand Union	100	Supermarkets	2,800
9. Robert Bosch GmbH	Germany	Borg-Warner American Microsystems Robert Bosch Corp.	10 10 100	Chemicals Computers Electronics	2,576
10. Philips	Netherlands	N. American Philips	62	Electronics	2,184
11. Unilever	Netherlands	Lever Brothers Thomas J. Lipton National Starch & Chemical	100 100 100	Consumer goods Food Chemicals	1,897
12. Seagram	Canada	Joseph E. Seagram & Sons	100	Liquor, oil, gas	1,887

$102

SOURCE: *Forbes*, April 2, 1979.

rently sold in the United States is going to foreign buyers, with up to 50 percent of the choice land in the Mississippi Delta and California's Central Valley being purchased by overseas interests.[5] Some American farmers have complained that foreigners are driving up prices and taxes by paying too much for land and are threatening the survival of small family farms. Predictions have even been made that if foreign acquisitions of farmland continue at the present pace, foreign ownership will eclipse American ownership in just a few decades and American agriculture will then be substantially controlled from abroad.[6]

The Foreign Investment Issue: A Tempest in a Teapot?

Whether based on fact or simply xenophobic-linked innuendo, foreign investment in the United States has emerged as a highly volatile public issue. Legislators in several states have already introduced bills which would severely limit or even curtail altogether nonresident alien ownership of farm and timber land. The Missouri legislature, for example, actually passed a bill in April 1978 which prohibits foreigners from buying more than five acres of agricultural land.[7]

In response to public concern over increased Japanese investment activity in Hawaii and a growing fear of the effect which OPEC money might have on the American economy, the Congress of the United States was prompted in 1974 to pass the Foreign Investment Study Act. This law stipulates that the Commerce and Treasury Departments will conduct periodic studies and subsequently submit reports to Capitol Hill on foreign "direct" and "portfolio" investment in the United States. Foreign direct investment is defined by the Commerce Department as "the direct and/or indirect ownership of 10 percent or more of the voting stock of a United States corporation—by a non-U.S. citizen."[8] In other words, a direct investment provides the foreign source with a participating or controlling interest in a U.S.-based firm, whereas a portfolio investment does not allow the investor such an interest because of the nature or the value of the holding.

In the spring of 1976, the Department of Commerce issued a massive nine-volume study touching on most dimensions of the foreign investment issue.[9] In the footsteps of this landmark study, other pertinent reports on foreign investment have been issued by Commerce, Treasury, Agriculture, and the General Accounting Office. On the whole, each of these studies has concluded that foreign investment for the moment does not constitute a danger to American national interests, although each admits its research was severely hampered by the paucity of information sources pertaining to the scope and magnitude of foreign investment activity. Specifically, these government-sponsored studies made the following observations:

1. Foreign direct investments in the United States are significant in size and scope, but are relatively a small factor in the nation's overall economy.[10]

2. The flap over massive foreign takeovers of U.S. industries, especially by the Middle East oil-producing countries, is unsubstantiated.[11]

3. The strong concern expressed about foreign ownership of agricultural land and other real estate does not appear to have a strong factual basis for the nation as a whole. However, the inadequacy of data in this field, together with the use of indirect means of obtaining ownership and techniques to avoid ownership disclosure, results in much uncertainty as to the amount and nature of land owned by aliens (except in a few local areas for which special investigations have been undertaken). This indicates a need for further investigation.[12]

4. Foreign direct investment is not the predominant vehicle for the transfer of technology into or out of the United States. However, technology transfers associated with such investment are significant. In the area of product and process technology, the net balance appears to be into the United States, but in the area of management innovations and marketing techniques the net flow of technology appears to be outward.[13]

5. National interests, and the need to provide adequate safeguards in the fiduciary and natural resources sectors of the economy, are served by federal laws restricting and regulating investments by aliens in the fields of transportation, communications, energy and natural resource development, and banking, as well as by the Department of Defense's industrial security program and broad presidential powers. Additional restrictions are imposed in some fields, e.g., land ownership, insurance, and banking by the states. This protective authority was developed over many years in response to perceived needs. Although diverse in many respects, collectively the measures provide the protection required.[14]

These official reports conclude that U.S. safeguards against "excesses" in the foreign investment domain are sufficient, but that the government should monitor investment activity more closely in the future.[15] In particular, the Commerce Department has recommended that the foreign investment data base be improved by conducting major benchmark surveys every ten years, by preparing analyses of trends and significant developments on a continuing basis and by commissioning special studies as needed, and by improving procedures for the collection and dissemination of investment data.[16] Commerce adds that much more information is currently needed on the labor effects of foreign direct investment, the impact of such investment on local communities, the relationship of foreign investment to incentive packages offered by the state and local governments, and the magnitude of foreign involvement in land purchases.[17]

In effect, the pertinent departments and agencies of the U.S. executive branch have concluded that foreign investment is in no way a threat to the integrity of the American economy or to American society as a whole. In fact, these studies point out that a significant number of positive economic benefits might accrue from an upsurge in overseas investment activity in the United States. For example, at the beginning of 1975, foreign-controlled firms accounted for 1.1 million jobs and 11.4 billion dollars in annual wages and salaries (see Figure 1-2).[18] More than 95 percent of the employees of these firms at that time were American citizens. Such investment also creates new technology, expands tax revenues, makes U.S. companies more competition-oriented to the benefit of the American consumer, creates new markets for supplier firms located in the United States, provides new products, and helps ease criticism of U.S. direct investment abroad, which is still four times as great as foreign investment in the United States. Indeed, foreign direct investment in the United

FIGURE 1-2
Foreign Direct Investment by Industry, 1976

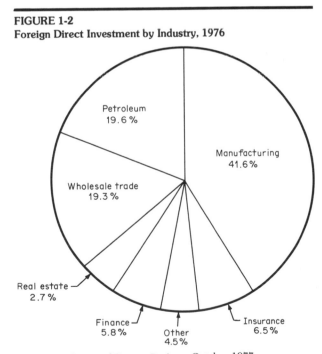

SOURCE: *Survey of Current Business,* October 1977.

States, which stood at 34 billion dollars at the end of 1977, is relatively small when compared to the U.S. investment of 33 billion dollars in Canada and 55 billion dollars in Western Europe.

In overall perspective, foreign-owned manufacturing plants account for less than 2 percent of all U.S. manufacturing establishments with 20 or more employees.[19] The New York-based Conference Board, which keeps track of manufacturing activities of foreign firms located in the United States, has also reported that the total sales of the 100 largest foreign-owned companies in the United States in 1975 added up to 44.7 billion dollars, less than the 47.8 billion dollars in sales of just the top U.S. company that year, Exxon. Surveys have also indicated that the foreign-owned companies doing business in the United States enjoy a large degree of autonomy in their day-to-day operations and that reinvested earnings in the U.S. economy are comparatively high among these firms, showing a significant measure of confidence in the growth and the stability of the American marketplace.[20] Moreover, these companies devote a higher percentage of their capital to research and development purposes within the United States than do their U.S. counterparts abroad.[21] Finally, the great bulk of the foreign investment emanates from Western Europe and Canada, traditional allies of the United States and regions where massive U.S. investment has already taken place (see Figure 1-3). In view of these statistics, one begins to wonder whether Americans should really be overly concerned about the recent upsurge in foreign investment activity in the United States.

A New Challenge to America?

In a very famous book, *The American Challenge,* first published in France in 1967, Jean-Jacques Servan-Schreiber warned: "Fifteen years from now it is quite possible that the world's third greatest industrial power, just after the United States and Russia, will not be Europe, but American industry in Europe. Already, in the ninth year of the Common Market, this European market is basically American in organization."[22]

In this book, Servan-Schreiber described the European Common Market as a new "Far West" for American business exploitation and warned that unless the Europeans began to confront this dramatic challenge, the Americans would eventually develop a monopoly on "know-how, science, and power."[23] The French author depicted his book as "a call to action" for the Europeans and he was successful in sparking numerous debates on both sides of the Atlantic concerning the effects on national economies of American overseas investment.[24]

In spite of the potpourri of arguments put forward to support the premise that foreign investment in the United States is a positive force, some Americans are extremely wary about the sudden rapid growth in investment activity and consider that the United States now faces its own "foreign" challenge. These people use the illustrations given in the first section of this chapter to buttress their point of view. They also point out that in the short period between 1974 and 1976, foreign banking activity in the United States escalated dramatically, with the number of bank

FIGURE 1-3
Foreign Direct Investment by Country, 1976

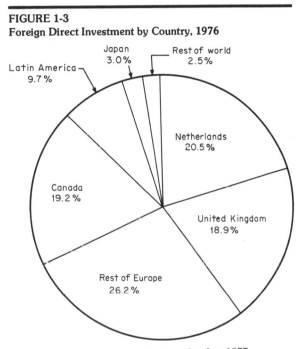

SOURCE: *Survey of Current Business,* October 1977.

branches of foreign firms more than doubling, bank agencies going up by more than one-half, and bank subsidiaries increasing by one-third.[25] In the important chemical industry, foreign firms doled out more than 1 billion dollars in 1977 alone to acquire existing U.S. plants.[26]

In certain extreme cases, xenophobic hackles have seemed to appear on the necks of some Americans opposed to foreign operations on U.S. soil. For example, Societé Imetal, a French company owned by the Rothschild family, made a bid a couple of years ago to acquire a controlling interest in the Copperweld Corporation, a specialty steel manufacturer with plants in Ohio and Pennsylvania. Workers and residents from nearby communities set up picket lines at the plants to protest the foreign conglomerate's takeover effort, sporting signs which read, "Go home, Frenchie." Groups of citizens also traveled to Washington, D.C., to seek redress from the Federal Trade Commission and the U.S. Congress, and picket lines were established in front of the French Embassy. Later, a well-organized letter and telephone campaign was undertaken in an effort to convince key public officials to halt the Société Imetal–Copperweld negotiations. In spite of the aroused feelings of many of the workers and local residents, Société Imetal eventually acquired two-thirds of the Copperweld stock.[27]

To say the least, the issue of foreign investment in one's homeland can be provocative and emotion-laden. Servan-Schreiber's assertions about the American multinationals' domination of the French economy stirred the passions of many of his countrymen. More than one-half million copies of *The American Challenge* were sold in France in its first three months in circulation. Heated discussions occurred in tiny provincial hamlets, and numerous student demonstrations protesting the perceived American domination took place in the famed Latin Quarter of Paris and in other major French cities.

In the late 1960s and early 1970s, America's expansive neighbor to the north, Canada, also reacted strongly to the foreign investment issue. Mel Watkins, a professor at the University of Toronto, and a select group of fellow Canadians began to complain vociferously about what they considered to be Canada's relegation to the status of a U.S. resource colony. Over 200,000 Canadians soon rushed to join Independent Canada Associations which were formed to fight against the influx of American and other foreign investment. The Canadian government eventually reacted to these protests and established a Foreign Investment Review Agency (FIRA) which currently screens foreign investment proposals and may recommend the rejection of any investment project considered to be detrimental to Canada's interests. Moreover, American magazines which published special editions in Canada were ordered by the Ottawa government to sell some of their stock to Canadian investors. *Time* magazine, for one, refused to comply with this order and shut down its Canadian operations altogether.

Will Americans in the 1980s react to the dramatic upsurge in foreign investment activity in the United States in the same way that Western Europeans did in the mid-1960s and Canadians did in the early 1970s? Why has the United States suddenly emerged as such an attractive haven for overseas investment money? What will be the impact on Wall Street of the vigorous foreign interest in the stock market and how will the average American investor be affected by the infusion of foreign funds into the U.S. financial markets? What are the implications for the American industrial and business communities of the recent investment activities by Volkswagen, Michelin, Bayer, Unilever, Sony, and other world corporate giants? Do foreigners threaten to monopolize certain sectors of the American economy and will the profits of foreign affiliates be siphoned off and sent back to the parent companies?

What will be the effect on rural America of massive foreign purchases of farm, timber, and ranch land? Will foreign owners of farmland help to precipitate the demise of the family farm and will they ship their farm products overseas and not make them available for domestic consumption? Does the United States need to formulate a long-range foreign investment policy which would impose major restrictions on certain types of investment activity? Should the American government create a foreign investment screening agency patterned after Canada's? And if the U.S. government does decide to clamp down on certain investment activities, would other governments retaliate by imposing strict limitations on U.S. investment abroad?

All of these questions will be carefully scrutinized in the chapters which follow. The next chapter explores the world of international investment and the rules of the game which typify foreign investment activity. The third chapter diagnoses why foreign investors have now become so enamored of the United States and examines the regulations which they must abide by upon entering the U.S. marketplace. Chapters Four through Six look very closely at recent foreign investment activity in the American manufacturing, financial, and real estate spheres. The seventh chapter concentrates on the geographic distribution of foreign investment in the United States and scrutinizes state and local government programs which have been established at the taxpayers' expense to attract overseas funding. Chapter Eight presents three case studies within the foreign investment sphere: Pennsylvania's successful effort in enticing Volkswagen to construct a 300 million dollar auto assembly plant at New Stanton; Spartanburg, South Carolina's special overseas recruitment program which has persuaded more than 40 foreign companies to establish facilities in that small Southern community; and the Amrex Corporation's ongoing quest to internationalize the American real estate market and thus make it much easier for foreigners to invest in U.S. properties. The final chapter will summarize the major points of the study and offer recommended courses of action for the United States to take in the face of the mushrooming growth in foreign investment activity.

TWO

New York to Bonn
to Riyadh to Tokyo:
An Introduction
to the World
of International Investment

Multinationals and Interdependency

As OPEC aptly illustrated in the period following the 1973 Middle East War, interdependency has become the key word in depicting contemporary international relations. In essence, the economies of individual nations have become increasingly vulnerable to the repercussions resulting from political and economic upheavals in distant lands. As Tables 2-1 and 2-2 indicate, the importing and exporting of goods constitutes a significant percentage of the overall gross national product for many of the West's most advanced industrial societies. Consequently, labor problems in France which foment a drop in purchasing power in that country may well trigger increased unemployment in Germany, simply because the economic well-being of many German industries is dependent on the steady exporting of products to France and to other nations. Indeed, the analogy of one nation sneezing and several others catching cold is not an absurdity within the context of the present international economic system.

The growth of multinational corporations in the latter half of the twentieth century has certainly contributed to the increasing economic interdependency in the world. In the early 1970s, approximately 15 percent of the 3 trillion dollar total value of world production was attributable to subsidiaries and branches which were not owned by the citizens of the countries in which they were located.[1] As an illustration, a company such as Nestlé, which limits its shareholders to Swiss nationals or residents, does 98 percent of its business *outside* of Switzerland.[2] Thus contemporary international relations can no longer be construed simply as interactions among national governments with diplomats occupying the center stage. Rather, multinationals such as International Business Machines (IBM) and Siemens, air transport cartels such as International Air Transport

TABLE 2-1   Exports as a Percentage of Gross National Product (GNP)*

Country	Value of exports, $ U.S. millions†	Exports as percent of GNP
Australia	13,119	13.9
Belgium‡	32,843	48.2
Canada	38,633	19.9
France	55,812	16.1
Germany	102,032	22.9
Italy	36,919	21.6
Japan	67,225	12.1
United Kingdom	46,263	21.1
UNITED STATES	114,997	6.8

*Includes goods only.
†Computed at winter 1978 prices.
‡Belgium-Luxembourg Economic Union.
SOURCE: *OECD Observer*, March 1978.

TABLE 2-2   Imports as Percentage of Gross National Product (GNP)*

Country	Value of imports, $ U.S. millions†	Imports as percent of GNP
Australia	11,184	11.9
Belgium‡	35,355	51.9
Canada	37,959	19.5
France	64,390	18.6
Germany	87,782	19.7
Italy	43,372	25.4
Japan	64,799	11.7
United Kingdom	55,967	25.5
UNITED STATES	121,793	7.2

*Includes goods only.
†Computed at winter 1978 prices.
‡Belgium-Luxembourg Economic Union.
SOURCE: *OECD Observer*, March 1978.

Association (IATA), or even international trade unions such as the World Auto Council, may well have a dramatic impact on the economic vitality and resiliency of foreign nations. For example, coordinated strike action against the French-based glass company, St. Gobain, was carried out simultaneously in several nations in 1969. Unhappy with various features of their existing contracts, union representatives from St. Gobain plants in France, the United States, Italy, Germany, Belgium, Norway, Sweden, and Switzerland assembled at the Geneva meeting of the International Chemical and General Workers Federation. As a result of a strategy session held at this meeting, an international strike plan was formulated and later implemented rather successfully. To say the least, the international repercussions resulting from the labor action went far beyond the boundaries of St. Gobain's home country, France.[3]

This chapter will briefly trace the historical development of international investment activities within an increasingly interdependent world, and will present case studies on how citizens of two nations, France and Canada, have responded to massive foreign investment in their own respective countries. Optimally, these case studies will provide some valuable insights on how the American public will react to increasing foreign investment in the United States in the early years of the 1980s. Many scholars have also recently asserted that an international code of foreign investment must be enacted within the next few years in order to (1) protect host countries from blatant multinational exploitation and (2) ensure that international firms are not subjected to unfair restrictions by national governments. In the final section of this chapter, the positive and negative features ascribed to international investment will be scrutinized, and an assessment made of the desirability and the practicality of a so-called international code of investment.

Foreign Investment within the Global Context

Action and reaction—the historical roots   Whether through the vehicle of colonialism or more subdued routes, foreign investment has historically played an integral role in the development of most national economies. Throughout its illustrious history, England has ventured forth to the far reaches of the world in search of investment opportunities. In 1600, Queen Elizabeth I granted the East India Company an "exclusive" right to conduct trade and build settlements in the Far East, a territory which had been reserved for Portuguese exploitation by papal edict. Eventually the East India Company, the Virginia Company, and the Hudson's Bay Company, among others, helped open up investment opportunities for Englishmen in a third of the world.

With the inclusion of India within the colonial fold, one could boast with great veracity that the sun never set on the British Empire. However, in the nineteenth century, British money sources turned increasingly to portfolio investment opportunities because businesses in the colonial world which needed capital were no longer so dependent on direct supervision or technology transfers from the mother country. Funds available for overseas portfolio investments swelled rapidly, and between 1870 and 1914 an astounding 40 percent of British savings was committed to foreign projects.[4]

Such foreign investment activity, although at times reaping magnificent profits, often proved to be a rather risky proposition. Even the British investment in U.S. railroads and other related transportation stocks, which was so instrumental in America's rapid expansion westward, sometimes fared badly because of the periodic economic depressions which afflicted nineteenth-century American society.

At the end of World War I, one-fourth of Great Britain's 4 billion pounds of foreign investment was lost. Across the Channel, cries of anguish from the Bourse district of Paris could be heard loud and clear when Lenin's new Bolshevik regime repudiated Russian foreign debts to the capitalist nations. Upwards of 1.5 million French investors had poured 12 billion francs into Russian enterprises prior to the commencement of the First World War. As a consequence of World War II, British and other European investors also forfeited billions of dollars in foreign investments.

Not only does foreign investment have deep roots in the developmental patterns of many nations, but so does national reaction against investment money which emanates from foreign sources. Several documented cases are on record showing disenchantment and outright suspicion toward foreign investment activity in the late eighteenth and early nineteenth centuries. For example, at an 1852 stockholder's meeting of an Essen coal company, a German stockholder bitterly complained about the entry of French, British, and Belgian investors into the coal industry of the Ruhr Valley. Similar expressions of acrimony were recorded by Germans toward U.S. electrical companies which had invested heavily in Germany in the 1890s. Americans were also openly accused of taking advantage of Germany's economic predicament by pouring money into key industrial sectors of the troubled Weimar Republic in the 1920s. Additional antipathy toward U.S. investment was recorded in Great Britain during the early years of the twentieth century and in France just prior to the Depression.[6]

The contemporary investment picture Although empirical evidence is somewhat scanty because a number of industrially advanced nations do not keep statistics on foreign investment activity, the post-World War II era may nonetheless be segregated into at least three distinct investment periods. For the decade following the cessation in wartime hostilities, investment was concentrated in the sphere of natural resources, particularly in the development of petroleum sources. U.S. investors were clearly the dominant force during this era as American money flowed into Canada, the Middle East, and Latin America. In the latter part of this period, Europeans also began to invest substantially in the Middle East and in Africa, whereas British investors specifically zeroed in on investment opportunities in Far Eastern countries which were once an integral part of the British Empire.[7] For Japan, Germany, and a few other countries, this early post-war period was consecrated to the rebuilding of their devastated economies and very little money was allotted for foreign investment activity. In Japan, for example, currency exchange restrictions did not end until the mid-1950s, thus precluding the opportunity for overseas investment by Japanese nationals.

From the late 1950s until approximately 1970, the manufacturing and trade spheres emerged as the prime target areas for foreign investors. Western Europe, by this time well along in terms of economic recovery and expansion, became the most attractive region for foreign money, much of which flowed eastward from the United States (see Table 2-3). The renewed vitality of the European economy, the restoration of currency convertibility, and the establishment of large geographical markets through the creation of the European Economic Community (EEC) in 1958 and the European Free Trade Association (EFTA) in 1960, all contributed to the transformation of Western Europe into an amazingly attractive investment haven. Moreover, in the face of stiffer international competition in the manufacturing sphere from the rejuvenated Europeans and Japanese, U.S. firms began to perceive a need to establish plants abroad in order to maintain the competitive advantage which heretofore had been sustained simply by exporting products from the United States. It was within the context of this dramatic upswing in U.S. investment in Europe that Jean-Jacques Servan-Schreiber wrote his famous *The American Challenge,* warning of the impending American business community domination of the European economy unless the Europeans responded boldly to the challenge and began to modernize their own industrial and business structures.

In the 1970s, however, other Western advanced industrial societies began to chip away at America's dominant position in the foreign investment sphere. In relative terms, the 1970s emerged as a decade of increasing European, Japanese, and OPEC investment abroad. In vivid contrast, the rate of U.S. investment overseas has declined vis-à-vis that of the other major countries, although the United States clearly retains its number one position in terms of having the most investment money committed abroad

TABLE 2-3 U.S. Direct Investment Abroad by Nation or Geographic Area, 1936–1976, $U.S. millions

Year	Canada	Latin America and other Western Hemisphere	Western Europe	Other world	Total
1936	1,952	2,847*	1,245	647	6,691
1940	2,103	2,771†	1,420	706	7,000
1950	3,579	4,576	1,733	1,900	11,788
1955	6,761	6,242	3,002	3,390	19,395
1960	11,179	8,365	6,691	5,630	31,865
1965	15,318	10,886	13,985	9,285	49,474
1970	21,015	12,962	25,255	16,248	75,480
1973	25,541	16,484	38,255	21,033	101,313
1974	28,404	19,492	44,782	17,494	110,172
1975	31,038	22,101	49,533	21,540	124,212
1976‡	33,927	19,918	55,906	27,493	137,244

*"Other Western Hemisphere" included with "Other world."
†"Other Western Hemisphere" included once again with "Other world."
‡Preliminary figures.
SOURCES: U.S. Department of Commerce, *Historical Statistics of the United States: Colonial Times to 1970,* and
Statistical Abstract of the United States, 1977.

(see Figure 2-1). Although it is still too early to say with certainty, it does appear as if a fourth post-World War II international investment phase is now in full swing. The most prominent feature of this new phase is the rapid emergence of the United States as the most attractive investment haven in the world, with billions of dollars of foreign money pouring into the country on an annual basis during the last half dozen years of the 1970s.

FIGURE 2-1
Comparison of Foreign Direct Investment in the United States and U.S. Direct Investment Abroad, 1937–1976

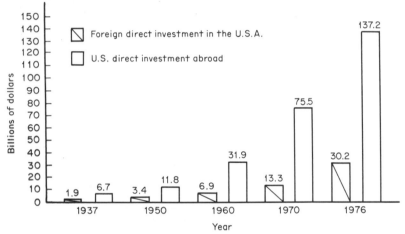

SOURCES: U.S. Department of Commerce, *Historical Statistics of the United States: Colonial Times to 1970,* and *Statistical Abstract of the United States,* 1977.

Host Country Reactions to Foreign Investment—Two Case Studies

The French example General Charles de Gaulle assumed the leadership of France during the turbulent Algerian crisis of 1958 and directed the affairs of the French nation from his Elysée presidential suite until 1969. During this period, De Gaulle was obsessed with the quest to restore France's past grandeur and to ensure that the French nation would once again play a pivotal role in world affairs. In order to demonstrate French independence, De Gaulle withdrew his nation from the North Atlantic Treaty Organization's (NATO) military command and ordered U.S. and other allied forces off French soil. At the same time, he vigorously pushed forward with the development of a *force de frappe* program which he hoped would provide France with a powerful nuclear capability.

De Gaulle also perceived that the role of the U.S. dollar in world monetary transactions was much too great and he launched a concerted campaign to weaken the dollar's hegemonic position by cashing in some of France's huge dollar reserves for U.S. gold. The French leader was also highly critical of U.S. involvement in Indochina and asserted that the United States was guilty of an "arrogance" of power which was dangerous to global stability and which would one day prove to be very costly for American society as a whole.

To say the least, Franco-American relations were severely strained during a large portion of De Gaulle's tenure in office. During the 1960s, of course, a steady stream of American investment money flowed into Western Europe and this became a major point of discussion in European circles, as manifested by the overwhelming reception given to Servan-Schreiber's *The American Challenge.*

During its first few years in office, the Gaullist administration actually welcomed U.S. investment as a means to modernize and invigorate the somewhat stale French economy. In July 1959, De Gaulle's hand-picked Premier and faithful disciple, Michel Debré, indicated that if "U.S. firms are going to set up plants in the Common Market, it is better, under any circumstances, that they choose France rather than her partners."[8]

This "open arms" policy espoused by the Gaullist government lasted until approximately 1963. At that time, American firms in France controlled 40 percent of the telecommunications industry, and were in the process of carving out large segments of other key industrial sectors as well.[9] Perhaps even more ominously in the eyes of General de Gaulle, U.S. businesses were thoroughly monopolizing the field of advanced technology in Europe as a whole, controlling 50 percent of the semiconductors, 80 percent of the computers, and 95 percent of the new market for integrated circuits.

The French President was far from thrilled when Chrysler assumed control of Simca, General Mills bought out Alsacienne, the largest French confectionary firm, and Libby forcefully entered and soon began to dominate a key sector in the French processed food industry. Finally, De Gaulle's temper erupted upon learning of General Electric's bid to take over the ailing Machines Bull Company, France's largest homegrown computer firm. At first, De Gaulle hoped to block the deal entirely, but eventually a compromise was reached whereby GE would assume control over a part of Machines Bull, but the French government would take over responsibility for the sensitive work Bull had been doing for the French defense community.

Through then-Premier Georges Pompidou, De Gaulle eventually invoked a moratorium on foreign investment in France, apparently with at least the tacit support of much of the French public. However, De Gaulle sadly learned that such a ban on foreign investment represented a grave tactical mistake. Soon after Pompidou's announcement, both General Motors and Ford, which had planned on expanding their operations in France, selected new plant sites in Germany and Belgium respectively. In effect, when the French government turned thumbs down to the requests by American companies to establish subsidiaries or to invest in existing firms in France, the American-based multinationals simply sought out similar opportunities in other parts of the European Community. As a result of France's membership in the EEC and the free trade provisions of that regional organization, an American company located in any other EEC country would still have open access for its products to the French market while depriving France of the employment and tax benefits accruing from having the firm situated on French soil. Eventually, the Gaullist administration saw the light and abandoned the strict investment restrictions. Beginning in 1966, France once again officially welcomed foreign direct investment on a "selective" basis.[10]

More than a decade has now passed since De Gaulle's departure from office, and American investment in France has continued to mount. U.S. investment in that country increased from 2.6 billion dollars in 1970 to 4.3 billion in 1973 and to 6.0 billion in 1976.[11] On the whole, the centrist leadership under the tutelage of President Valéry Giscard d'Estaing has continued to welcome foreign direct investment from the United States and from other nations.

However, France has now developed a very sophisticated set of regulations involving foreign direct investment. Investment proposals must now be submitted to the government in advance and are then carefully scrutinized. Although most proposals have thus far been given the green light to proceed, some have been turned down on the basis of being "incompatible" with France's overall economic priorities. The screening agency within France's Ministry of Finance has particularly welcomed those projects which introduce new technology into the French economy, involve vigorous research and development pursuits, and create new jobs and exports in certain designated product areas or regions.[12] Nevertheless, this agency will often seek to find a French company to substitute for the foreign firm and if this search proves to be fruitless, will still frequently place strict limitations on the scope and the nature of the foreign acquisition. In addition, the foreign investors are required to abide by comprehensive legal disclosure regulations and must file an annual confidential statement on profits and losses with the Finance Ministry. French authorities also warn potential foreign investors that French-owned companies will at times be given preference in the procurement of government contracts.

There is, however, one area in which French authorities are very lenient vis-à-vis foreign investment activity. Through the Regional Development

Agency (DATAR), French officials have actively encouraged both domestic and foreign investors to establish firms in the economically depressed regions of Southwestern and Western France and in Corsica. DATAR has even gone so far as to establish offices in the United States and other developed nations to attract such investment. This organization has been given the authority to put together investment "inducement" packages which may include a combination of loans or cash grants, tax incentives, job training, employee relocation and housing subsidies, and favorable long-term leases on facilities.[13]

Thus, foreign investment in France is now welcomed and even openly encouraged in certain economic and geographical sectors. On the other hand, all foreign direct investment proposals are screened by a Finance Ministry agency with authority to reject applications deemed as incompatible with French interests. French public opinion seems to support the current policy, even though newspapers have often been critical of the employee layoff practices of foreign-owned firms operating in France. To say the least, the current investment atmosphere in France certainly differs dramatically from that which existed 15 years ago. At that time, during the mid-1960s, the Gaullists were extremely wary of the consequences of massive foreign investment, and the official government policy for a while was to bar almost all types of investment activity. Ironically, this earlier policy was strongly supported by the political left and the right in France and even centrist elements tacitly accepted the edict. In contrast, the current French policy permits the government to screen out undesirable foreign investments, while at the same time allowing the nation to take advantage of employment and revenue opportunities made available by "acceptable" investment proposals from abroad.

It is highly doubtful that the U.S. government would react to foreign investment in the same fashion as the Gaullist government did several years ago. However, if the investment flow into the United States continues to grow steadily stronger, Washington may indeed consider certain controls on foreign investment in the future; and there are several lessons to be learned from the French policies of both the 1960s and 1970s.

On the other hand, what about America's own investment abroad? Specifically, will American money continue to flow into France and other parts of Western Europe? The French government formulates five-year Economic and Social Development Plans for the nation and has had the tendency in recent years to interfere with some of the activities in the private economic sector in order to force compliance with the plans' objectives. For example, several foreign-owned firms have been jawboned by the Paris government and convinced not to lay off employees, even though market conditions seemed to warrant such a move. In addition, the French and other European governments have increasingly offered subsidies to indigenous marginal businesses in order to avoid the loss of jobs. Such government practices make it more difficult for U.S.-owned firms to compete successfully with their European-owned counterparts. Because of the U.S. government's own jawboning practices, many Western European governments have recently signed an Organization for Economic Cooperation and Development (OECD) pledge to curb state support of such marginal industries, but domestic pressure for job preservation may well counter the intent of the pledge.[14]

U.S.-owned firms are also concerned about the impact of worker participation schemes which have slowly gained momentum in France and in certain other Western European nations. Worker participation programs permit labor representatives to take an active part in the management decision-making process and in decisions pertaining to the dissemination of profits. Although such a concept in some modified form may well be the wave of the future, many U.S. companies remain extremely leery of the whole notion.

Moreover, the specter of an eventual leftist government in France still bothers many foreign investors, in spite of the recent problems which have plagued the French Communist Party (PCF) and the French Socialist Party (PS). A few years ago, the Socialist leader, François Mitterand, came within a percentage point of defeating Giscard in the race for the presidency and the Communist-Socialist alliance was narrowly beaten in the 1978 parliamentary elections. Moreover, Communists and Socialists remain dominant forces in France's local and regional governments. Equally as important, various sectors of the left remain dedicated to the pre-1978 Common Program of the PCF-PS which demanded the nationalization of key industries, a goal which naturally receives little sympathy from the foreign investment community and which still worries many potential American investors.

Because of the more stringent government regulations, the malaise linked to future political uncertainty, and the fact that French production costs now rival or even surpass American costs, it is quite possible that the pace of American investment in France and in the neighboring European countries may slow down appreciably. If such a trend does emerge, it is likely that these American investors will earmark more of their funds for investment opportunities in their own home country, the United States.[15]

The Canadian example The Canadian economy has been penetrated by foreign investment to a larger extent than that of any other advanced industrial society in the Western world. Fifty-eight percent of the Canadian manufacturing sector is foreign-controlled, as are 61 of the 102 largest corporations in the manufacturing, resources, and utilities fields. Three-fourths of the capital in the key Canadian oil and natural gas industries comes from foreign sources, and American companies produce and refine over 90 percent of the Canadian petroleum products.[16] By the end of 1976, Americans alone had pumped 34 billion dollars in direct investments into the Canadian economy, appreciably more than the estimated 30 billion dollars of total foreign investment in the United States that same year. Canada, in fact, has been referred to as "the most extreme example of an industrial country where the production plans, pricing policy and capital movements of American corporations have largely made the local economy and monetary system an extension of the American."[17]

In the 1960s, a significant number of Canadians began to express deep concern about the vast amounts of American money flowing into the country, fearing that Canada was being mortgaged to the hilt to American investors and that the northern nation was being transformed into an economic colony of the United States.[18] In addition, Canadians were visibly upset with the extraterritorial nature of American antitrust laws, the Trading with the Enemy Act, and the Foreign Assets Control Regulations.[19] For example, when the Congress decided that U.S. companies should withdraw from the radio patent pool in the 1950s, U.S.-owned firms in Canada were also expected to comply, even though the pool was still legal in Canada. The U.S. government also ordered affiliates of U.S. firms located in Canada to desist from trading with Mainland China, Cuba, and certain other Communist nations, during a period when Canada continued to have normal diplomatic and trade relations with these nations.

Independent Canada Associations began to spring up throughout the nation and pressure mounted to force the national government to modify drastically Canada's traditional "open door" policy to foreign investment. In reaction to this organized protest, the Trudeau administration established a task force in 1970 to survey the problem of foreign investment in Canada. Recommendations from the task force prompted the passage in 1973 of a parliamentary bill to create the Foreign Investment Review Agency (FIRA).[20]

As part of the Ministry of Industry, Trade, and Commerce, personnel in FIRA have the responsibility of screening all new foreign direct investment proposals in Canada, as well as proposed expansion plans into "new" economic sectors by foreign-owned firms already operating in the nation. However, the expansionary activities of established foreign-controlled companies into related activities are exempt from review.[21]

An American or any other foreign group which is contemplating a direct investment in Canada is sent a Foreign Investment Review Agency information kit which is almost an inch thick. This kit provides an application form, an overview of pertinent legislation and regulations, and two booklets entitled "A Businessman's Guide to the Foreign Investment

Review Act" and "A Guide to Filing Notice with FIRA." In addition, specific guidelines for transactions involving real estate, venture capital, corporate reorganization, and oil and gas reserves are included in the packet.

Once the interested foreign investment group submits the formal application to FIRA, approximately 100 days are needed before the proposal will be fully processed.[22] Although FIRA conducts the investigation, it is the Federal Cabinet in Ottawa which renders the final verdict on whether the proposal is accepted or denied. Oftentimes, before rendering the decision, federal officials will first discuss the proposal with authorities in the province or provinces which will be directly affected by the investment activity. A proposal may not be turned down without first allowing the investment group to submit a brief on why the investment will be beneficial for the Canadian economy. Moreover, even though the Cabinet's determination of what is of "significant benefit" to Canada cannot legally be questioned, all other elements of the screening and decision process may be challenged in the Canadian federal court system.

In accepting a proposal, the Canadian government may insist that certain "undertakings" be performed by the investment group within a specified period of time. These undertakings represent a binding contract between the investor and the Canadian government and a suit may be initiated if compliance is not forthcoming. Aside from these undertakings, however, foreign investors are only subject to the same reporting requirements that apply to indigenous Canadian firms, a feature which contrasts quite vividly with the current investment regulatory practices of the French government.

A few foreign investment groups have claimed that the FIRA process is quite arbitrary and that some foreign companies have been blatantly discriminated against in their efforts to conduct business in Canada. For example, the review process may be invoked in the transfer of assets or stock between two non-Canadian firms if the transfer involves the takeover of a Canadian subsidiary. A few years ago, Ohio-based White Consolidated Industries made a bid to acquire a division of Westinghouse. Even though both companies were of American origin, the Canadian government officially denied the takeover of Westinghouse Canada by White's own subsidiary in Canada.

Furthermore, in order to encourage the use of Canadian-owned or at least Canadian-based media facilities, the Canadian government no longer permits tax deductions for advertising in "non-Canadian" media sources such as U.S.-owned magazines or U.S. border stations which transmit television signals into Canada. In the magazine sphere, a "Canadian" publication must be 75 percent Canadian-owned or differ in content by 80 percent from its foreign parent publication. These restrictions forced *Time Canada* to shut down operations in a celebrated incident a few years ago, although an arrangement was made whereby the *Reader's Digest* could continue to publish its French language magazine after complying with certain conditions.[23]

Restrictions on certain types of foreign investment have also been instituted by provincial governments which wield much more discretionary power than their state government counterparts in the United States. These restrictions have been most noticeable in the sphere of land investment. The province of Ontario has imposed an extremely high tax on the transfer of land title to non-Canadians in order to dissuade land speculation on the part of foreign interests. Prince Edward Island also makes it virtually impossible for nonresidents of that province to acquire land. Alberta, Saskatchewan, and Manitoba have also implemented less severe land ownership restrictions.[24]

On the other hand, critics of FIRA claim that the only U.S. proposal which would not be given the go ahead by the agency would be one submitted by Murder, Inc.[25] It is true that approximately 80 percent of all proposals are given the green light by the Federal Cabinet. In addition, the number of proposals submitted to FIRA continues to spiral upward. The number of applications to establish new businesses in Canada in 1977 was up 74 percent over the previous year and the number of requests to acquire a controlling interest in Canadian enterprises was up 56 percent.[26]

A policy which closely parallels that of the French government is Ottawa's encouragement of foreign investment in economically depressed areas. The Department of Regional Economic Expansion (DREE) was established in 1969 to promote such regional development. Through the Regional Development Incentive Program, DREE officials may offer cash grants and loan guarantees to both domestic and foreign investors. Since its creation, DREE has dispensed 600 million dollars through the incentive program to encourage manufacturing activity in Newfoundland, Nova Scotia, New Brunswick, Prince Edward Island, Manitoba, Saskatchewan, and specially designated parts of the other provinces.[27]

Provincial governments have also developed their own individual incentive programs and often join with the federal government to put together a "packaged" deal for certain highly coveted investment projects. As an illustration, the French-based Michelin tire firm was persuaded to construct facilities in Nova Scotia after Ottawa kicked in a 14.4 million dollar grant and the provincial government came up with a 45 million dollar low-interest loan. Recently, a great deal of publicity was accorded to the packaged deal which prompted the Ford Motor Company to choose southern Ontario over Ohio as the location for a 535 million dollar engine plant. In order to entice Ford, the Canadian federal government provided a 40 million dollar grant and the Ontario provincial government put up another 28 million dollars. The deal prompted U.S. Treasury officials to "express concern" over such transactions, but was generally supported by most elements in the Canadian mass media.[28]

The momentous victory of the Parti Québécois (PQ) in Quebec's 1976 provincial elections has had both a positive and a negative impact on foreign investment activity in Canada. Under the leadership of Premier René Lévesque, the PQ has pushed for political sovereignty for Quebec and is dedicated to the establishment of a separate French-speaking nation on the North American continent. Lévesque knows that if the francophone citizens of Quebec are to accept such a proposition, they must be assured that the Quebec economy will remain relatively stable and prosperous. After getting off to a rocky start in a speech before the Economic Club of New York, Lévesque firmed up his own game plan and began to encourage most types of foreign investment activity in Quebec as a means to ensure economic prosperity. In particular, millions of dollars have been earmarked by the Quebec government for public relations forays into the United States to explain PQ objectives to the American public and to assure the American business community that its investments in Quebec will continue to be welcomed and protected. For the moment, 25 percent of Quebec's employees in the manufacturing sector work for American-owned industries and an additional 9 percent for other foreign-controlled firms.[29] Thus as a consequence of the PQ victory, some potential foreign investors have shied away from Canada because of the resulting political uncertainty, whereas others have entered Quebec because of the assurances and the guarantees provided by the PQ leadership.

In summary, Canada reassessed in the early 1970s its traditional open door approach to foreign investment which both it and its neighbor to the south had followed for many years. Through FIRA, the Canadian government now screens most types of foreign direct investment activity and may ultimately reject any proposals which are considered as nonbeneficial to the Canadian economy. In spite of these new controls, the uncertainty associated with the Quebec situation (which will remain even if the PQ government does not continue in office), and the fact that both federal and provincial governments have lately become more directly involved in the economic sector, foreign direct investment continues to flow into Canada. Public opinion polls show that this foreign investment phenomenon is now a matter of concern for a majority of the Canadian people.[30]

At the very least, the Canadian government has established a mechanism which is designed to ensure that foreign direct investment will benefit Canadian society as a whole and not just the foreign groups which put up the investment money. Both the Foreign Investment Review Agency and the Department of Regional Economic Expansion might well provide useful models for the United States if and when Washington decides to formulate a comprehensive U.S. policy toward foreign investment. The need for and the particulars of such a future U.S. policy will be examined in the concluding chapter of this book.

The Differing Perceptions of the Value of Foreign Investment

Does foreign investment by powerful multinational corporations threaten the sovereignty of national governments? Indeed, have the multinational corporations grown so powerful that they are now beyond the control and jurisdiction of any national or international regulatory body?

Within the American context, does foreign investment abroad precipitate the loss of jobs at home, as the AFL-CIO has consistently claimed? Does such investment drain the U.S. Treasury of valuable tax dollars? Moreover, will the transfer of American technology which often accompanies investment overseas lead to the loss of any competitive edge which U.S.-based firms might once have enjoyed in the international marketplace?

There is not a solid consensus of opinion in the United States or elsewhere concerning the virtues and the vices of direct investment abroad.[31] In his book *The Nation and Athenaeum* even John Maynard Keynes hedged somewhat on the issue of international investment. Although admitting that such investment had certain attractions, Keynes argued that foreign investment involved a "national" cost that the investors themselves did not compute into their private calculations. In other words, Keynes in the end evinced a modest bias in favor of domestic investment, believing that the commitment of money abroad deprived the home country of a resource that could be used to create jobs and expand domestic market opportunities.

As a prominent group within America's so-called radical left movement, the neorevisionist school has long viewed foreign investment with extremely jaundiced eyes. The neorevisionists insist that large corporate entities actually determine the priorities of the U.S. government and that U.S. investment abroad is designed to make as much of the world as possible vulnerable to capitalist exploitation. In particular, insist the radical leftists, investment abroad is one tool in the kit of the large capitalists to guarantee a constant supply of cheap natural resources for American industry as well as the continued presence of foreign markets within which American products can be dumped at exorbitant prices.[32]

At the opposite end of the political spectrum, far right critics contend that foreign investment is an important weapon in the hands of a clique of ultrarich and ultrapowerful people who are determined to dictate the structure of the world economic order and to impose their own special brand of socialism on the Western nations. Authors within the far right often identify the Bilderberg Group, an association of international financiers and industrialists, and the Trilateral Commission, an organization composed of well-known statesmen, academicians, and business leaders which meets periodically to discuss problems common to the United States, Western Europe, and Japan, as the core of this international political and economic conspiracy.[33]

Even within the confines of less extremist circles, opinions concerning the pros and cons of foreign investment vary dramatically. Some liberals, for example, are sympathetic with certain arguments put forward by the "global reach" and the "sovereignty-at-bay" proponents. The global reach thesis asserts that multinational corporations have been transformed into global or international business monoliths which have formulated a set of interests and goals totally distinct from those of any single national government.[34] According to this perspective, these global entities are now more powerful than most national governments and dominate three of the fundamental resources of international economic life: production technology, finance capital, and marketing.[35] Through foreign direct investment, these expansion-oriented corporations muzzle local initiative and preclude the development of local entrepreneurial talent.[36] Unless something drastic is done to check the growth and freedom of latitude of these global corporations, both the global reach and sovereignty-at-bay theorists predict that the integrity of national governments will be undermined and that national economic planning will become subservient to the ambitions of these international oligopolies.[37]

In sharp contrast to these rather alarmist perspectives, many within the centrist political spectrum consider that foreign investment has been a positive force in modernizing national economies and in providing people in most parts of the world with higher standards of living. In addition, the upsurge in foreign investment is perceived as just one more indicator of the increasing interdependency of the modern world and that in most cases, the goals of international investors and of national governments are not incompatible. For example, within certain reasonable limits, multinationals can feel comfortable with national policies which encourage the redistribution of personal income and the enlargement of social services, the development of economically depressed areas, and the protection of local jobs. Moreover, foreign investors can be empathetic with and supportive of national efforts to maintain a healthy balance of payments situation. In effect, within the specific American context, these centrist and moderately conservative elements believe that U.S. investment abroad has not had a deleterious impact on American jobs, the U.S. balance of payments picture, the overall functioning of the international economic system, nor the foreign policy goals of the United States.[38]

Even some of these sources fear, however, that national governments may become overly suspicious of international investment activities and begin to manifest an economic nationalism which would be counter-productive in an increasingly interdependent world.[39] In order to avoid such a scenario, even some of the most ardent supporters of foreign investment activity are now pushing for the adoption of an international investment code of ethics. Is such a code feasible, and if so, how might it affect future American reaction to increased foreign investment in the United States, investment which now ranks ahead of all other nations in the world except Canada?

The practicality and desirability of an international code of ethics   Recent history has vividly shown that some activities by foreign investment groups or multinational corporations may not be totally beneficial to the interests of host countries. In the past few years, more than 300 corporations have publicly admitted paying bribes of half a billion dollars in order to further their interests in host countries. Governments in the Netherlands, Italy, Belgium, Honduras, and Japan have been badly shaken or even toppled because of the revelations of questionable payments by foreign corporate entities operating in these countries.[40]

On the other hand, the specter of expropriation in developing nations obviously disturbs all foreign investors. As a lucid example, U.S. companies alone have 1.6 billion dollars in claims lodged against Cuba because of the Castro administration's nationalization of "capitalist" enterprises. In the advanced industrial world, the fear of unfair competition from government-owned industries also hangs over the heads of many international corporations. Moreover, national policies pertaining to antitrust regulations, securities provisions, export controls, balance of payments stipulations, and tax procedures have all at one time or another infringed on the business plans of foreign firms. In effect, the national interests of individual countries may at times be on a collision course with the overriding profit considerations of international investors.[41] The host country in most cases desires foreign investment but does not want in the process to forfeit any of its sovereignty in the economic and the political spheres.[42]

In order to minimize the possible sources of conflict between national governments and international investors, several attempts have been made in the post-World War II period to formulate an international investment code of ethics which would be binding on both the investors and national governments. Representing a step in this direction, the Havana Charter was consummated in 1948 with the intent of establishing an International Trade Organization. In the Havana document, national governments pledged to provide "reasonable opportunities for investment acceptable to them and adequate security for existing and future investment."[43] These governments also promised to "give due regard to the desirability of avoiding discrimination" in their attitudes toward foreign investors.[44] However, a great deal of uncertainty enshrouded the entire Havana Charter because nation-states were granted the latitude to ensure that foreign investment did not interfere in the conduct of internal affairs or national policies, to determine whether and to what extent they would allow future foreign investment, and to prescribe the terms of ownership of existing and future investments.[45]

The International Chamber of Commerce and many other business-linked organizations complained that these stipulations left foreign investors vulnerable to the arbitrary actions of national governments.[46] Most governments, in fact, have gone ahead and placed major restrictions on certain types of foreign investment activity. Many of the developed nations limit or prohibit altogether foreign investment in communications, finance, public utilities, and defense industries, all of which are considered as crucial to the maintenance of national sovereignty. In Canada, Japan, and the United States, the exploitation of certain raw materials is off limits to foreign investors. In the United Kingdom, Italy, France, and several other major industrial nations which have extensive sectors of the economy under direct state control, foreign investment in these specific sectors is also restricted.[47]

The developing nations have also instituted numerous controls on foreign investment within the past few years. For example, several countries in Latin America have banded together to formulate the Andean Code.[48] The Andean provisions prohibit new foreign investment in public utilities, transportation, communications, finance, insurance, advertising, marketing, and publishing. The code also provides for the phased divestiture of certain foreign investments already made in these Latin American countries. However, the member governments have frequently differed in their application of the code and have at times permitted case-by-case waivers of these rather stringent provisions.

Meanwhile, the quest for an international investment code has continued on a sporadic basis. In 1958, the Swiss government and a British parliamentary group proposed a formal charter on world investment and five years later the Organization for Economic Cooperation and Development (OECD) issued a draft convention on the protection of foreign property. On the whole, however, very little has been done to formulate an international code of foreign investment which would parallel the General Agreement on Trade and Tariffs (GATT) for world trade, and the International Monetary Fund (IMF) regulations for international monetary transactions. Perhaps a small step in this direction was taken when the OECD ratified a Declaration on International Investment and Multinational Enterprises in the mid-1970s (an excerpt from this declaration is found in Table 2-4). A United Nations' committee also recommended in 1977 the implementation of extensive new disclosure rules for multinational corporations. This proposed UN Charter, which has been publicly supported by Secretary-General Kurt Waldheim, would require the multinationals to divulge financial data, labor practices, environmental policies,

TABLE 2-4   OECD General Policies on Multinationals and International Investment

Enterprises should:

- Take fully into account established general policy objectives of the member countries in which they operate.
- In particular, give due consideration to those countries' aims and priorities with regard to economic and social progress, including industrial and regional development, the protection of the environment, the creation of employment opportunities, the promotion of innovation and the transfer of technology.
- While observing their legal obligations concerning information, supply their entities with supplementary information the latter may need in order to meet requests by the authorities of the countries in which those entities are located for information relevant to the activities of those entities taking into account legitimate requirements of business confidentiality.
- Favor close cooperation with the local community and business interests.
- Allow their component entities freedom to develop their activities and to exploit their competitive advantage in domestic and foreign markets, consistent with the need for specialization and sound commercial practice.
- When filling responsible posts in each country of operation, take due account of individual qualifications without discrimination as to nationality, subject to particular national requirements in this respect.
- Not render—and they should not be solicited or expected to render—any bribe or other benefit, direct or indirect, to any public servant or holder of public office.
- Unless legally permissible, not make contributions to candidates for public office or to political parties or other political organizations.
- Abstain from any improper involvement in local political activities.

SOURCE: *OECD Observer,* July 1976.

organizational structures, and investment programs. The International Chamber of Commerce, the International Organization of Employers, and the U.S. representatives to the United Nations have all opposed the committee recommendations, contending that individual countries might be tempted to use the proposed code as a model for mandatory regulations.[49]

In the absence of an international investment code, national governments have as a minimum expected foreign-owned firms within their jurisdictions to be good corporate citizens and to uphold the laws of the nation. Many of these governments support in spirit the so-called Calvo Doctrine which stipulates that foreign-owned subsidiaries should not be allowed to seek diplomatic support from the government of the country in which the parent company is located. The Canadian government, for example, has issued the following "Guiding Principles for Good Corporate Behavior" for foreign-owned subsidiaries situated in Canada:

> Firms are to strive for "maximum competitiveness" and "appropriate specialization" within the international firms. Market opportunities are to be exploited at home and abroad, natural resources processed in Canada where economic to do so, and Canadian procurement sources searched out and developed. A pricing policy fair to both the company and to Canadians is to be pursued, "including sales to the parent company and other affiliates." R and D capacity is to be developed. Sufficient earnings are to be retained to support the growth of the Canadian operation. Firms are to work toward a Canadian outlook within management, and include "a major portion of Canadian citizens on its Board of Directors." Firms are "periodically to publish information on the financial position and operation of the company" and "to have the objective of a financial structure which provides opportunity for equity participation in the Canadian enterprise by the Canadian public." They are to recognize and share "national objectives" and "encourage and support Canadian institutions directed toward the intellectual, social and cultural advancement of the community."[50]

Frankly, there is little likelihood for the time being that the major Western, Socialist, and Third World nations could agree on enough points to piece together a comprehensive international investment code. Even if such a code could be devised, which international regulatory body would have adequate enforcement power to require compliance with the code's provisions?

On the other hand, economic nationalism may well intensify and foreign investment activities in many countries may become a very risky proposition at best.[51] Moreover, without a general world consensus on investment practices, illegal and even malicious conduct on the part of certain multinationals will certainly continue. Unfortunately, little will be accomplished toward creating a meaningful investment code until the problems of international investment have been exacerbated. Ironically, if the uncertainty shrouding the investment picture intensifies, complicated further by monumental monetary exchange problems, then the United States may well become the preferred sanctuary for even more foreign money. After all, the United States remains the bastion of capitalism in the world and maintains an open door policy toward most types of foreign investment. In view of these conditions and others which will be discussed in the next chapter, Americans should perhaps brace themselves for even greater foreign investment activity in the 1980s.

THREE

Why Invest in the U.S.A.?
The Foreigner's
Point of View

Introduction

Foreign direct investment in the United States climbed to an all-time record high of 34 billion dollars by the end of 1977, up more than 150 percent since the beginning of the decade. In covering the foreign investment issue, media sources have had the tendency to concentrate on Arab transactions in the United States and have given a great deal of attention to the potentially awesome economic impact which OPEC surplus funds might have on the U.S. marketplace.[1] In spite of all the ink accorded to this "Arab" dimension, the fact remains that an overwhelming percentage of the money flowing into the United States for direct investment purposes continues to emanate from the advanced industrial societies in Western Europe, Canada, and Japan (see Table 3-1).

This chapter will examine why the United States has recently emerged as a tremendously popular haven for foreign investment funds and why this investment from abroad is expected to accelerate even further in the years to come. In addition, the latter part of the chapter will discuss the rules and regulations established by the federal government which are pertinent to foreign investment activity in the United States.

TABLE 3-1 Foreign Direct Investment in the United States, 1977; $ millions

	Total	Percent increase end 1973–end 1977	Manufacturing	Petroleum	Trade	Finance	Insurance	Real estate	Other
All countries	34,071	65.7	13,706	6,566	7,208	2,154	2,275	779	1,385
Europe total	22,666	62.6	8,405	5,520	4,916	1,270	1,772	196	588
Netherlands	7,091	76.5	1,677	*	288	427	*	38	308
United Kingdom	6,337	17.3	2,247	485	1,977	249	1,176	81	124
Germany	2,494	158.4	1,313	−6	962	122	56	30	17
Switzerland	2,400	69.0	1,513	3	339	181	300	7	56
France	1,793	116.9	906	*	486	177	27	−1	*
Other Europe	2,549	95.3	752	*	866	*	*	*	*
Canada	5,999	42.7	3,437	710	754	160	185	104	649
Japan	1,741	1045.4	325	48	824	493	38	31	−19
Latin America	3,287	59.5	1,449	272	643	*	*	339	122
All other countries	379	85.8	*	16	69	*	*	109	*
Memorandum:									
OPEC nations	157	70.6	24	4	−8	29	4	102	1

*Withheld by Commerce Department to avoid disclosure of information on individual foreign-owned firms.
SOURCES: U.S. Department of Commerce and the *Morgan Guaranty Survey*, September 1978.

The Luring Appeal of the U.S. Market

The growth of foreign multinationals The booming development of the domestic economies of Western Europe and Japan in the 1960s was accompanied by a noteworthy expansion in trade and financial interactions among the advanced industrial world. Part of this rapid expansion is definitely attributable to the undervaluation of most of the major world currencies vis-à-vis the American dollar beginning in 1965. This undervaluation made exports from these countries much more cost competitive with U.S. products and prompted the major industries in Europe and Japan to switch their exporting activity into high gear.

The trend toward corporate mergers and consolidations in Western Europe and Japan during the late 1960s also enhanced the capability of these companies to exploit economies of scale in production, marketing, and research and development. In 1964, the 200 largest foreign industrial corporations had total sales of 108 billion dollars, only 45 percent of the 239 billion dollars in sales tallied by America's 200 largest companies. In 1969, the 200 largest foreign-based corporations had moved up to 62 percent of the total sales of their U.S. counterparts, and by 1974, they were up to 89 percent. In the decade following 1964, the foreign group's sales increased nearly twice as fast as the U.S. group's.[2]

As a further illustration of the growing strength of foreign-based enterprises, the sales of Japanese-based multinationals catapulted from 15 billion dollars in 1964 to 113 billion dollars in 1974. German multinationals were up from 23 to 111 billion dollars and British multinationals from 26 to 107 billion dollars during the same period.[3] Even though sales growth is not necessarily equivalent to earnings growth and the figures quoted above are subject to general inflation and currency revaluation considerations, the sales figures do serve as a good indicator in showing that the large foreign-based multinationals are rapidly reaching parity with their U.S. counterparts. As a result of their rapid development and the valuable experience gleaned from years of international trading activity, these giant foreign multinationals were at last ready and prepared to tackle a new and rather awesome challenge. In effect, these foreign giants had finally gained enough confidence to compete head-on with American firms in the richest and most integrated market in the world, the United States.[4]

Moreover, some foreign governments have even openly encouraged their respective business communities to expand into the American and other overseas markets. This new thrust, of course, differs dramatically from the earlier national exchange control programs which severely limited international investment opportunities. Under the leadership of President Giscard and Premier Raymond Barre, French officials have actively supported certain types of investment activity abroad in order to ensure that French companies will remain competitive with the major multinationals from the United States, Germany, and Japan. In line with this way of thinking, France's giant tire producer, Michelin, has decided to spend more than 400 million dollars to produce radial tires in four U.S. plants.

The Japanese government is also actively encouraging overseas investment with the lure of low interest loans to companies contemplating such a move. Government officials have estimated that Japan's total overseas direct investment could spiral from the present 19 billion dollars to as high as 80 billion dollars by 1985. Although a somewhat deceptive figure because of the low initial base, Japanese investment in the United States has nevertheless increased by more than 1,000 percent in the period between 1973 and 1977, and it is highly probable that the United States will remain as a principal target for future Japanese investment activity.[5]

The West German government has followed suit and has praised the efforts of German companies which have been seeking new investment opportunities overseas. In particular, these German investors have been very active in the U.S. market. In 1976 and 1977, more than a billion dollars of German money entered the United States in the form of direct investments, an amount equivalent to one-half of German direct investment in the North American nation in the preceding 25 years. For the first time in 1977, German direct investment in the U.S. market was greater than the combined investments of that country in all of the other European Community nations.[6]

The dollar's woes   Direct foreign investment in the United States became increasingly attractive in the 1970s in part because of the Nixon administration's decision to end the convertibility of the dollar into gold and the subsequent devaluations of the dollar in 1971 and again in 1973. For example, in the period between April 1, 1971, and April 1, 1978, the dollar plummeted 63 percent in value vis-à-vis the Japanese yen, 81 percent vis-à-vis the German mark, and 131 percent vis-à-vis the Swiss franc (see Table 3-2 for a more extensive look at the dollar's woeful performance). Prior to President Carter's bolstering efforts in the autumn of 1978, the dollar sank to record post-war lows against several major world currencies, thus making these currencies much more valuable in the American market. As an illustration, Thyssen AG, the number one steel producer in West Germany, offered to pay 275 million dollars in January 1978 for the Budd Company, a U.S. automobile and railroad car supplier. Only six months earlier, the deal would have cost Thyssen an additional 28 million dollars. Why? In the interim period, the value of the U.S. dollar had dropped dramatically in relationship to the German mark.[7] Even the British, whose economy has lagged during the past several years and has

TABLE 3-2   Revaluation of Major World Currencies against the 1965 American Dollar, Percentages

	German mark	Dutch guilder	French franc	Swiss franc	British pound	Canadian dollar	Japanese yen
1965	*	*	*	*	*	*	*
1968	0.8	−0.4	−0.4	0.6	−14.0	−0.3	−0.3
1970	9.6	−0.8	−11.6	1.0	−13.8	0.6	1.0
1972	26.8	12.6	−2.6	13.4	−6.2	8.2	19.2
1973	41.4	22.4	8.1	34.1	−11.2	8.1	37.1
1974	59.1	34.1	2.7	44.5	−14.2	11.0	30.8
1975	71.3	50.3	16.5	71.6	−13.8	7.6	22.8
1976	58.1	34.0	4.7	71.5	−31.3	9.7	20.5
1977	68.0	44.5	−1.4	71.0	−38.4	2.3	30.1
1978	101.8	69.0	8.2	138.9	−33.2	−4.9	64.0

* Symbolizes the base year from which figures for other years were computed.
SOURCE: *The Wall Street Journal.* April 1st was used as the benchmark for each year.

ranked with the Italian economic system as the two "weak sisters" of the European Community, have recently found it quite advantageous to invest in the United States. As the *Economist* pointed out in December 1977:

> The cheapening dollar has made American industry still more of a steal for foreigners. So, in relative terms, has the better performance of other stock markets. For example, sterling has appreciated against the dollar by 18 percent since the pound's low point in late 1976 and the London Stock Market has risen by 47 percent in the past year while Wall Street has fallen by 16 percent. Anybody switching out of a typical share in British industry will therefore find that a typical share in American industry *costs him less than half as much* during this dollar crisis as it did in the 1976 sterling crisis.[8] [Author's italics.]

The relatively low status of the American dollar in relation to other world currencies will probably persist as long as the United States continues to suffer from an anemic trade imbalance. Even though the drop in the dollar's value should make U.S. exports much more competitive on the world market and increase the demand for American products by consumers in other nations, the U.S. trade deficit continued to drift upward during the latter part of the 1970s. In 1977, the United States suffered through its worst trade performance in history. The staggering 26.7 billion dollar deficit in that year was four times higher than the previous record deficit registered in 1972. However, 1978 was even worse, and the December 1978 deficit marked the thirty-first consecutive month of trade deficits for the United States. The total U.S. foreign trade deficit for 1978 was a dismal 28.5 billion dollars.

Partially as a result of this huge trade deficit, billions of "surplus" dollars have been accumulating in the hands of investors in Europe, Asia, and the Middle East. As long as this less than enviable trade performance persists, the American dollar will have problems keeping pace with many of the other major currencies of the world, thus providing foreigners with an added incentive to invest in American industrial, commercial, and real property as a hedge against both general inflation and the further erosion in the dollar's value. Furthermore, the inclination of foreigners to acquire a piece of the American market with the excess dollars becomes even stronger when stock prices on Wall Street plummet, as occurred in 1969–1970, 1973–1974, and during part of 1978.

Expansiveness and unity of the American market   Another important reason why foreign investors have cast a covetous eye on the United States is because of the vastness and inherent unity of the American marketplace. The United States offers the largest, most cohesive market in the world. The gross domestic product of the United States in 1977 was 1,881 billion dollars, a figure which dwarfs Japan's 680 billion, Germany's 510 billion, and Great Britain's 243 billion.[9] In addition to its size, the American market is also intensely competitive, representing the ultimate testing ground for the most up-to-date technological, marketing, and managerial innovations. With little exaggeration, what transpires today in the American market will likely be the precursor of what will occur later on in the other markets of the world.

Moreover, the United States is blessed with a marketplace in which one dominant language is used and which has a fairly uniform and consistent code of business regulations from one end of the country to the other. Although Americans often take these advantages for granted, contrast this situation with the European Economic Community (EEC). The EEC, which for the moment consists of nine Western European nations, was created in 1958 and currently rivals or even surpasses the United States in terms of overall gross domestic product and the production of certain key industrial goods. Remarkably, in the face of the differing national traditions of each of the member countries, the EEC has been able to mold part of Western Europe into a free trade zone which shares common external tariff policies. However, ultimate decision making on important matters within the EEC still resides with the nine sovereign governments, and standardized agreements are often difficult, if not impossible, to formulate. With the additional impediments of a potpourri of cultural practices, six different working languages, and eight different currencies, the EEC must struggle along and hope to achieve unitary market conditions on an incremental basis. In comparison, the United States is fully integrated as a nation and as a marketplace, sporting almost 220 million relatively affluent consumers. Consequently, the United States has naturally emerged as a very fertile area for overseas investment activity.

The stability of the American capitalist system In comparative terms, U.S. government intervention in the American economic system has been quite negligible and the United States clearly reigns as the "Great Protector" of world capitalism. Coming from Western nations in which the governments have been much more directly involved in economic affairs in the post-World War II period, overseas investors greatly appreciate capitalism's durability in the United States. As Arthur Fürer, President of Nestlé S. A. of Switzerland, has concluded: "We believe that free economies have a much better future than planned ones. The U.S. seems likely to continue along the path of economic freedom, while Europe risks going in a more socialistic direction."[10] Furthermore, as Figure 3-1 clearly illustrates, definite tax advantages exist for those people conducting business in the United States when compared to the rather onerous tax burdens placed on citizens of most of the world's other major industrial nations.

Since 1970, unit labor costs have increased less rapidly in the United States than in almost all other major industrial nations and the United States has also done a fairly decent job of controlling inflation (see Tables 3-3 and 3-4). In addition, salaries have spiraled up more rapidly in most

FIGURE 3-1
Comparative Tax Costs and Government Expenditures

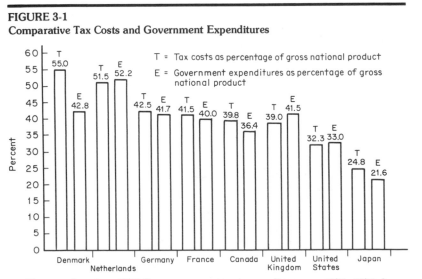

*Tax costs based on 1974 figures, government expenditures, on 1975–1976 data
SOURCES: *Economic Trends,* November 1976; *OECD Observer,* March 1977; and Bank of America statistics, 1974.

of the other industrial societies. As an example, according to Conference Board statistics, a beginning engineer in Denmark in 1975 received a 37 percent higher salary than his counterpart in the United States. In fact, the U.S. engineer's beginning salary also ranked behind that of his colleagues in West Germany, Switzerland, Norway, and Belgium.

Moreover, the United States has not been decimated by the wildcat strikes and other forms of labor unrest which have rocked several of the other major Western industrial nations. American labor unions are only moderately involved in political activities and the American working man and woman have never had the love affair with socialism which has so often typified the working class in other countries. As a stark illustration, France's largest and best organized trade union is the Confédération générale du travail (CGT). The CGT has close links with the French Communist Party and has periodically been used as a tool by the French Communists to further their own political aims. In Great Britain, the worker groups aligned in the Trade Unions Congress (TUC) are closely identified with the British Labour Party and officially, the policy priorities of the Labour Party are supposed to be decided at the party's trade union-dominated Annual Conference. Even though American labor unions have been perennially identified with the Democratic Party, the linkages to political decision making are much more tenuous on the American

TABLE 3-3   Foreign Unit Labor Costs as a Percentage of U.S.
Unit Labor Costs, 1965 – 1974, Percentages

	1965	1970	1973	1974
Japan	57	51	84	91
Canada	85	85	96	99
Germany	55	58	95	99
United Kingdom	107	94	120	122

SOURCE: U.S. Bureau of Labor Statistics, *Monthly Labor Review.*

TABLE 3-4   The Consumer Price Index, 1970 = 100.0

	1972	1973	1974	1975	1976	1977
Germany	111.1	118.8	127.1	134.7	140.8	146.3
United States	107.8	114.4	127.0	138.6	146.6	156.1
Canada	107.8	116.0	128.6	142.5	153.2	165.4
France	117.7	119.9	136.3	152.2	166.8	182.7
Japan	110.9	123.9	154.2	172.4	188.4	203.6
United Kingdom	117.2	128.0	148.4	184.4	214.9	249.0

SOURCE: *OECD Main Economic Indicators,* 1972–1978.

scene than in most other major nations. Foreign investors seem to appreciate this fact and ironically, large sums of money from the British trade union pension funds are now flowing into the United States to be placed in real estate and commercial transactions. Furthermore, foreign investors, who have traditionally been wary of labor unions in their own countries, also have the option of setting up facilities in states where worker unionization is a rare phenomenon. This definitely helps to explain why so many foreign enterprises have headed directly to the right-to-work states in the American South.

Nor can the stability of the American political system be underestimated as a motivating force for increasing foreign investment activity. With Western Europe worried about Eurocommunism and other forms of leftism and Canada transfixed with the Quebec situation, the United States is in a rather unique position of having a moderate and stable system of government which remains highly supportive of the capitalist ethic. The enviable stability of the American governmental system, which is buttressed by a middle-of-the-road, consensus-oriented citizenry, certainly helps convince troubled foreigners that their investment funds will be fully protected in the United States.

American Incentive Programs for Foreign Investment and the Specter of Protectionism

The fact that the U.S. government is nondiscriminatory toward most types of foreign investment is also a plus in the eyes of overseas investors. In effect, the federal government's open door attitude toward foreign investment has undoubtedly contributed to the increase in the foreign money flow into the United States, while at the same time helping to subdue criticism of America's own massive investment abroad.

Although the United States has been officially neutral toward foreign investment, state and local governments and private groups have swung into high gear in an effort to attract overseas investment to their specific regions. The activities of the state governments will be highlighted in Chapter Seven, but it should be mentioned at this juncture that most states have now set up international trade and investment divisions which have incentive packages designed to entice foreign investment money into the state. Civic groups have also become integrally involved in this process as is illustrated by the recent visit of San Diego Chamber of Commerce representatives to Tokyo and Osaka. The purpose of the visit was to invite Japanese industries to join with the already committed Sony Corporation, Kyota Ceramic Company, and a handful of other Japanese firms in setting up plants in the San Diego area.[11]

From a different angle, there has been growing pressure on the U.S. federal government to place controls on the importation of a wide range of foreign-made products, including textiles, shoes, color televisions, and other finished goods. At the 1977 annual convention of the AFL-CIO held in Los Angeles, George Meany forcefully advocated a protectionist policy against foreign imports, stating that the United States should "do unto others as they do to us, barrier for barrier, closed door for closed door." At least five states have already passed variations of "Buy American" laws. Indiana, for example, now offers a 15 percent price advantage to domestic steel bidders over foreign firms in the issuing of contracts. Under the Trade Act of 1974, U.S. workers who lose their jobs because of foreign competition are entitled to special federal government benefits, including 70 percent of their average weekly wage for up to 52 weeks, job training, and placement and relocation services. Fearing that national and state officials will increasingly buckle under to pressure from domestic industries which have been outflanked by overseas competitors, foreign firms have been rushing to set up facilities within the American market as a safeguard against U.S. import protectionism.

The new American land rush Seemingly, the purchase of American land has become an almost uncontrollable obsession with certain foreign buyers, and with good reason. First of all, recent history has clearly borne out that owners of real property have stood an excellent chance of keeping pace with or even outdistancing the rate of inflation. Thus for the foreign investor possessing either a huge surplus of American dollars or funds in a currency which has recently outpaced the American dollar, U.S. land has become particularly attractive. Moreover, the price of land in the United States is still generally well below that being asked for comparable pieces of real estate in most other parts of the industrialized world, sometimes as much as 10 to 20 times less costly in the United States than in Japan, Switzerland, and various other parts of Europe. Furthermore, many of these countries are "land poor" in comparison to the United States, a phenomenon of which most Americans are unaware. Great Britain, as an example, is only the size of the state of Oregon but has a population of 60 million as compared to Oregon's 2.3 million. West Germany is smaller in size than Montana, but has 70 times the population of that Western state. In fact, the largest nation of Western Europe, France, is not as big as Texas. Japan is also somewhat smaller than Montana in geographic terms but has well over 100 times Montana's population. Thus the relatively land-starved Europeans and Japanese can find real estate deals in the United States which are often dirt cheap in terms of their own countries' prices and which still provide an excellent hedge against inflation.

In a related sphere, the uncertainty associated with the lack of raw materials in many of the Western nations has also precipitated a great deal of investment in the United States. America continues to be blessed with an abundance of many natural resources, and foreign industries must have assured access to some of these materials in order to produce their finished products. Consequently, many foreign firms have been prompted to set up plants in the United States adjacent to where the raw materials are located. The outright purchase by foreign interests of property containing some of these natural resources, such as farm, timber, and mineral land, has been accelerating dramatically in recent years.

Future projections Most projections of economic growth in the 1980s among the major Western nations are more bullish toward the United States than toward Japan, Canada, and the Western European countries. In the official U.S. Department of Commerce study dealing with foreign direct investment, personal interviews were conducted with representatives of 72 foreign companies headquartered in West Germany, the Netherlands, Switzerland, the United Kingdom, Japan, and Canada. With few exceptions, these executives predicted that the United States would attract in the future an increasing share of the worldwide direct investment flow because the American market could provide: (1) better profits, (2) faster productivity growth, (3) less labor unrest, (4) increasingly more favorable labor and production costs, (5) comparatively less government intervention in the economic sector, (6) greater investment security, and (7) improved access to raw materials.[12] In the intervening years since this Commerce study was completed, predictions of persistent growth in foreign investment activity in the United States have continued to be made, often premised on the reasons just listed. Indeed, the United States will soon outdistance Canada as the number one host nation in the world for foreign direct investment funds.

Methods of investment Much of the foreign direct investment flowing into the United States has come from the largest foreign multinational firms and there has recently been a marked increase in their acquisitions of existing American companies with book values of more than 100 million dollars.[13] For example, citizens of the Netherlands currently rank as the number one investors in the United States. It is estimated that 85 percent of the Dutch direct investment in the American marketplace comes from just six companies. Three of these, Royal Dutch Shell, Unilever, and Philips, rank in *Fortune's* top 20 list of the world's largest industrial corporations. Switzerland has been most visibly represented by such giants as Nestlé Alimentana, Hoffman-LaRoche, and Ciba-Geigy; the United Kingdom by British Petroleum, Burmah Oil, British-American Tobacco, Imperial

Chemical Industries, and Dunlop-Pirelli; West Germany by Bayer, BASF, Hoechst, and Siemens; Japan by Mitsubishi, Sumitomo, Mitsui, Matsushita, and Toyota; and Canada by Alcan, Massey-Ferguson, and International Nickel.[14]

These foreign investments have generally been in the form of new ventures, joint ventures, and outright acquisitions, with financing arranged through cash offerings, commercial bank loans both in the United States and abroad, debt securities, and equity offerings.[15] As an illustration of a typical foreign direct investment transaction, take the case of a large British company which acquired a small U.S. firm back in 1973. One hundred percent of the common stock of the U.S. company was acquired through an offering of cash for stock. The cash for the acquisition was provided by a consortium of London banks. The financial affairs of the new U.S. acquisition were then quickly merged with those of the other U.S. subsidiaries of this British conglomerate. Eventually, long-term loans for the construction of an additional manufacturing facility for the acquired company were arranged through U.S. banks with loan guarantees provided by the British firm's other American subsidiaries.[16] In the acquisition of U.S. firms, the British giant and other foreign investors have shown a strong favoritism for companies with good track records and with solid management, management that will remain in place even after the takeover is consummated.[17]

The Government's Position Toward Foreign Investment

The historical setting In his famous Farewell Address to the American people, President George Washington warned that the newly formed nation sequestered in the New World should steer clear of the political intrigues which were then so commonplace in Europe. By following a policy of "no entangling alliances," the first President contended that the young American nation would stand a much better chance of prospering and of firming up national solidarity.

Up until World War I, American Presidents remained fairly faithful to Washington's admonitions, at least insofar as American political and military involvement outside of the Western Hemisphere was concerned. Even after the conclusion of the First World War, America "came home" and returned to the relative safety of its friendly shores protected by the expansiveness of two mammoth oceans. In essence, the United States reaffirmed its traditional isolationist foreign policy preference and the Senate even refused to permit American participation in the League of Nations, Woodrow Wilson's own brainchild which was later to be succeeded by the United Nations.

Although he adamantly spoke out in opposition to American military and political involvement overseas, George Washington had positive comments about foreign economic ties which would help to nourish America's fragile economic structure. Washington's Secretary of the Treasury, Alexander Hamilton, stated in a message to the Congress that instead of viewing foreign investment in the United States as a rival, it ought to be welcomed with open arms because it would permit "an increased amount of productive labor and useful enterprise to be set to work."[18] Through the next 188 years of American history, government officials generally went along with Hamilton's way of thinking and placed very few restrictions on incoming investment from abroad. Moreover, as both Washington and Hamilton had anticipated, foreign funds were an instrumental factor in the development of the infant economy which early on was hampered by a dearth of domestic capital support.[19] In the early part of the nineteenth century, approximately one-fourth of all the business equity holdings in the United States was controlled by foreign investors.[20] In 1869, foreign investment in the United States reached 1.5 billion dollars and spiraled upward to 7.2 billion dollars at the start of World War I. In contrast, U.S. investment abroad was only 100 million dollars in 1869 and only 3.5 billion dollars in 1914.[21]

In particular, European investment was a pivotal force in the westward expansion of the railroads, and huge chunks of Western real estate were swallowed up by investors from the British Isles and from the European continent. In 1857, for example, the Dubuque and Pacific Railroad sold 500,000 acres to English investors. By 1880, the Texas and Pacific Railroad had relinquished 640,000 acres to foreigners; and in the 1880s, the Sioux City and St. Paul Railroad sold an additional 40,000 acres of choice Iowa farmland to a London holding company which in turn developed the land for tenant farming.[22]

Eventually, enterprising American firms began to dispatch agents to Europe in order to drum up land sales. In addition, foreigners often invested in state bonds and when some of the states were unable to honor their financial commitments, these investors were reimbursed with state land. Alabama followed just such a policy in 1876 when it offered land in exchange for 8 percent state bonds which had defaulted.[23]

Foreign mortgage firms were integrally involved in providing much-needed credit for land purchases in the West during the last three decades of the nineteenth century. Large European-owned cattle ranches were also established in the West in the wake of the anthrax epidemic of the 1860s which had decimated the cattle industry in Great Britain and on part of the continent. Just prior to World War I, alien owners had managed to accumulate between 30 and 35 million acres of U.S. land. However, this early onslaught by foreign investors into the real estate domain sparked a great deal of criticism in the American West and precipitated some major restrictions on foreign ownership in several states. In 1887, the Illinois legislature passed a series of bills prohibiting nonresident aliens from acquiring further land and preventing alien landlords who had previously purchased land from requiring their tenants to pay taxes on that land. Legislatures in Minnesota, Wisconsin, Nebraska, Colorado, Iowa, and Missouri passed similar laws during the next decade, and a handful of other states passed less restrictive legislation pertaining to absentee foreign land ownership. In 1887, the U.S. Congress entered the controversy by restricting land ownership in the American territories to U.S. citizens or aliens seeking U.S. citizenship.

Legislation with clear racist overtones also affected foreign ownership in a few other Western states. California's 1882 Chinese Exclusion Act was designed to remove people of Chinese ancestry from over 500,000 acres of farm land. Anti-Japanese initiatives passed in California in 1913 and 1920 and related legislation ratified in certain other states also denied this ethnic group the right to acquire land.

Many of these restrictions directed at aliens and certain ethnic groups were repealed or fell into complete disuse after World War II. As will be discussed in a later chapter devoted to foreign investment in the real estate sector, only a few states currently have laws on the books which severely limit alien land ownership. At the federal level, Congress enacted in 1917 the Trading with the Enemy Act which enables the President, in times of war or national emergency, to greatly restrict or even prohibit banking, manufacturing, commercial, or other types of activity being carried on in the United States by foreign nationals, if this activity is considered as detrimental to American interests. In addition, the Chief Executive is empowered to confiscate the property belonging to aliens from designated "enemy" nations. In the aftermath of the German invasion of Denmark and Norway in April 1940, President Roosevelt issued an executive order freezing the U.S. assets of Danish and Norwegian citizens. Although the United States had not yet entered the war effort at that time and was still officially neutral, Roosevelt's action was designed to prevent Hitler's regime from exploiting the U.S.-based possessions of citizens from the occupied Scandinavian nations. During both World Wars, enemy property in the United States was confiscated by the federal government and more than 440 million dollars worth of this property was sold at public auction during the Second World War. In the post-World War II era, property belonging to nationals residing in Mainland China, North Korea, Vietnam, Cuba, Cambodia, and Rhodesia has been frozen by federal authorities. To keep things in perspective, however, one should remember that the vast majority of foreign investment transactions in the United States have not been affected at all by this extraordinary federal legislation.[24]

Contemporary Restrictions on Foreign Investment Activity

The open door emphasis In general, the U.S. government has continued to treat foreign investment in the same manner as domestic investment and historically has not discriminated solely on the basis of the overseas citizenship of the investor.[25] In clear contrast to the French and Canadian cases discussed in the second chapter, foreign investors in the United States are not presently required to apply to federal authorities for permission to proceed with their investment plans.[26] Likewise, once the investment has been made, the federal government endorses a hands-off policy toward the activities of the foreign firms conducting business in the United States. Resident and nonresident aliens with business interests in the United States are also entitled to equal protection under the law.[27] Furthermore, these investors are not subject to exchange controls, are free to convert the U.S. dollar into other currencies, may have a 100 percent interest in U.S. firms and are not compelled to participate jointly with domestic investors or government agencies, and may freely remit profits, dividends, and interest which accrue from their investments in the United States.[28]

At the state level, the principle of comity is usually observed vis-à-vis foreign investment. In effect, state government regulations treat foreign firms in the same fashion as companies organized in other parts of the Union. Once admitted to the state, the foreign-based firms are regarded as having the same rights and duties as any other company doing business within that state.

Recent government activities Because of rising public concern associated with the rapid upsurge in foreign investment, the U.S. Congress passed the Foreign Direct Investment Act in 1974. This document authorized a thorough study of most facets of foreign investment in the United States to determine whether the overseas-originated activity should be subject to greater regulation on the part of federal authorities. Two years later, the International Investment Survey Act was passed on Capitol Hill. This act stipulated that studies on foreign direct and foreign portfolio investment in the United States, as well as U.S. investment abroad, should be made at least every five years and that confidential data on such investment should be gathered on an even more regular basis. These surveys are currently being completed by several executive agencies, although nonresident investors have not been required by law to furnish information requested by these agencies.[29]

Sandwiched between these two congressional acts was the Ford administration's 1975 Executive Order establishing the Committee on Foreign Investment in the United States. Theoretically, this executive branch committee is empowered to monitor foreign investment activity and may even consult in advance with foreign governments concerning certain proposed investments. Quite frankly, this committee has only convened on a very sporadic basis and has had few consultations with governments in other nations.

In the summer of 1978, Congress moved somewhat more assertively into the real estate investment sphere by requiring foreign investors to disclose their purchases of land to government agencies. Prompted by outcries protesting the rapid increase in farmland transactions involving foreign nationals, the law itself does not interfere with the investment activity per se. However, because of the stiff disclosure regulations, the new law may dampen the enthusiasm shown by publicity-shy foreigners to buy into the huge U.S. agricultural property market.

If negative public reaction continues to intensify as a result of the noticeable escalation in foreign activity within the American marketplace, the 1978 disclosure law may well be a precursor of more stringent regulatory action on the part of the U.S. government. Already bills have been introduced on Capitol Hill which would severely restrict or prohibit altogether certain types of foreign investment in the United States. One such piece of legislation, the Dent-Gaydos Bill, would flatly prohibit foreign direct investment in excess of 5 percent of the voting stock of any publicly traded corporation. Another bill would ban nonresident aliens from acquiring U.S. farmland. Yet, in spite of these restrictive measures which have been introduced on the Hill, it is highly unlikely that Congress would act too drastically because of the fear of foreign government retaliation against U.S. investment abroad.

Restricted investment spheres   Certain segments of the American economy are restricted or are totally off-limits to foreign investors, although many loopholes do exist which permit foreigners to have at least an indirect interest in many of these economic sectors. The restrictions that do currently exist are rationalized by the U.S. government in the following manner:

> The applicable restrictions on foreign investment in the U.S. relate to certain categories of enterprises which are considered sensitive either: (1) because of a close relationship with national defense; (2) because they involve the exploitation of certain natural resources, wherein there has historically been some degree of alien disability; or (3) because they play a peculiarly fiduciary role.[30]

Antitrust regulations   Along with the usual staffing, labor, and financing problems commonly associated with the establishment of facilities in a foreign nation, overseas investors have been particularly perplexed by U.S. antitrust laws. In fact, a recent survey of European executives who had coordinated new projects in the United States indicated that several had to alter their original investment plans because of what they considered to be uncertainties associated with the U.S. antitrust labyrinth.[31]

In effect, the U.S. antitrust regulations have few parallels in other advanced industrial societies and are thus viewed with a mixture of anxiety and suspicion by investors from abroad. This foreign investor perplexity is compounded by the fact that U.S. authorities have tried at times in the past to give American antitrust provisions an extraterritorial dimension. As Professor Charles Kindleberger has noted, U.S. law has periodically assumed that "both U.S. companies abroad and foreign companies in the U.S. direct the operations of their subsidiaries in ways that conform to U.S. purposes."[32] In 1955, for example, the U.S. Department of Justice attempted to interfere with the long-established trade practices of the Swiss watchmaking industry on the basis that some of the watches were being sold in the United States and thus watchmaking trade practices in general were subject to U.S. antitrust regulations. The Swiss government eventually interceded in the case and was able to bring about a termination of the Justice Department's planned assault on the watchmakers of that Alpine nation.[33] As a consequence of this and other related incidents, foreign investors who penetrate the American market have at times feared that the U.S. government might attempt to use antitrust provisions in order to regulate some of their activities in other countries. On the other hand, most of the investors latch on quite early to competent American lawyers steeped in antitrust rules and regulations, and some of the initial foreign trepidation toward the U.S. antitrust syndrome has now dissipated.

Transportation   Nonresident aliens are currently excluded from engaging in coastal or inland water shipping activities. The Merchant Marine Act of 1920 stipulates that all freight and passengers transported between points in the United States or its territories must involve vessels built and registered in the United States and owned by American citizens. In order to register a ship for such activity, all of the principal officers of the company must be Americans and 75 percent of the company's voting stock must be domestically controlled.[34]

U.S. laws do permit aliens to have a controlling interest in domestic corporations operating fishing boats and international shipping lines, but foreign nationals are not entitled to construction and operating subsidies which are available to U.S. citizens and U.S.-controlled firms. Furthermore, Section 37 of the Shipping Act requires prior approval by the Secretary of Commerce for most forms of alien investment in the U.S. ship construction and repair industry.

In the domain of air transportation, the Federal Aviation Act of 1958 limits the registration of commercial aircraft to individual American citizens, partnerships in which all of the participating parties are citizens, and domestic corporations in which a minimum of 75 percent of the voting shares is in citizens' hands and the president and two-thirds of the board of directors are U.S. citizens. In other words, aliens may own up to 25 percent of U.S.-chartered corporations controlling airline-related firms. For example, even though plans were eventually scuttled, the Shah of Iran did enter into preliminary negotiations in 1974 to purchase 13 percent of the shares of Pan American Airlines. Yet even if this transaction had proceeded beyond the initial stages, the Civil Aeronautics Board (CAB) would have first had to sanction the deal, for it must approve any domestic or foreign company's efforts to acquire more than a 5 percent interest in a domestic air carrier. Furthermore, the CAB must first grant permission before any foreign individuals or firms can acquire any phase of the aeronautics industry, including aircraft manufacturing, servicing, or refueling.

A combination of national and state laws also makes it extremely difficult for foreign firms to penetrate the railway industry. Thus, in overall perspective, foreign investors are fairly well restricted in the acquisition of a direct and controlling interest in many sectors of the U.S. transportation industry. On the other hand, some foreign involvement in most transportation spheres is tolerated under current U.S. federal and state regulations.

Communications The Radio Act of 1927 prohibits foreign-owned or -controlled businesses from operating "an instrument for communications" in the United States. The Federal Communications Act of 1934 amplifies upon this earlier legislation by forbidding alien nationals from owning radio stations or holding operator licenses. Foreigners may own up to 25 percent of U.S.-chartered corporations in most spheres of the communication's industry, with only 20 percent allowed in the telegraph and communication satellite sectors. Moreover, the Federal Communications Commission has an overseer role over the communication's industry in general and is charged with the responsibility of protecting the interests of the American public.

The development of natural resources In accordance with the Federal Power Act of 1920, the development of hydroelectric power facilities on navigable streams is open only to U.S. citizens, associations of U.S. citizens, and domestically organized corporations. Conversely, associations composed in whole or in part of aliens, corporations formed in other nations, and foreign governments are prohibited from participating in the development of the U.S. hydroelectric facilities. A major loophole does exist, however, because there is no limitation on the percentage of foreign ownership of corporations registered in the United States. As a result, foreign investors may purchase shares in a domestic corporation and thus have an impact on developments in the hydroelectric field.

The provisions of the Geothermal Steam Act of 1970 closely parallel those in the hydroelectric sector in that the exploitation of this resource is theoretically limited to U.S. citizens and corporations, but alien investment is once again permitted in domestically organized corporations.

The Mining Law of 1872 stipulates that U.S. citizens and aliens who have declared their intention to become citizens may acquire federal land having valuable mineral deposits. However, loopholes do exist and foreign nationals are permitted to obtain leases on federal land if (1) the exploitation is open to U.S. citizens and corporations and (2) the alien's home country permits U.S. nationals situated in that country to exploit the same resources. The United States has reciprocal agreements in this sphere with most other advanced industrial nations and, consequently, foreign firms are granted the opportunity to exploit America's valuable coal, oil, gas, and other natural resource reserves. In addition, the leasing or transfer of federal lands in general is open to citizens of foreign nations which have reciprocal agreements with the United States.[35]

For evident reasons, the most serious restrictions on foreign investors in the natural resources area are in the domain of atomic energy. Aliens, foreign corporations, foreign governments, and corporations dominated by foreign interests are expressly precluded by the Atomic Energy Act from obtaining licenses to operate facilities for the utilization or the production of atomic energy. Any foreign investments in domestic corporations which are currently engaged in such activities are closely monitored by federal authorities and the continued involvement of these corporations within the atomic energy sphere is decided by the federal government on a case-by-case basis.

Banking, insurance, and securities   Federal laws generally lump the commercial operations of foreign-owned banks into the same category as domestic-controlled banking operations. However, the local bank chartering provisions found in many state laws have precluded alien control of deposit banks in many states. To be more precise, the direct entry of alien banks into retail banking activities is prohibited in approximately three-quarters of the American states. In addition, a 1978 bill enacted by the U.S. Congress has tightened up some of the options available to foreign-owned firms which are currently operating or are considering operating banks in the United States (see Chapter Five for a closer examination of this new law and its probable effects on foreign banking activity in the United States).

Foreign-controlled insurance companies are also closely regulated by the state governments and special mandatory deposit requirements are often placed on the foreign firms. Frequently, trustee deposits must be established by these insurance companies in an amount equal to their outstanding liabilities. The rationale for these special restrictions is to guarantee that these firms will have enough money available within the state to fulfill their short- and long-range commitments to the citizens of that state.

In the securities' field, the Securities and Exchange Commission (SEC) requires full disclosure of the "character" of securities sold publicly in the United States in order to dissuade any fraudulent activity. Foreign corporate issues are generally treated in the same manner as domestic issues, but the foreign entities are not usually accustomed to such a comprehensive disclosure policy in their own home countries and have at times been hesitant to venture into the U.S. stock market because of the SEC regulations. On the other hand, a 1964 amendment to the Securities Exchange Act of 1934 does permit the SEC to grant certain special exemptions to the issuers of foreign securities if such exemptions are clearly in the interest of the American public and are consistent with the protection of U.S. investors.

National defense stipulations Foreign-owned companies may generally conduct business with the U.S. government on the same basis as domestic companies. However, these foreign-controlled firms must comply with the provisions of the Buy American Act of 1970 which stipulate that the federal government may purchase only items which have at least a 50 percent U.S. product content.

Alien-owned firms are not prohibited from attempting to secure contracts for defense-related work, but they are usually precluded from winning the contract because they cannot receive the necessary security clearances enunciated in the Armed Services Procurement Act of 1947 and the Federal Property and Administrative Act of 1949. Moreover, foreign investors are not barred from buying into companies that are already performing contract work for the Defense Department, but they do run the risk of having these contracts cancelled as a result of the foreign takeover.

To a limited extent, foreign investors can comply with the security restrictions by making sure that all of the major officers of the company in which they have invested are American citizens. However, such activity is once again monitored on a case-by-case basis and assertions that national defense may be jeopardized by allowing foreign access to defense contracts seem to be overly exaggerated.[36] Although action should perhaps be taken to strengthen even further precautionary measures, the U.S. Defense Industrial Security Program has generally functioned satisfactorily in protecting classified information and materials, in enhancing the U.S. defense industry capability, and in safeguarding the principle that U.S. defense policies should be free from foreign influence. This Department of Defense-administered program scrutinizes all foreign-controlled or foreign-influenced firms which seek to do classified contract work for the U.S. government. If the foreign connection is judged to be potentially dangerous to U.S. interests, then security clearance for the firm will simply be denied and the contract work assigned elsewhere.

The tax dimension   The Foreign Investors Tax Act was passed by the Congress in 1966 to ensure that foreign investors would be duly taxed on income derived from their operations in the United States, but not in a manner or to an extent that such investment from abroad would be discouraged. Moreover, the laws of most states stipulate that foreign firms located within the state will have to pay taxes only on the income earned within the state's boundaries. Thus, whereas domestic companies may be taxed on their total income derived from almost all sources, whether at home or abroad, foreign conglomerates are usually taxed only on the income they gain from their U.S. subsidiaries.

For the most part, foreign direct investment in the United States is subject to the same tax provisions imposed on domestic investment. Foreign investors may be subject to a special withholding tax, but even this tax may be reduced or eliminated altogether, depending on the tax treaties which the United States has with more than 25 other nations. Foreign investors from various parts of the world may also channel their funds through the Netherlands Antilles, the Bahamas, or certain other tax havens which offer advantageous tax provisions for the penetration of the U.S. marketplace.

The 1974 Commerce study looked very closely at the tax provisions pertaining to foreign investment and concluded that the United States has no need for additional special regulations which would either attract or deter future investment from abroad. The report asserted that:

> An advantage to foreign investments in the U.S. would be unfair and intolerable to domestic investors, and a disadvantage to foreign investments is difficult to reconcile with principles of nondiscrimination, policies favoring the free flow of capital, and the needs of the U.S. for additional capital.[37]

Despite the fact that American tax provisions are highly complex because of the existence of separate national, state, and even local tax regulations, the foreign investors hire competent U.S. tax attorneys and are generally in agreement that the American tax system is quite fair to investors from abroad.[38] In fact, significant loopholes currently exist which permit many foreign nationals to avoid paying U.S. capital gains taxes, providing them with a major advantage over their American competitors. This capital gains dimension will be discussed in a later section.

Foreign investment restrictions in perspective In spite of the literal potpourri of restrictions which have just been highlighted, equality of treatment definitely continues to characterize federal and state government policies toward foreign investment in most spheres of economic activity. Some of the restrictions which do exist date from the 1920s, and even the official Department of Commerce study on foreign investment admits that some of these provisions may well be anachronistic and are terminologically vague. As the Commerce report concludes:

> If present restraints are retained, clarification of the legislative intent underlying them and the circumstances under which aliens may and may not invest is minimally in order.[39]

The study also asserts that:

> Although restraints in defense and energy resources seem called for by current United States interests, in contrast, certain other industries can be identified as areas where the variables suggest that restraints, at least in their present form, may be outdated. Present restraints in the transportation industry constitute barriers to competition and capital markets in an industry which has been described as lacking in competition and capital intensive. The military significance of aviation and the maritime industries may call for some separation of aliens from the objects of investment; for example, the planes and seacraft, in the case of war, but restraints on alien investment may be unnecessary to accomplish that separation. Restraints on investment in the manufacture of those objects, however, may continue to be justified for reasons explored in the Defense Industry Section of this report. Presidential power to take over facilities in other industries—for example, power and common carrier communications—may obviate the necessity for restraints on alien investment in those industries.[40]

In effect, official U.S. government sources assert that current restrictions on foreign direct investment are adequate and some of the regulatory provisions now on the books could easily be scrapped without doing any significant damage to American economic interests.

Enticing Foreign Investors—The Invest in U.S.A. Program

Not only has the government's regulation of foreign investment in the United States been rather lax, but U.S. authorities have even gone out of their way to entice foreign money to America's shores. If one were to visit the main Department of Commerce building in Washington, D.C., he would discover that it is a large edifice situated just a few blocks from the White House. Visitors to the building are required to sign in at a desk in the main lobby and are then given detailed instructions on how to reach the office which they are seeking. These instructions are vital because once beyond the main floor, the visitor is confronted with a veritable maze of corridors which, if placed in miniature, would drive even the most intelligent of mice berserk. After trekking along a few of these corridors which measure several football fields in length, the mouse's human counterpart might be fortunate enough to stumble upon Room 4020, the rather tacky headquarters for the Invest in U.S.A. program. Throughout the 1960s and the early 1970s, the Invest in U.S.A. project sponsored seminars in Europe, Asia, and Canada for the purpose of informing foreign nationals about investment opportunities in the United States. In the early 1960s, a branch office for the program was opened in Paris and during the Nixon years, slick brochures were produced in several languages bearing the title: "Investment in the United States: An Invitation from the President of the United States."

The Invest in U.S.A. program has undoubtedly helped to facilitate the entry of several billion dollars of foreign capital into the American marketplace. In particular, state agencies have often extolled the program for facilitating state-level opportunities to attract foreign firms. Jack Cawthorne, the executive director of the National Association of State Development Agencies (NASDA), has offered the following opinion concerning Invest in U.S.A.'s special rapport with state governments:

> The states have had fantastic results working with Invest in U.S.A. This is the logical place to pinpoint regions of the U.S. where a foreign company may invest. Then the states can move in and do their own selling job.
>
> I'll give you a good example. Recently a Canadian firm came to us about putting a plant in the United States, but said it didn't want to deal individually with each of the 50 states. We suggested the firm go to Commerce and talk with Invest in U.S.A.
>
> We have had a continuous dialogue with this office, and it provides a service that is vitally needed by the states.[41]

In spite of this praise emanating from state development officials, the Ford administration seemed to have a different opinion about the value of Invest in U.S.A. and decided not to seek funding from the Congress for the renewal of the program. An official executive branch report released at the beginning of 1977 made the following points:

> The fundamental policy of the U.S. government toward international investment is neither to promote nor discourage inward or outward investment flows or activities.
>
> This policy is consistent with and reaffirms our long-standing commitment

to a generally open international economic system. The government, therefore, should normally avoid measures which would give special incentives or disincentives to investment flows or activities and should not normally intervene in the activities of individual companies regarding international movement.[42]

At the time of the publication of this book, the Invest in U.S.A. program was still in a state of limbo and its staff had been pared down to the skeletal level of three officers. The program is still hoping for renewed funding, and President Carter has traditionally been an active supporter of most types of foreign investment activity. As Governor of Georgia, he personally led several delegations abroad in the search for foreign manufacturers who would be willing to set up facilities in his home state. In a letter to the annual meeting of NASDA officials, President Carter also stressed that "investment from other countries continues to benefit the United States."[43] Perhaps in anticipation of a renewal of support from the White House, Invest in U.S.A. officials joined with other Commerce personnel to sponsor direct investment seminars in Osaka and Tokyo during the first two weeks of October 1978.[44] This seminar was the first overseas endeavor for the program in more than two years.

Even with the skeletal staff, Invest in U.S.A. continues to handle an average of 50 telephone calls a day and greets numerous delegations from abroad.[45] The program places interested foreign investors in touch with pertinent representatives at the state and local levels and provides advice on visa regulations and on other related matters which foreign firms will encounter in establishing facilities in the United States.[46] In effect, Invest in U.S.A. stands out as the prime symbol of the benevolent open door policy which has for so many years characterized official U.S. reaction to foreign investment activity. Moreover, even with its scanty resources, Invest in U.S.A. has served as an important catalytic force in the ultimate decision made by scores of foreign firms to set up facilities in the United States.

Beyond the Open Door

On the whole, foreign investors believe that they have been given a fair shake by national, state, and local government units and are particularly impressed by the comparative lack of red tape involved in entering the U.S. marketplace. As a French investor explained in a Conference Board interview:

> We were impressed by the lack of government regulations regarding investment in the United States. If we had made a similar investment, even in France, we would have had to get approval from the Ministry of Finance and the 'Ministry of this and the other.' In the United States, we had no dealings whatsoever with government agencies.[47]

In fact, none of the 40 foreign executives interviewed by the Conference Board felt that the regulations governing the entry and operation of businesses in the United States were discriminatory.[48] These views seem to echo the sentiments of the foreign investment community as a whole. Consequently, the government regulations which do exist in the domain of foreign investment are not a major deterrent to most types of investment activity and generally sustain the image that Washington continues to keep the welcome mat out for investment from abroad.[49] In an era when many regions of the world are rocked by deep-seated cleavages and major upheavals, the United States has become increasingly attractive as a safe and fertile haven for foreign investment money. When this phenomenon is combined with the government's open door emphasis, it becomes apparent that the overseas investment money which has poured into the United States during the last decade represents only a trickle and that, potentially, America faces in the next few years a financial deluge of unprecedented proportions.

FOUR

The Beetle Has Landed in Pennsylvania: The Impact of Foreign Investment on America's Business and Industrial Communities

America "Going Cheap"?

In what undoubtedly ranks as the most publicized foreign investment deal of 1976, Volkswagen announced from its Wolfsburg, West Germany, headquarters that it would construct a 300 million dollar assembly plant in New Stanton, Pennsylvania, which would provide as many as 4,500 new jobs by the end of 1978. This transaction consummated by Volkswagen was one of more than 200 announced foreign investments in the U.S. manufacturing sphere in 1976.[1] The number climbed to 274 in 1977, representing an all-time annual record, and during the five-year period ending with the third quarter of 1978, foreign investors had purchased interests in 1,114 American companies.[2]

In an editorial entitled "American Going Cheap," the London-based *Economist* magazine urged foreign central banks, whose vaults were overflowing with American greenbacks, to spearhead greater investment in the United States, particularly in the manufacturing field. The editorial bluntly stated that "American industrial corporations are on offer this Christmas at clearance sale prices."[3]

As discussed in the previous chapter, many foreign executives agree that the U.S. industrial milieu currently offers attractive investment opportunities because of steady productivity growth, increasingly more favorable labor costs, greater investment security, more secure sources of raw materials, fewer labor problems and fewer worker holidays, and less government interference in the economy in general. Energy costs have also increased more rapidly in Western Europe and Japan than in the United States. In addition, U.S. Orderly Trade Agreements (which are synonymous with the concept of "import quotas") and U.S. tariff policies have convinced many foreign executives of the wisdom of establishing facilities within the American market as an alternative to the growing uncertainty associated with exporting products to the United States.

The manufacturing sector has clearly attracted the largest chunk of foreign direct investment over the years and more than half of the transactions have been in the form of acquisitions of existing companies rather than the establishment of new subsidiaries (see Table 4-1).[4] These investments are certainly attributable in part to the recent fragility of the dollar and the periodic softness of the stock market. Yet, perhaps an even more persuasive motivating force is the desire of these foreign manufacturing firms to acquire existing technological, marketing, and administrative expertise in the United States.[5]

As Table 4-2 aptly illustrates, European, Canadian, and Japanese companies dominate foreign investment in U.S. manufacturing. German investors have been especially active in the past few years, spurred on by the strength of the German mark vis-à-vis the dollar and the fact that German labor costs in early 1978 were already 6 percent higher than comparable U.S. costs.[6] For the first time in many years, German direct invest-

TABLE 4-1 Value of Foreign Direct Investment in the United States by Industry, 1937—1977, $ millions

Year	Manufacturing	Petroleum	Insurance	Other*	Total
1937	729	283	412	458	1,882
1941	741	222	521	855	2,312
1950	1,138	405	1,065	783	3,391
1955	1,759	853	1,499	965	5,076
1960	2,611	1,238	1,810	1,251	6,910
1965	3,478	1,710	2,169	1,440	8,797
1970	6,140	2,992	2,256	1,882	13,270
1973	8,559	3,768	2,854	2,222	17,403
1974	10,387	5,614	2,723	6,420	25,144
1975	11,386	6,213	3,152	6,911	27,662
1976	12,550	5,901	3,722	8,009	30,182
1977	13,706	6,566	4,429	9,370	34,071

*Includes industries such as mining and smelting, transportation and utilities, trade, and miscellaneous industries which have been subsumed within the three main categories.

SOURCES: *Historical Statistics of the United States: Colonial Times to 1970,* and U.S. Department of Commerce annual statistics.

ment in the United States in 1976 surpassed U.S. investment in Germany, and in 1977 Germans invested 826 million dollars in the United States as compared to the 265 million dollars invested by Americans in Germany. In all, approximately one-fifth of recent investment in the American manufacturing sphere has emanated from German sources. Some of the recent deals have included Bayer AG's acquisition of Cutter Laboratories and Miles Laboratories, the makers of Alka-Seltzer, Hoechst AG's takeover of Foster Grant, the largest U.S. manufacturer of sunglasses, Bertelsmann's purchase of Bantam Books, and Siemens' absorption of Litronix and Micro Devices, two electronics firms.

Investors from the British Isles have also consummated a large number of deals in the manufacturing and commercial fields. British-American Tobacco has purchased Kohl Corporation, a large Midwest food, drug, and department store chain, and the tobacco conglomerate has also acquired ownership of the trendy Gimbels and Saks Fifth Avenue stores. A fellow United Kingdom company, Cavenham, has purchased a 51 percent share of the Grand Union supermarket chain, and J. Lyons, a restaurant firm, has latched on to an 83 percent chunk of the Baskin-Robbins ice cream parlors.

Table 4-3 gives a sampling of just a few of the thousands of firms from many countries of the world which have recently invested in the American

TABLE 4-2   National Origins of 2,053
Foreign-Owned Manufacturing Plants
Listed by the Department of Commerce,
1974

Nation	Number of plants
Canada	457
United Kingdom	358
Germany	282
Japan	199*
France	170
Netherlands	158
Switzerland	150
Sweden	47
Binational	65
Unknown	15
Others	152

*May be understated because data were not obtainable from California, where significant Japanese investment is known to exist.
SOURCES: U.S. Department of Commerce, *Foreign Direct Investment in the United States,* 1976, and the Conference Board.

TABLE 4-3 A Sampling of Foreign Firms Involved in the American Manufacturing Sector

Country of origin	Foreign firm	U.S. affiliate	State location	Product line
Australia	Kiwi Polish	Kiwi Polish	Pa.	Shoe polish
	Mainline	Honolulu Iron Works	Hawaii	Metal fabrication
Austria	Koreska, W.	Kores Manufacturing	N.Y.	Carbon paper, ink
	Plasser Railway Machinery	Plasser American	Va.	Railroad equipment
Bangladesh	Jolil	Georgia Synthetics	Ga.	Carpet backing
Belgium	Agfa Gevaert	Agfa Gevaert	N.J.	Photo supplies
	Sidal-Société de l'Aluminium	Sidal Aluminum	Md., Wis.	Aluminum processing
Canada	Alcan Aluminum	Alcan Aluminum	Several	Aluminum fabrication
	Crush International	Crush International	N.J.	Soft drinks
	Distillers Corp. Seagrams Ltd.	Joseph E. Seagram & Sons	Several	Whiskies, wines, liqueurs
	Grampion Marine	Grampion Marine	N.C.	Sailboats
	Massey-Ferguson	Massey-Ferguson	Iowa, Mich., Ohio	Farm tractors
	Moore Corp.	Moore Business Forms	N.Y., Wis.	Business forms
	Northern Electric	Northern Telecom	Fla., Mass., Mich.	Telephone equipment
	Thomson Newspapers	Thomson Newspapers	Ohio	Publisher
	Walker (Hiram) & Sons	Hiram Walker & Sons	Calif., Ill., Mich.	Distillers
	Weston (George) Ltd.	Loblaw Inc.	N.Y.	Food products
Chile	Baterias Metropolitanas	International Battery	P.R.	Batteries
Denmark	DAK Meat Packers	DAK Foods	N.J.	Canned meat
	Royal System	Royal System	N.Y.	Furniture

TABLE 4-3 A Sampling of Foreign Firms Involved in the American Manufacturing Sector *(Continued)*

Country of origin	Foreign firm	U.S. affiliate	State location	Product line
Finland	Valmet Oy	Savage Arms	Miss.	Shotguns
	Oy Visko	Hormel-Visko	Wis.	Food products
France	Air Liquide	Liquid Air	Ga., S.C.	Industrial gas, welding equipment
	Bic	BIC Pen	Conn.	Pens
	Compagnie Industrielle des Télécommunications	Intercontinental Electronics	N.Y.	Transformers
	Comptoir de l'Industrie Textile de France	Christian Dior-New York	N.Y.	Clothing
	Guerlain	Guerlain	N.Y.	Clothing
	Michelin	Michelin Tire	Ala., S.C.	Tires
	Rossignol	Rossignol Ski	Vt.	Skis
	Saint-Gobain-Pont-à-Mousson	Certain-Teed Prod.	Pa.	Building materials
	Société Imetal	Copperweld	Ohio, Pa.	Metals, wire
	Source Perrier	Poland Spring Bottling	Mass.	Mineral water
Germany, Federal Republic of	AEG-Telefunken	AEG-Telefunken	N.J.	Electronic items
	Agfa-Gevaert	Agfa-Gevaert	N.J.	Photo supplies
	BASF	Dow-Gadische	Ala., N.C., Va.	Chemicals
	Bayer	Cutter Laboratories	Calif.	Pharmaceuticals
	Robert Bosch GMbH	Robert Bosch	Ill.	Automotive equipment
	Henkel	Henkel	N.J.	Chemicals
	Hoechst	American Hoechst	Several	Chemicals, dyes, plastics, and synthetic fibers
	Kraftwerkunion	Allis-Chalmers Power Systems	Wis.	Thermal electric power generating equipment
	Siemens	Siemens Components Group	Ariz.	Computer parts
	Volkswagenwerke	Volkswagen Products	Pa., Tex.	Auto accessories

Country	Parent Company	U.S. Company	State	Product
Greece	Petzetakix	Cosmoflex	Mo.	PVC hose
Hong Kong	Reynard Sportswear	Don Sophisticates	N.Y.	Clothing
Iran	Pahlavi Foundation	Union Carbide Caribe	P.R.	Petrochemical
Italy	Fiat	Fiat-Allis	Ill., Wis.	Earthmoving equipment
	Ing. C. Olivetti & Co.	Olivetti Corp. of America	Pa.	Office machines
	Liquigas	Ronson	Ca., N.J.	Lighters, appliances
Japan	Hitachi Metals	Hitachi America	Ga.	Communications equipment
	Matsushita Denki Sangyo	Matsushita Electric (Panasonic)	Mass.	TV receivers
	Mitsubishi Shoji	Centrecon Inc.	Wash.	Concrete
	Sony	Sony	Calif.	TV receivers
	Teac	Teac	Calif.	Recorders
	Toyota Jidosha Hambai	Toyota USA	Calif.	Truck assembly
Mexico	Fertilizantes Fostados Mexicanos	USAMEX Fertilizer	La.	Fertilizer
Netherlands	Akzo	American Enka	N.C.	Synthetic fibers
	Philips	Alliance Manufacturing	Several	Motors
	Royal Dutch Petroleum	Shell Oil	Tex.	Petroleum
	Unilever Org.	Thomas J. Lipton	N.J.	Tea, soup mixes
		Kind & Knox Gelatine	Iowa	Gelatine
		Good Humor	N.J.	Ice cream
Norway	Jac Jacobson	Luxo Lamp	Calif., N.Y.	Lamps
Saudi Arabia	Pyah	Pyah Industries	N.J.	Plastic houseware
South Africa	Anglo American Corp. of South Africa	Terra Chemicals International	Iowa	Fertilizer
Spain	Piher	Piher Corporation	Miss.	Electronics
Sweden	Electrolux	National Union Electric	Conn.	Vacuum cleaners
	Svenska Kullager-fabriken	SKF Industries	N.C., Pa.	Ball and roller bearings

TABLE 4-3 A Sampling of Foreign Firms Involved in the American Manufacturing Sector *(Continued)*

Country of origin	Foreign firm	U.S. affiliate	State location	Product line
Switzerland	Ciba-Geigy	Fiberite	Calif., Minn., Pa.	Molding compounds
	Nestlé Alimentana	Nestlé	N.Y.	Food products
	Sandoz	Sandoz-Wander	Ill., Neb., N.J.	Chemicals, dyes
Taiwan	Taiwan Glass	Pacific Tempered Glass	Oreg.	Glass
United Kingdom	British-American Tobacco	Brown & Williamson Tobacco	Ky.	Tobacco products
	British Oxygen	Yardley of London	N.J.	Perfumes, soaps
		Airco	N.J.	Industrial gases
	Coats Patons	Coats & Clark	N.Y.	Yarn
	Dunlop Holdings	Dunlop Tire & Rubber	Several	Tires, tubes
	EMI	Capitol Industries-EMI	Calif.	Recording
		Capitol Records	Conn.	Recording
	ICI	Atlas Chemical Industries	Del.	Chemicals
	Imperial Tobacco	Imperial Tobacco	N.C.	Tobacco
	J. Lyons & Co.	J. Lyons & Co.	N.Y.	Foods
	S. Pearson & Son	Penguin Books	Md.	Publisher
	United Biscuits	Keebler	N.Y.	Bakery
	Wilkinson Match	Wilkinson Sword	N.J.	Razor blades, razors
	Yardley & Co.	Yardley of London	N.J.	Perfumes, soaps
Yugoslavia	Slovenijales	S.K. Products	Ga.	Furniture

SOURCE: U.S. Department of Commerce, *Foreign Direct Investors in the United States*, March 1976.

manufacturing and commercial spheres. This foreign investment onslaught is expected to continue unabated, particularly in the petroleum, chemical, food and beverage, primary and fabricated metal, electrical and nonelectrical machinery, and lumber and paper industries.[7] As a possible harbinger of things to come, Bayer announced in 1977 that it would invest as much as 500 million dollars in the United States over a five-year period.[8] Although far less precise in terms of money estimates, many other foreign companies have also stated their firm intentions to increase their investment activities in the American manufacturing sphere.

Investment on a Sectoral Basis

Chemicals In the five-year period beginning in 1973, investment in existing U.S. chemical firms by foreign-owned companies increased by more than 50 percent. In 1977 alone, foreign investors doled out more than 1 billion dollars for chemical-related mergers in the United States.[9] Of the 274 foreign investments in the entire manufacturing sphere in 1977, 59 were in the chemical industry, the highest of any industrial sector. Once again, this accelerating investment trend is expected to continue as some of the foreign giants have already announced their mid-range ambitions in the U.S. market. Bayer insists that it will increase its U.S. sales to more than 1 billion dollars by 1980.[10] The Japanese-owned firm Shintech, a major producer of polyvinyl chloride, has also pledged to boost its sales within the U.S. domestic market from 100 million dollars to 500 million dollars in just seven years.[11] Obviously, much more direct investment in the United States will be necessary in order for these companies to reach their projected goals.

Some of the most noteworthy deals in the chemical sector include Bayer's acquisition of 97 percent of Miles Laboratories for 47 dollars a share, a transaction which cost the German conglomerate 54 million dollars. Henkel, a German detergent maker which manufactures the popular Persil laundry soap for the European market, bought out General Mills' chemical operations. Unilever, the Dutch-British giant which has consummated deals in a wide variety of sectors, plunked down 482 million dollars to acquire National Starch and Chemical. Perhaps somewhat surprisingly at first glance, the Swiss-based Nestlé Company, which has long been renowned for its chocolates, but which also owns Stouffer Foods, Libby, and Crosse & Blackwell, continued its diversification campaign by offering 276 million dollars for Alcon Laboratories, a pharmaceutical manufacturer. Nestlé and Unilever are the two largest food manufacturers in the world, and Nestlé employs 137,000 people in 50 countries spanning the globe. The Swiss firm already pockets 2 billion dollars in annual sales in the United States alone and with the acquisition of Alcon, the conglomerate is seeking a slice of the action in the American chemical sector. ELF Aquitaine, the large French company, has also begun to make inroads in the American market through the purchase of American Can's M & T Chemicals facilities.[12]

As discussed earlier, conditions both within the United States and within the advanced industrial world are conducive for a further escalation in foreign investment in the U.S. chemical industry. Fears of protectionism, coupled with the growing insistence by U.S. buyers that they have a more secure access to foreign-made chemical products than the overseas shipping process now affords, will undoubtedly provide additional impetus for foreign penetration of the U.S. market. Moreover, the prime investors in the chemical sphere are the giant multinationals which have already had significant trade experience in the United States and are thus well aware of the idiosyncrasies and special marketing conditions prevalent in the United States. The names of Bayer, Unilever, and Nestlé certainly bear out this point. Although these foreign-controlled firms have accounted for a relatively small percentage of the sales in the very diversified U.S. chemical industry, their impact on this field has grown steadily over the past five years. In certain sectors of the chemical industry, such as pharmaceuticals, foreign firms already account for up to 25 percent of the total sales in the U.S. domestic market.[13]

Electronics As an executive from Siemens, the world's fifth largest electronics firm, has aptly stated, the U.S. represents the "Mecca of world electronics" and more and more foreign firms are expected to make the pilgrimage in quest of a larger piece of the American pie.[14] Overall, the United States accounts for more than one-quarter of the world's 400 billion dollar annual turnover in electronic equipment.[15] Even though it ranks fifth in size in the world, the Munich-based Siemens firm currently controls less than 0.5 percent of the vast and lucrative U.S. market. However, Siemens has moved aggressively in recent months to rectify this situation. In July 1977 the German conglomerate finalized a deal with Allis-Chalmers which provides the Munich-based firm with a 20 percent interest in the Allis-Chalmers Electrical Products Group. Siemens paid 19 million dollars for this one-fifth share, and at the end of 1978 had the option of picking up another 30 percent of the company. This joint venture has recently resulted in the construction of a large electronics factory in Florida.

In the search for additional technological inroads, Siemens later acquired a 17 percent interest in Advanced Micro Devices, a Sunnyvale, California, semiconductor firm. Siemens has also agreed to enter into a joint venture with this firm to produce and to distribute microprocessors. Siemens continued to look for investment opportunities in the Bay Area and soon after announced the purchase of 80 percent of the shares of the Litronix company, a firm involved extensively in optoelectronics.[16] Siemens' American beachhead was expanded even further when an agreement was signed between the Munich company and Corning Glass to produce "Siecor" optical cables. Siemens now has operations in several American states and all indications point to further activities by the German giant in the U.S. electronics field.

The Japanese have also been very active in this sector, as manifested by heavy Japanese investment in the "Silicon Valley" along the San Francisco peninsula. Nippon Electric Company, the world's third largest independent semiconductor maker, agreed recently to buy Electronic Arrays of Mountain View, California. A few hundred miles down the California coast, Sanyo announced its intentions to build an electronics plant in the San Diego region. Halfway across the continent, Toshiba unveiled plans for a similar plant in the Nashville region and Matsushita Electric Industrial Company acquired the ailing Motorola television manufacturing division in Illinois. Matsushita shelled out 108 million dollars for this acquisition back in 1974 and has funneled millions more into the renovation of the Illinois-based plant. Matsushita's ultimate objective is to make the televisions and other electronic equipment produced at the American facility competitive with the products manufactured by fellow Japanese firms such as Sony and Panasonic. Under the new name of Quasar Electronics, Matsushita's Illinois company has now apparently turned the corner and is beginning to show a profit.[17] Meanwhile, the other major Japanese electronics firms have either constructed new plants on American soil or have such plans on the drawing board. Sony, for example, currently supplies two-thirds of the American demand for its televisions from its San Diego manufacturing facility. Another Japanese firm, Sharp, will build its first U.S. plant near Memphis in order to produce color televisions and microwave ovens. One of Sharp's and Sony's major Japanese competitors, Hitachi, has agreed to coproduce color TV sets with General Electric at GE's huge Syracuse, New York, and Portsmouth, Virginia, facilities. However, the Justice Department has at least temporarily put a halt to the Hitachi-GE project, claiming that Clayton Antitrust Act provisions have been violated.

Senator Gaylord Nelson, Chairman of the Senate Select Committee on Small Business, has publicly expressed fears that the United States may be "losing the cream of its new technology" because small, high technology companies are finding it extremely difficult to raise venture capital domestically. Just such a predicament forced KMS Industries of Ann Arbor, Michigan, a research firm involved in the development of a laser-fusion power generator, to sell out to a group headed by Canadian investors.[18] Amdahl Company of California was also forced to raise venture capital by selling 36 percent of the business to Fijitsu, the Japanese giant. Amdahl has been involved in the design and the manufacturing of large-scale computers.[19]

Senator Nelson has been so concerned about this trend in the electronics and other high technology fields that he has discussed the issue directly with the White House. In Nelson's opinion, foreign buyers will be able "to take these new products and their technology and exploit them abroad for the benefit of foreign jobs, foreign profits, foreign exports, and foreign economic and military strength."[20]

Automobiles The number of imported automobiles in the United States doubled from 1955 until 1970, and doubled once again from 1970 to 1975. In effect, Americans have seemed to evince a special type of "love affair" with the passenger vehicles produced overseas.

However, as a result of the strength of the major European and Japanese currencies vis-à-vis the dollar and a sharp increase in labor and transportation costs, the sticker prices of foreign automobiles have risen sharply in the past few years and some of these foreign companies are definitely feeling the crunch. As an example, the price of Japanese cars spiraled dramatically upward in the first nine months of 1978, representing an increase of 18 to 21 percent from just January of that year. As a consequence, Toyota, Nissan (the makers of Datsun), Honda, and Toyo Kogyo (the makers of Mazda) have been seriously considering following in the footsteps of Volkswagen and constructing assembly plants in the United States.[21] However, the Japanese assert that the cost and stability of an American work force is a prime factor in making the ultimate decision to head across the Pacific to the United States. Consequently, the Japanese were very disturbed by the "no money, no bunny" wildcat strike which broke out at the Volkswagen plant only six months after its opening. The workers demanded a pay scale and fringe benefits comparable to those offered by General Motors, Ford, and Chrysler.[22] Volkswagen officials claimed, and were generally supported by the United Autoworkers' top brass, that the high start-up costs of establishing a new facility in a foreign country precluded the possibility of immediately offering Detroit-style benefits. The UAW leadership, which has consistently encouraged the Japanese auto giants to set up facilities in the United States, dispatched emissaries to Tokyo to assure the Japanese car executives that such wildcat actions are an isolated phenomenon and should not detract from their investment plans. Moreover, through decisive UAW lobbying in New Stanton, the strike was settled within a few days.

Simply to remain competitive within the American market under current international economic conditions, the major foreign car producers may well be forced to establish automobile assembly plants and parts facilities in the United States. The French government-owned Renault firm has already agreed on a limited partnership arrangement with American Motors, and Volvo has done some work on an assembly plant in Virginia. Toyota builds 60,000 truck beds a year at a Long Beach, California, site, and Honda is currently completing a 24 million dollar motorcycle assembly facility near Allen Township, Ohio. Honda has made sure that it has an option on enough acreage adjacent to the facility to construct an auto assembly plant in the future. Within the next decade, many of these giant foreign auto producers may well be competing head-to-head with Detroit's Big Three on U.S. turf, and it is difficult to prognosticate what the overall impact on the American market will be, other than the immediate employment opportunities which will be available for thousands of American autoworkers.

Retailing Of the 50 largest retailing firms in the United States listed by *Fortune* in 1978, three were foreign-owned: Grand Union, National Tea, and Gimbels. In the past few years, foreigners have expanded their involvement in this sphere, as is exemplified by the activities of German entrepreneur Hugo Mann. Mann owns a chain of huge self-service discount stores in West Germany known as "hypermarkets." These hypermarkets are approximately three times the size of most big U.S. discount outlets, and cases of food and general merchandise are stacked along aisles in metal racks from which the shoppers pick out what they want. Labor costs are reduced by this format, and because of the chain's high volume and quick turnover, Mann's pet project has made him a millionaire many times over.[23]

Impressed by the retailing opportunities in the United States, Mann acquired a 68 percent share of the Fed-Mart Corporation, a 48-store supermarket and general merchandise chain with outlets mainly in California and Texas. Mann's next venture was to buy a huge chunk of Vornado, Incorporated, owners of the 140 Two Guys discount outlets and the Builders Emporium home repair centers. In 1976, the combined sales of Mann's U.S. retailing group was an impressive 1.4 billion dollars. He is now testing his hypermarket concept in the San Diego region and hopes eventually to establish a series of such stores nationwide. The German entrepreneur has also begun to branch out in his American pursuits, because Vornado recently announced plans to construct a casino and entertainment complex in Atlantic City.

Table 4-4 presents a partial list of foreign-owned food and nonfood retail establishments in the United States, as compiled by the Commerce Department, using 1975 data. The foreign-controlled Big Three in *Fortune's* top 50 accounted for 3.5 percent of the group's total U.S. retail sales; and on a nationwide basis, foreign-owned retail establishments have

TABLE 4-4   Major Foreign-Owned Retail Establishments, 1975

U.S. company	Foreign owner	Date of initial acquisition	Percent owned
Food-related establishments			
Grand Union	Cavenham, U.K.	1973	51
National Tea	Loblaw, Canada	1955	84
Loblaw	Loblaw, Canada	1939	100
Kohl	British-American Tobacco, U.K.	1972	80
Food Town Stores	Delhaize Frères, Belgium	1975	33
Baskin-Robbins	J. Lyons, U.K.	1973	100
Nonfood-related establishments			
Gimbel Brothers Saks Fifth Avenue	British-American Tobacco, U.K.	1973	100
Fed-Mart	Hugo Mann, Germany	1975	64
Kay	Bowater, U.K.	1975	72
Ohrbach's	Brenninkmeyer Family, Netherlands	1965	100
Kohl	British-American Tobacco, U.K.	1972	80
Bond Industries	Seamar, Netherlands	1974	23
Heath	Schlumberger, France	1962	100
F.A.O. Schwarz	Franz Carl Weber, Switzerland	1974	91
S. Klein	Julio Tanjeloff, Argentina	1975	100
George Jensen	Julio Tanjeloff, Argentina	1975	100
Rosenthal Studio-Haus	Julio Tanjeloff, Argentina	1975	100
Astro Minerals	Julio Tanjeloff, Argentina	1963	100

SOURCE: U.S. Department of Commerce, *Foreign Direct Investment in the United States,* Vol. 3, 1976.

still had little impact on the U.S. marketplace.[24] Nonetheless, judging from the activities of Mann and other overseas investors who have been greatly impressed by the size and the affluence of the U.S. retail market, foreign-owned businesses should make steady inroads in this sphere for many years to come. As an apt illustration of the developing trend, the Tenglemann Group of West Germany purchased in 1979 a controlling interest in the Great Atlantic & Pacific Tea Company (A&P), America's second largest supermarket chain and Brascan of Canada made an unsuccessful 1.1 billion dollar bid to acquire F. W. Woolworth.

Publishing   Because of government-imposed restrictions in certain sectors of the communications industry, foreign investors have had to be content with penetrating the U.S. newspaper, magazine, and book markets.

Recognizing that the United States has by far the largest population among the Western advanced industrial nations, foreign publishing firms which have been eminently successful within their own national markets have yearned for the opportunity to gain a foothold on American soil. In the past two or three years, literally scores of transactions have been consummated and several well-known American firms have been swallowed up by foreign competitors.

In the newspaper arena, much attention has been accorded to Australian tycoon Rupert Murdoch's acquisition of the *New York Post, The Village Voice, San Antonio Express, The Star,* and a handful of other newspaper-related publications. However, outside of the immediate New York area, Thomson Newspapers, Ltd., of Canada has certainly had the greatest foreign impact on the U.S. newspaper community. Thomson, which also controls one-third of the papers published in Canada, owns 57 U.S. papers scattered throughout the United States. In all, the Thomson papers in the United States have a combined daily circulation of more than 1 million.

Books and magazines have also become a favorite target of foreign investors. In 1974, the Agnelli family of Italy, the owners of Fiat, doled out 70 million dollars to acquire Bantam Books. Recently, the Agnellis have sold a majority interest in Bantam to West Germay's Bertelsmann Group, the world's largest publishing company. Viking Press is also 66 percent British-owned and the Bonnier Group, Sweden's largest publishing house, has recently purchased a 50 percent interest in the 13-30 Corporation of Knoxville, Tennessee, with the intent of turning out consumer-oriented books and magazines for the American market.

Gruner and Jahr, Germany's largest magazine publisher, which is 75 percent controlled by Bertelsmann, has agreed to buy *Parents'* magazine and will soon be turning out a U.S. version of *Geo,* a very popular West German periodical which is somewhat akin to *National Geographic.* Gruner and Jahr's chief German rival, Alex Springer Verlag, has also begun operations in New York and is reportedly seeking out major investment opportunities.

The Associated Newspapers Group, Ltd., of London acquired *Esquire* in the fall of 1977 and a few months later, the publisher of France's famous *Paris-Match* announced plans to resurrect the old *Look* magazine. Daniel Filipacchi, the owner of *Paris-Match,* has also bought out *Argosy, Camera 35,* and *Railroad.* Moreover, Murdoch, the new owner of the *New York Post,* has branched out into the magazine trade through his ownership of *New West* and *New York.* In order not to be left out of the swift foreign rush into the American marketplace, the London-based *Financial Times* and the *Economist* have also publicly disclosed plans to seek new outlets in the United States.[25]

Conducting Business in the U.S.A.— Characteristics of Foreign-Owned Firms

Surveys have shown that the employment created in the United States as a result of foreign direct investment is of a higher skill level than currently exists on the average in indigenous U.S. manufacturing firms.[26] Moreover, foreign firms usually reinvest at least one-half of their U.S.-based earnings back into the American economy for the first six or seven years after making their initial investment, appreciably higher than their U.S. counterparts with operations overseas. A National Science Foundation sample study has also determined that the foreign-owned companies spend significantly larger portions of their research and development budgets on basic and applied research than do U.S.-owned companies, particularly in the chemical-related industries.[27]

In reference to the management and employment practices of the foreign-owned firms doing business in the United States, the landmark U.S. Department of Commerce foreign investment study offers some interesting insights.[28] This study, which examined the prevailing business practices and procedures of 100 U.S. subsidiaries of foreign-owned firms, concluded that the foreign investors who acquired existing companies in the United States were very reluctant to undertake major shake-ups in the managerial and technical ranks of the enterprises. With little doubt, the foreigners prefer to take full advantage of the expertise available in existing U.S. management circles. Moreover, they do not want to attract adverse publicity which might be associated with wholesale firings of the carryover personnel. On the other hand, many of the foreign firms have been very wary about accepting the unionization of their working force, particularly the Japanese companies.

The survey of the 100 subsidiaries also revealed that the number of jobs available to American workers often increased after the new start-up or the acquisition, at times by as much as 50 percent, Moreover, prospects for job security and additional employee benefits often improved, especially in those firms which had only been marginally profitable before being taken over by a foreign company. A majority of the American workers surveyed in the study generally did not perceive any major differences existing between their foreign-owned firms and American-owned companies in the same industrial sector. When differences were perceived, the American employees tended to evaluate their own foreign-controlled enterprise in more positive terms than the U.S.-owned counterparts.

As a specific example of foreign management practices, one might look at Matsushita's takeover of the Motorola facility in 1974. Upon learning of the transaction, the workers at the Franklin Park, Illinois, plant were very apprehensive about their future employment status. Plant morale dipped even further when Matsushita, which considered that Motorola's existing management structure was somewhat flabby, dismissed some of the top and middle management personnel. On the other hand, the lower echelons were not affected by this limited housecleaning operation.

The name of the plant's product line was soon changed to Quasar, and Matsushita has had to struggle along as millions of dollars were pumped into sorely needed plant and assembly line renovations. Prior to the Japanese takeover, as many as 50 percent of the Motorola televisions had been returned by customers for repairs. In contrast, Quasar has aimed for less than a 1 percent return rate. Seemingly, the company has now turned the corner and has shown some black ink on the ledgers. The workers, who are all nonunion, have expressed great satisfaction with the new ownership and insist that worker-management communication lines are now infinitely better than those which existed under the former Motorola management. The chief executive officer of the company is now an American and the marketing division has been almost totally left in the hands of American employees, with only one out of a 400-member marketing team being Japanese.[29]

In contrast, Hoechst of Germany seemed to botch employee relations when it took over control of Foster Grant; and some American executives working for Japanese-owned firms have complained about discriminatory practices, prompting numerous lawsuits in the U.S. court system. These executives insist that they receive lower pay and fewer fringe benefits, and have the path to promotion blocked because they are not Japanese citizens. For example, Japanese staff transferred to the United States from the parent corporation always retain the customary lifetime employment security, and are often offered two yearly bonuses and lucrative relocation benefits. In addition, other incentives available to Japanese executives usually include complete medical and dental coverage for employee and family, reimbursement for private automobile insurance premiums, and salary increases of up to 50 percent when the employee marries and an extra 5 to 10 percent for each child. In comparison, U.S. staff of the Japanese normally receive one annual bonus, are entitled to fewer fringe benefits, and are very seldom guaranteed lifetime job security.[30]

The Japanese and other foreign investors are quite sensitive to these host country criticisms and have begun to emulate some of the recent practices of U.S. multinationals abroad. In particular, workers and top management are, whenever possible, selected from the nation in which the subsidiary is located. Although certain complaints persist, foreign investors do attempt to make sure that their American employees are relatively satisfied. As an illustration, the Japanese-owned Texprint Corporation of Macon, Georgia, has not turned a profit in several years, but the company has refused to fire anyone. At times, the paternalistic-oriented top management has requested that certain personnel accept lower paying positions, but these workers have not been asked to seek employment opportunities elsewhere. On an average, Japanese-managed U.S. firms invariably report labor turnover and absenteeism rates at least 50 percent below those of comparable U.S. firms.[31] Other foreign-owned establishments have also seemed to do a better job in this sphere than their U.S.-owned counterparts.

Manufacturing and Commercial Investment in Perspective

The official Commerce Department study of foreign direct investment in the United States reached the following conclusion:

> Foreign direct investment occurs in virtually all the broad sectors of the U.S. economy, but its role in all of these sectors is relatively small.
>
> In manufacturing, foreign investment is identified as significant in some subsectors. The number of such subsectors in which foreign presence is of major importance, however, is not large in relation to the total number of subsectors that exist in the tremendous and diverse U.S. economy. Among the fields where foreign investment is relatively large are newsprint and several chemical industries (e.g., the manufacture of dyes, pharmaceuticals, and synthetic fibers).
>
> Some foreign-owned companies were found to be among the three or four largest U.S. producers of certain products, e.g., agricultural chemicals, building and construction supplies, and phonograph records. Such high rankings, however, do not necessarily mean that the individual company's share of the total U.S. market for a particular product is high, since most of the industries are large and consist of many producers. Moreover, even where a foreign-owned company ranks second or third, in most instances a considerable gap exists between it and the leading U.S. producer.[32]

In an appearance before a Congressional committee in early 1974, Peter Flanigan, then Assistant to the President for International Economic Affairs, also downplayed the impact of foreign investment on the overall U.S. commercial and manufacturing sectors:

> Foreign investment in the United States is not a significant factor when compared with the vast size of our economy. . . . For example, at the end of 1973, foreign direct investment in the United States was around 16 billion dollars and the growth in such investment in 1973 was only two percent of the amount spent in the United States on business plants and equipment.[33]

Even today, at the dawn of a new decade welcoming in the 1980s and ushering out the 1970s, foreign direct investment in the U.S. manufacturing and commercial fields is still relatively small when viewed within the overall context of total investment activity in these spheres. However, foreign transactions in these sectors have increased dramatically since the time Flanigan testified before Congress and the Department of Commerce issued its famous report on foreign investment. In an admittedly incremental fashion when placed within the context of overall investment activity in the United States, foreign investors are nevertheless acquiring larger shares of the U.S. industrial and commercial business. As David Bauer of the Conference Board commented in mid-1978: "As recently as 1974, employment in foreign-owned manufacturing plants in this country represented less than three percent of all manufacturing jobs. If foreign investment activity continues at its recent pace, the figure will soon approach five percent."[34] In effect, the foreign investment trend is definitely swinging upward; and on a sectoral basis, such as in certain chemical and high technology fields, foreign-owned firms have already captured significant portions of the U.S. market. Moreover, the foreign firms have seemed to have been fairly well assimilated into the mainstream of the American business community. For example, the U.S. Department of Commerce recently authorized a loan guarantee of 21.3 million dollars to help preserve jobs in Korf Industries' steelmaking facilities in Georgetown, South Carolina, and Beaumont, Texas. These jobs were threatened largely as a result of overseas competition in the steel industry, particularly from Japan. Somewhat ironically, however, Korf, the company receiving the loan guarantee from the federal government to help protect it against the increased competition from abroad, is 70 percent controlled by German sources and 30 percent by Kuwaiti investors.[35]

FIVE

Foreign Money on Wall Street: Implications for the American Investor

Introduction

Several months ago, a loan officer from a small Texas bank made a routine visit to a construction firm located in an isolated hamlet in the eastern part of the state. Upon exiting from the office of the company's treasurer, the loan officer noticed a very urbane man, sporting a European-style pinstriped suit, calmly sitting in the lobby. Several days later, the bank officer learned that the well-dressed man represented the Union Bank of Switzerland, prompting the Texan to observe wryly: "If they've made it out there, they must be everywhere."[1]

From the plush offices of Wall Street to the dusty streets of a small southwestern town, foreign investors have made their presence keenly felt in the banking, securities, and insurance fields. Even the Narodny Bank of Moscow in the U.S.S.R. was rumored to be seeking a piece of this U.S. action by negotiating the purchase of three northern California banks.[2]

Foreigners in the Banking Sector

In most parts of the United States, banking activity is a localized phenomenon, and thus foreign-controlled banks which are permitted to function in some of the states may exert a great deal of influence over the economic vitality of local communities and the individual businesses within these communities. In this respect, the small U.S. regional banks, to a much greater extent than the large American international banking institutions, have expressed alarm over the rapid escalation in foreign investment in this sphere. As the Commerce Department study reported:

> It is feared by some that these may be the forerunners of a large-scale foreign invasion of U.S. banking and, in particular, that some of the oil-exporting nations may use their enormous earnings to buy control of important sectors of the industry, thereby acquiring a significant influence over the economic, and perhaps even political, life of the United States.[3]

Recent foreign activity Some foreign banks can actually boast of long-established roots in the United States, having opened up American branches in the nineteenth century. In addition, some major U.S. banking institutions, such as the Bank of America, were originally organized with foreign capital. However, persistent growth in foreign banking operations did not begin until after World War II, spurred on by the emergence of the dollar as the world's major currency and New York City as one of the two major centers for international capital. Many of the giant foreign banking institutions do as much as one-third or more of their world business in dollars and thus consider that having facilities in the United States will ensure that a stable supply of dollars will always be available for international banking purposes.

For a variety of reasons, a great spurt in foreign banking activity in the United States occurred in the early 1960s, picked up even greater momentum in the 1973–1974 period, slowed down somewhat in 1975–1976, and then accelerated once again during the rest of the decade (see Figure 5-1). Having accumulated vast dollar deposits, the large foreign banks wanted to put this money to work by gaining direct access to the huge and lucrative U.S. market during a period when certain U.S. bank securities were depressed. Some of these banks have also been spurred on by high liquidity in their own national currencies but a paucity of domestic investment opportunities linked to rather stagnant economies. For example, German banks have recently accumulated huge reserves in domestic savings accounts while offering relatively low interest rates. However, these banks have found few opportunities to invest this money in Germany because of the lagging level of economic growth.

The large international banks have also been attracted to the American market for the simple reason that they want to service the financial needs of the giant foreign multinationals which have recently migrated to the United States. At the same time, of course, they hope to capitalize on the stability and the growth potential of the U.S. economy by enticing American homegrown enterprises into their banking fold. Moreover, an added incentive for establishing beachheads on American terra firma during the mid-1970s was linked to an abiding fear that the U.S. Congress would finally pass a bill on its agenda since 1974 which would significantly restrict *new* foreign banking operations in the United States.[4]

At the end of 1972, 52 foreign banks had established approximately 100 facilities in the United States. By early 1977, the number of facilities

---

FIGURE 5-1

Assets of Foreign-Owned Banks in the United States

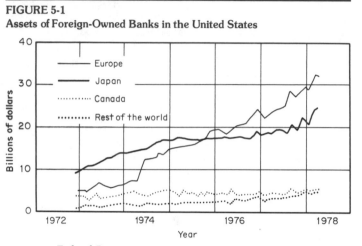

SOURCE: Federal Reserve System.

---

had more than doubled and foreign banks had increased their assets by 175 percent. In comparison, the assets of the major American banks which report on a regular basis to the Federal Reserve System rose only 40 percent during this period.[5] As of April 1978, 122 foreign banks, including the 50 largest banks outside the United States, had established several hundred offices in the United States with assets totalling more than 90 billion dollars. Transactions completed during the first three-quarters of 1978 pushed this assets level up to close to 95 billion dollars. Moreover, in 1977 alone, 22 new foreign banks began operations in the United States.[6]

A flock of foreign acquisitions of American banks has occurred in the middle and late 1970s, even though most foreign banks have expressed a preference for setting up their own facilities rather than acquiring existing U.S. firms. The European-American Bank and Trust, a consortium of six European banks, received headlines when it acquired control of the New York-based Franklin National Bank, an institution with 4 billion dollars in assets. In 1972, an Italian holding company had taken over control of the Franklin Bank by purchasing 21.6 percent of the bank's common stock. As a result of gross mismanagement and illegal foreign exchange speculation, Franklin went bankrupt and European-American stepped in to secure a chunk of the assets and liabilities in 1974. During the same year, Lloyd's Bank of London purchased from World Airways the California-based First Western Bank and Trust Company, a 1.1 billion dollar operation with 94 branches. Across the continent, the United Kingdom-based Barclay's organization acquired the Westchester National Bank of New Rochelle, New York.

In 1975, California was again the scene of a major banking transaction as the Bank of Tokyo assumed control of the Southern California Bank of San Diego, an organization with 70 branches and 800 million dollars in assets.[7] In 1977, Sumitomo Bank of California, a subsidiary of the Sumitomo Bank group of Japan, announced that it would acquire 19 branches from the Bank of California. By the end of that year, Japanese-owned state-chartered banks in California numbered seven, as compared to only two in 1970.

The foreign blitz has continued; and in 1976 New York City alone issued licenses for 22 foreign bank branches, boosting the total assets of the group of foreign banks situated in New York by nearly 40 percent to 23 billion dollars. In 1977, the Bank Leumi Le-Israel acquired New York's American Bank and Trust, with assets of 1.3 billion dollars. In fact, there was some talk in only a semifacetious vein that the foreign banks should have come to the rescue of the Big Apple and bailed it out of its financial crunch. Indeed, between June 1977 and June 1978, 60 representative or branch offices of foreign banks were opened in New York City alone, joining the 157 foreign offices which were already there.

In April 1978 the HongKong and Shanghai Banking Corporation announced that it had agreed to dole out 262 million dollars to acquire a 51 percent share of the ailing Marine Midland Bank, America's fifteenth largest bank holding company with assets in excess of 12 billion dollars.[8] London's National Westminster Bank also confirmed that it would pay 300 million dollars for a 75 percent chunk of the New York-based National Bank of North America, the fortieth largest in the nation. Another London institution, the Standard Chartered Bank, joined the takeover party by going public with plans to pay 372 million dollars for the thirty-second largest U.S. banking organization, the Union Bancorp. Investors from Venezuela, Colombia, Panama, Ecuador, and Spain have also recently purchased banking operations in South Florida; and farther north, the Bank of Montreal, the third largest in Canada, has offered approximately 50 million dollars to buy 89 of the 104 branches of New York's Bankers Trust Company.[9]

Arab investors have also received a great deal of publicity for their activities in the banking field. In 1973, Adnan Khashoggi, the Saudi Arabian business entrepreneur famed for his middleman role between American corporate giants and potential Middle East buyers, acquired a controlling interest in two Walnut Creek, California, banks. He soon completed some other deals in the Golden State but eventually decided to back out of a transaction to acquire control of the First National Bank of San Jose because of adverse stockholder and customer reaction to the proposed change in ownership.

Ghaith Pharaon, another Saudi financier, also captured a spot in the headlines when in 1975 he purchased a controlling interest in the Bank of the Commonwealth of Detroit, an institution with more than 1 billion dollars in total assets. However, as in the case of his fellow countryman Khashoggi, Mr. Pharaon received adverse publicity in his attempt to buy into the Community National Bank of nearby Pontiac, Michigan. The negotiations for this takeover were swiftly terminated when a union pension fund group decided not to provide some of the capital necessary for Pharaon's tender offer.[10]

The Saudi Arabian national was understandably miffed by the Pontiac incident and later divested himself of his controlling share in the Bank of the Commonwealth. Pharaon moved southward to warmer climates and joined with John Connally and a few other influential investors in the purchase of a 20 percent interest in the Main Bank of Houston. In January 1978 he arranged to buy 10 percent of the stock of the Bank of Georgia from Jimmy Carter's confidant, Bert Lance. Later in June, Pharaon completed a tender offer which provided him with a 60 percent share of this Georgia bank. From all indications, Pharaon continues to have his eyes open for attractive banking operations within the United States. Some even conjecture that Saudi Arabia's National Commercial Bank, the second largest in the Middle East and a financial backer of Pharaon, strongly pushed for the Bank of Georgia takeover bid. Allegedly the Saudi Arabian institution viewed the Georgia bank as providing it with an opportunity to enter the U.S. market and gain a share of the lucrative letters-of-credit and bond guarantee business for construction projects carried out in the Middle East and other parts of the world.[11]

Bert Lance has also allegedly been involved with foreign investors in a rather questionable takeover bid of Financial General Bankshares, a 2.2 billion dollar holding company that controls banks in New York, Virginia, and the District of Columbia. Lance reportedly submitted a secret bid to acquire a controlling interest in Financial General on behalf of Pakistani banker Agha Hasan Abedi, a consortium of Arab investors, and Lance's wife. Lance later asserted that it was not necessary for the group to comply with the Williams Act of 1968 which requires disclosure to the Securities and Exchange Commission of any acquisition in excess of 5 percent of the stock of a company. By assigning each member of the consortium 4.9

percent or less of the stock, the Lance group reasoned that the Williams Act was not applicable in this particular case, a way of thinking that raised many eyebrows among personnel in Washington's regulatory agencies.[12]

Restrictions on foreign banking operations The strong populist inclinations which permeated much of American society in the second half of the nineteenth century helped to bring about in 1863 the creation of a dual federal-state regulatory system over banking activities. The populist doctrine was inherently suspicious of both "Big Government" and "Big Business" and this philosophy has left an indelible imprint on the banking laws of most American states. In effect, populists perceived that banks should have strictly local roots, and state laws mirrored this perspective by denying banks the opportunity to expand outside of the state or even at times outside the county of their original operation. This severe state-imposed limitation certainly helps explain why the major U.S. banking institutions in the post-World War II era have sought out new clientele through overseas offices.

America's dual federal-state bank regulatory system is unique among the major industrial nations of the world and this overlapping jurisdiction has undoubtedly caused moments of befuddlement for many foreign banking operations considering penetrating the U.S. market. In actuality, most banking regulations are determined by state legislatures, and as Table 5-1 illustrates, banking provisions may vary dramatically from one state border to the next. At the federal level, the Comptroller of the Cur-

TABLE 5-1 State Restraints on Foreign Banking Activity, 1975

State	Direct entry of alien banks permitted	Direct entry of alien banks forbidden	Limited authority for alien banks to make loans	Out-of-state domestic banks may branch into the state	State banks may branch out of the state
Ala.		x			
Alaska	x		x	x	
Ariz.		x			x
Ark.		x	x		
Calif.	x			x	
Colo.		x	x		
Conn.		x	x		
Del.		x			
D.C.		x			
Fla.		x	x		
Ga.		x			
Hawaii		x	x		
Idaho		x	x		
Ill.	x		x		

State	Direct entry of alien banks permitted	Direct entry of alien banks forbidden	Limited authority for alien banks to make loans	Out-of-state domestic banks may branch into the state	State banks may branch out of the state
Ind.		x		x	
Iowa		x			
Kan.		x	x		
Ky.		x	x		
La.		x			
Maine		x			
Md.		x	x		
Mass.	x			x	
Mich.		x			
Minn.		x	x		
Miss.		x			x
Mo.	x		x	x	
Mont.		x	x		
Neb.		x			
Nev.	x			x	
N.H.		x		x	
N.J.		x			
N.Mex.		x	x		
N.Y.	x		x	x	x
N.C.		x			
N.Dak.		x			
Ohio		x			
Okla.		x			
Oreg.	x		x	x	
Pa.		x			
P.R.	x			x	x
R.I.		x			
S.C.	x				
S.Dak.		x			
Tenn.		x			
Tex.		x			
Utah		x			
Vt.		x	x		
V.I.	x			x	
Va.		x			
Wash.	x		x	x	
W.Va.		x			
Wis.		x			
Wyo.		x	x		

SOURCE: U.S. Department of Commerce, *Foreign Direct Investment in the United States,* Vol. 7, 1976.

rency, the Board of Governors of the Federal Reserve System, and the Board of Directors of the Federal Deposit Insurance Corporation (FDIC) are the key forces in regulating foreign operations. For example, federal laws permit foreign banks to set up subsidiary banks in the United States by obtaining special charters from the Comptroller of the Currency. However, most foreign banks have found this invitation unattractive because of the requirement that they join the Federal Reserve System and guarantee that all members of the subsidiary bank's board of directors are U.S. citizens. As of 1975, only one foreign bank had decided to seek the federal charter, although certain foreign operations have purchased existing banks which had previously secured the federal permits.[13]

Even certain activities of state-chartered subsidiaries are subject to federal regulation. For example, under the provisions of the 1966 Bank Merger Act, the Justice Department may institute antitrust action against a foreign bank-initiated merger or acquisition which would "substantially" decrease competition or tend toward monopolistic practices. The Federal Reserve System may also exercise "moral suasion" over foreign banks in order to ensure that recommended reserve requirements are satisfied and the Fed may "jawbone" the foreign firms into complying with certain management practices. Moreover, the Federal Reserve has been granted the authority to monitor foreign banking activities in the United States and to require all foreign operations except representative offices to submit monthly reports.[14] Federal regulations have also prevented most foreign-owned banks from obtaining FDIC insurance, a major handicap for those seeking deposits from the general public. On the other hand, most of these banks have dealt almost exclusively with large U.S. and foreign multinationals, so the $40,000 FDIC deposit guarantee has had little relevance.

Because of the passage of the 1978 International Banking Act which will be discussed shortly, the Federal Reserve will exercise even greater supervisory authority over foreign banking operations in the future. To a large extent, however, the foreign bank activities remain under the direct regulatory power of the individual state governments. Quite often, upon entering the U.S. market, foreign banks establish initial operations in New York City, the unquestioned financial capital of the nation. The penetration of the New York area is done with a representative office which acts as a liaison for the home bank, helps home country clients to conduct their business affairs in the United States, and assists in the development of correspondent relations with U.S. domestic banks. Perhaps equally important, the New York operation allows the foreign bank to survey the American scene firsthand and, so to speak, get a real feel for the turf before venturing forth into other parts of the country.

State laws normally deny the representative offices of foreign banks the privilege of engaging in retail banking activities. Consequently, the representative office functions as an information conduit for the foreign parent, spreading the good word about the home bank and arranging for loans and deposits directly on behalf of the parent institution. However, in order to build up a clientele of U.S. corporations and foreign multinationals, the U.S. operations of foreign banks must have the flexibility of providing some localized banking services, services denied to the representative offices. Thus the next step in upgrading its U.S. presence is for the foreign bank to seek an agency or a state-chartered branch status. An agency may engage in most banking pursuits except those dealing with the acceptance of domestic deposits subject to withdrawal, or the selling of certificates of deposit, or the exercising of trust powers.[15] Because of these restrictions, the agency banks are severely hampered in their efforts to engage in retail banking or to deal directly with the general public. As a consequence, the agencies usually concentrate on arranging credit market and business loans and on financing transactions of a purely international nature. To their benefit, agencies are normally not restricted in terms of the size of the individual loans which they may arrange.

Unlike the agency banks, state-chartered branches may accept domestic deposits and therefore may engage in many general retail banking practices so familiar to the average American consumer.[16] Relatively little capital is needed to start up a branch operation because the branch is considered as being directly supported by the parent bank. In addition, there is no stipulation that the branch must have stockholders or a board of directors totally composed of U.S. citizens. Another attractive feature to the foreign investor is that the branches may make relatively large loans because their loan limits are computed on the basis of the total capital assets of the parent bank, which may run into tens of billions of dollars. Because of the relative ease in establishing such branches and the business advantages available from this format, many foreign banking operations have preferred to go the branch route in expanding their activities in the United States.

Subsidiary banks are the last major organizational form which foreign investors may use in the United States. Subsidiaries may be chartered at the federal or state levels, but the latter route entails far less red tape and is overwhelmingly preferred by the foreign companies. In contrast to the representative offices, agencies, and branches, subsidiaries are separate legal entities chartered in the United States and subject to most of the same restrictions as domestic banks. Although control of the subsidiary remains in the hands of the foreign parent, the subsidiary may accept domestic deposits, obtain deposit insurance, and perform trust functions. On the other hand, more capital is needed to start up such an organization and the size of loans which may be made is often severely limited because computations are based only on the subsidiary's assets, and not on the total assets of the parent firm. In addition, a large cadre of U.S. citizens must be included among the subsidiary's stockholders and on the board of directors. As a result of the loan restrictions and the high U.S. citizen involvement, the subsidiary structure has not been overly attractive to foreign investors.

A few foreign banks have also established investment companies and securities affiliates in the United States, predominately in the state of New York which has liberal laws concerning the formation of such entities. A handful of these affiliates also provide general banking services at the same time. For example, the aforementioned European-American Bank group which was involved in the Franklin Bank deal, has banking subsidiaries and investment affiliates in New York, agencies in Los Angeles and San Francisco, and a partly owned branch in Chicago.[17]

The type of organizational structure adopted by the foreign bank will, of course, vary depending on the goals and resources of the bank within the American market and the specific type of banking activity it hopes to emphasize. The foreign firm will also be heavily influenced in its decision by the regulations enunciated by the government of the state in which it intends to operate. As of the beginning of 1974, 41 of the 50 states had no alien banks operating in any form within their borders. As of 1975, New York, Illinois, California, Washington, Oregon, Hawaii, Massachusetts, and the dependencies of Puerto Rico and the Virgin Islands permitted foreign banking operations beyond the representative office stage.[18] In 1976, Georgia liberalized its banking provisions in order to allow foreign banks to establish agency offices with the capability of granting loans. This major change in the banking law by the Georgia legislature helps to explain why several foreign institutions have flocked to Atlanta in recent months. Commonly, these states which do welcome foreign banking institutions require certain capital and liquidity levels, interest rate limitations, and reciprocity arrangements with the foreign firm's national government. Furthermore, as a growing point of controversy, some of these states, such as California, have introduced a "unitary" system of taxation which computes the foreign bank's tax liability on the basis of the parent bank's worldwide earnings, prorated according to the extent of the bank's sales, payroll, and property within the state. Some foreign banks have clamored that they are being unfairly ripped off by this unitary tax formula.[19]

Of all the states, New York has had the most liberalized provisions toward foreign banking activities. Subsidiaries, branches, and agencies are allowed to conduct business within the state, and even foreign-owned investment companies are permitted to offer certain limited banking services. As an additional incentive aimed at attracting more banking operations to New York, the state legislature has recently passed a bill establishing an offshore banking zone in New York. In effect, banks would be allowed under this provision to create International Banking Facilities (IBFs) which could accumulate foreign source deposits and book foreign loans while being exempt from paying state or local taxes on this income. With the exclusion of this state and local tax burden, the tax bite would decrease to a maximum of 48 percent, 4 percent below the current tax liability in the other major world financial center, London. Proponents of the measure claim that 6,000 new jobs would be created in New York City because of the expanded banking activity and the local payroll would climb by as much as 90 million dollars annually. Moreover, the decreased tax liabilities might attract a good share of the estimated 66 billion dollars in American bank assets now held in the Bahamas. However, there is a hitch in New York's plan, because before the IBFs can be fully implemented, the Federal Reserve System must first exempt them from reserve requirements on deposits and limitations on interest rates, waivers which the Fed has thus far been reluctant to grant.[20]

According to the Commerce Department study of all state regulations, the statutes of Nevada, Alaska, Utah, and South Carolina would probably permit the entry of foreign banks into those states. On the other hand, 30 states prohibit altogether the entry of out-of-state banks, although certain loopholes might exist insofar as foreign operations are concerned. The statutes of eight other states do not refer directly to the entry of out-of-state or out-of-country banks. However, most of these 38 states were considered as leaning toward the rejection of foreign penetration whether as a result of statute or administrative decree.[21] As an illustration of the state-originated limitations, Houston has become a very attractive area for many foreign banks because of the oil and natural gas dimension. However, Texas state law permits the foreigners only to set up representative offices and Edge Act corporations on Texas soil, and directly prohibits the formation of agencies, branches, or subsidiaries.

Government favoritism toward foreign banking?   In spite of the "off-limits" signs put up by most states, sectors of the American banking community have vociferously complained that government regulations favor foreign banking operations over U.S. banking enterprises. Often these charges have been directly linked to the provisions of the Glass-Steagall and the Holding Company Acts. These acts, coupled with certain state provisions, prohibit U.S. banks from carrying on operations in more than one state. However, in the past foreign banks have been exempted from this restriction. Consequently, the British-owned Barclay's firm maintains operations in California, Illinois, Massachusetts, New York, and the Virgin Islands, whereas the world's largest bank, the Bank of America, is limited to providing retail banking services in California. As another illustration, Chase Manhattan is limited in its U.S. operations to the state of New York, whereas the HongKong and Shanghai Bank and the Standard and Chartered Bank have banking institutions in New York, California, Illinois, and Washington. Federal legislation also prohibits domestic commercial banks from entering into investment banking activities in the United States, such as the underwriting and the brokerage of corporate securities. Once again, foreign banks have traditionally been exempted from complying with this provision.

In an effort to standardize the domestic and foreign bank competitive rules of the game, the Federal Reserve System asked Congress to pass the following proposals: (1) the Comptroller of the Currency would be permitted to license branches of foreign banks to operate in any state, even those in which state laws currently prohibit such operations; (2) all new state-chartered banks of foreign institutions would first have to receive a green light from the Comptroller of the Currency and the Secretary of the Treasury; (3) the prior exemptions given to foreign operations to conduct business in more than one state and to engage in investment banking activities would be ended, except for those foreign banks already having such operations in the United States prior to the passage of the bill; (4) U.S. branches, agencies, and subsidiaries of foreign banks having worldwide bank assets exceeding 500 million dollars would be required to join the Federal Reserve System; (5) the FDIC would be required to insure the deposits of the U.S. branches and agencies of the foreign banks; (6) up to 50 percent of the directors of the banking operations in the United States would be allowed to be foreign nationals; (7) foreign banks would be permitted to establish Edge Act corporations (for international transactions) without having majority control of these corporations in the hands of U.S. citizens; and (8) the federal supervisory agencies would be permitted to exchange periodic banking information with their counterparts in foreign countries.[22]

These recommendations were duly considered by the solons on Capitol Hill for several years, and finally an International Banking Act was passed by both chambers of Congress on August 17, 1978. Just a few weeks prior to the passage of the bill, Chairman G. William Miller of the Federal Reserve specifically asked a Congressional subcommittee for greater federal regulation and monitoring of foreign banking activity in the United States because of the tremendous growth in foreign institutions in the past few years. Miller made the following observation during his subcommittee appearance:

> I should like to review some of the reasons why the Board has for several years supported legislation that would provide a federal presence in the regulation and supervision of the operations of foreign banks in the United

States. These reasons lie in the growth in number and size of foreign bank operations, and their ever-increasing importance to the structure of the banking system and to the functioning of money and credit markets. The latter has obvious implications for the conduct of monetary policy. . . .

When the Board was developing its legislative proposals at the end of 1973, there were about 60 foreign banks operating banking offices in the United States with combined assets of about 37 billion dollars. Growth of these operations had been swift in the preceding years, and, as the Board stated at the time, that trend was clearly bound to continue. Those expectations have been more than fulfilled. As of April 1978, 122 foreign banks operated banking facilities in the United States with total assets of 90 billion dollars.[23]

The act which was finally passed on the Hill in 1978 does provide the Federal Reserve System with the principal authority over foreign banking operations, a dimension of the bill which did not particularly please many state governments. The Fed has also been authorized to set reserve requirements for both federal and state branches of foreign banks which have 1 billion dollars or more in worldwide assets. Moreover, the foreign-owned institutions must now obtain FDIC insurance if they accept customers with accounts of less than $100,000. In the future, foreign banks will also be prohibited from acquiring a "substantial" interest in banks in more than one state and will be prevented from buying or selling stocks within the United States. However, in order to leave the door open for more foreign capital to flow into the United States, foreign banks already operating in one state may still form branches in other states, a privilege which continues to be denied to domestic banks.[24] Conversely, any new interstate branches of foreign banks will be limited to accepting deposits from foreign sources and to conducting bank business which has a strictly international connotation. This provision was inserted into the new law in order to avoid giving the foreign banks an edge over their domestic competitors in the constant search for deposits from U.S. residents.

Foreign banking competition in perspective   Although admitting that the foreign presence in the U.S. banking sector has grown steadily, various sources still perceive that the foreign banks have had only a marginal impact on this sphere of activity. As an illustration of this point of view, the Commerce Department has observed that the 184 foreign banking operations reporting in 1975 represented little more than 1 percent of America's 14,600 commercial banks. The American affiliates of the foreign firms accumulated a total of 64 billion dollars in assets at the end of 1975, less than 7 percent of the 958 billion dollars in assets held by U.S. commercial banks.[25] Some insiders in the banking business also believe that foreign investors have made a serious tactical mistake in purchasing some of America's most gravely ill banking institutions, such as the Franklin and the Marine Midland Banks.

Still others assert that a large percentage of the commercial loans arranged by the U.S. affiliates of foreign banks go strictly to foreign-based multinationals and thus have only a modest impact on the U.S. domestic loan market. One source estimates, for example, that up to 95 percent of the commercial loans made by the U.S. affiliates of Japanese banks go directly to Japanese multinational corporations with facilities in the United States.[26]

Many also believe that the U.S. banks have risen to the challenge presented by the foreign competitors on American soil and have even begun to make significant inroads in prying away some of the foreign multinational business which has traditionally gone to the U.S. affiliates of foreign banks. As an executive of the Sony Corporation of America bluntly stated in reference to the U.S. operations of Japanese banks:

> At one time, Japanese banks had all of our business. We still have a strong loyalty to them because they gave Sony its start in America. But we're doing less and less business with them. Only two of our six main banks now are Japanese. The Japanese banks have felt that loyalty would cover them over the long haul. But as the Japanese subsidiaries have expanded into many different fields, the Japanese banks just weren't capable of handling the problems. They are trying to catch up and become competitive. But you can only learn how business is done here with years of experience.[27]

Conversely, if one flips the coin and looks at foreign banking from another vantage point, one discovers that these foreign banking operations have made very noteworthy progress on the American scene. Roger Anderson, the chairman of the Continental Illinois Bancorp, flatly admits that "the most intense competition we face in the commercial side of our business is coming and will continue to come from the foreign banks, here in the U.S. and abroad."[28] Stephen S. Gardner, vice chairman of the Federal Reserve System, has publicly stated that he expects the assets of the foreign banks in the United States to at least double during the next decade, a prognostication which may even be somewhat conservative based on recent banking data.[29] A foreign banking executive has also pinpointed the area in which he anticipates the greatest growth activity: "In the future, we will be concentrating our efforts on the smaller U.S. companies that are neophytes in the international trade arena. And if we can compete for their trade business, we can compete for their domestic business."[30]

The expertise of the foreign banks in the international trade arena is certainly much greater than that of a vast majority of all American banks, a feature which should certainly open some doors to American businesses which have had little exposure to the importing-exporting game. For potential importers, the U.S. affiliates of foreign banks can offer foreign exchange trading facilities and logistical assistance from the foreign parent. For the U.S. exporter, these banks can provide valuable advice on tracking down possible foreign buyers and up-to-date information on foreign financial and marketing conditions. Oftentimes, the foreign parent's facilities abroad may also be placed at the disposal of the U.S. customer.

The foreign banks have also consistently offered lower interest rates for commercial and industrial loans than their American counterparts, frequently pegged at ½ percent below the domestic competition.[31] These foreign banks seem to be willing to accept a lower profit ratio in order to attract U.S. businesses and have been assisted in this effort by the past advantages of not having to post non-interest bearing loans with the Federal Reserve and not having to provide FDIC insurance.[32]

Since the Fed first began to keep track of foreign bank assets in late 1972, these assets have expanded at twice the pace of American bank assets within the U.S. market. These assets jumped from 18 billion dollars at the end of 1972 to approximately 95 billion dollars six years later.[33] Of the 122 foreign banks which had entered the United States by mid-1978, all but a handful had worldwide holdings of at least 1 billion dollars and 45 had assets exceeding 10 billion dollars.[34]

With the exclusion of investments, foreign institutions now account for one out of every five dollars of big bank deposits and loans in the United States.[35] Among the large banking establishments in the United States, the foreign banks make approximately 20 percent of all the business loans in the nation and this figure jumps to 33 percent in California and 37 percent in New York, America's two largest financial centers.[36]

On the world scene, only 15 U.S. banks currently rank among the top 100 in terms of deposits, and only 31 are among the top 200. In 1968, 26 U.S. establishments were in the top 100 and 68 in the top 200.[37] The large fluctuation in the value of the dollar vis-à-vis other major world currencies helps to explain some of this slippage in the U.S. world rankings. Nevertheless, the point should be sufficiently clear that many banking giants exist in the world and almost without exception, these giants consider that the United States for the time being offers a safe and attractive market for their funds. As a consequence, foreign investment in the key banking sphere should continue to accelerate and it is highly unlikely that Congress will go beyond the limiting provisions for foreign banking contained in the 1978 International Banking Act. After all, there are more than 750 affiliates of U.S. banks scattered around the world and protectionism on the part of the U.S. government would undoubtedly have adverse repercussions for these American operations abroad. Thus the prospects are good that the invasion of the U.S. market will continue and that the U.S. government will maintain a posture of nondiscrimination toward these foreign banks.[38]

Foreigners on Wall Street

At the end of 1977, the holdings of foreign investors in the U.S. stock market had climbed to 5 percent of the total value of listed American equities. During the bullish spring of 1978, overseas money continued to pour into the stock market and was considered as a prime ingredient in Wall Street's upward surge.

The foreign attraction to the U.S. stock market is buttressed by the belief that the American economy will remain a stable force in the foreseeable future and will retain its essentially capitalist framework while other Western economies drift ever closer to socialism. In addition, the American stock market offers much greater variety and more depth than markets in other countries. As an illustration, the market value of equities listed on American exchanges at the end of 1977 equaled 834 billion dollars. In comparison, the world's second largest market, the Tokyo Exchange, had equities totalling 215 billion dollars and the London Exchange trailed farther behind at 116 billion dollars.[39]

Events in other countries have also triggered greater interest in the U.S. market, events which go beyond the simple drift to the left in various parts of the world. In an effort to hold down the value of the soaring franc, the Swiss government has enacted very restrictive measures to dissuade certain types of foreign investment activity in that country's securities market. Helped along by the economic stimulation provided by the North Sea oil, Great Britain has removed recent controls on British Isles investors desiring to invest abroad. On the opposite side of the globe, the Japanese Finance Ministry has also made it much easier for Japanese nationals to invest in foreign stocks and bonds. Whether it be a result of the Swiss government's cold shoulder to outside money, or the greater latitude available to the British and the Japanese investors to send their pounds and yen abroad, Wall Street should wind up as the recipient of more foreign funds.

Frankly, in spite of their recent avid interest in U.S. securities, foreign investors have not always found a bed of roses awaiting them in the American stock market. Not only must these investors be concerned with the ups and downs of the stocks which they purchase, but they must also be wary of the fluctuations of the dollar against their own native currencies. The impact of this double jeopardy game may be illustrated by the following hypothetical case. If a Swiss investor had bought the Dow Jones industrial average at the end of 1972 and cashed it in in June 1978, he would have lost 19 percent of his investment because of the Dow's decline during this period, and an additional 39 percent loss would have had to be tacked on because of the erosion of the dollar vis-à-vis the Swiss franc.[40] As a concrete example of the foreign investor's "daily double" dilemma,

Japan's Asahi Investment Trust Management Company decided to double its stake in the U.S. market from early 1977 until early 1978 and did reasonably well in terms of its selection of stocks. Unfortunately, the Japanese firm wound up losing money in the overall process simply because of the precipitous decline of the dollar in relationship to the yen.[41]

Cynics might conclude that foreign investors from the developed nations are gluttons for punishment, but in spite of the perils of Wall Street, these overseas residents have remained enamored of the Big Board. This love affair has become so serious in recent months that many large investors from abroad have been involved in "currency swaps" in order to get their hands on dollars to invest in the U.S. market. During the bull market of early 1978, U.S. multinationals provided millions of dollars in hard cash to foreign firms desperate to get a piece of the action. The currency swap is basically a simple exchange of dollars for British sterling or other foreign currencies. Of America's 300 largest corporations, at least 50 have entered into such swaps in the past year or so. A recent example of a typical swap transaction involved the U.S. affiliate of Joseph E. Seagram & Sons. The Seagram's firm arranged to supply 84 million American dollars to four large British money funds which had been actively involved in the U.S. stock market. In return, Seagram's would eventually receive 46 million British pounds to be used to finance the purchase of a distillery in Scotland.[42] The Barclay's Bank pension fund, British Airways pension fund, and interestingly enough, some of the socialist-oriented British labor pension funds have been among the top foreign investors in the American market.

For the sake of fair play, the U.S. Securities and Exchange Commission (SEC) ordered the New York Stock Exchange in 1976 to abolish its limitations on foreign firm participation in the exchange's activities. In 1977, both the New York and American Stock Exchanges complied with the order but have adamantly insisted that foreign firms be willing to open their books and records to the exchanges' representatives.[43] Such a requirement is very rare in the equity markets of other Western nations and foreign firms have been very reluctant to go along with this thorough inspection practice. Nevertheless, in February 1979, two European-owned securities dealers, EuroPartners and Transatlantic, became members of the New York Stock Exchange, marking the first time since before World War II that European firms have been allowed on the floor of the exchange.

However, as Table 5-2 indicates, the foreigners have been very active in the acquisition of interests in several U.S. brokerage houses which are well versed in Wall Street procedures. As an example, Baron Leon Lambert of Belgium, a relative of the Rothschilds, has moved swiftly into the Wall

TABLE 5-2 Foreign Ownership of U.S. Brokerage Houses

Company	Foreign investor	Percent ownership
Amivest Corp.	Morgantos, Curaçao	10
Becker-Warburg Paribas	S.G. Warburg, United Kingdom, Banque de Paris et des Pays-Bas, France	50
Blyth Eastman Dillon	Compagnie Financière de Suez, France	20
Ivan F. Boesky	Several European investors	Minority
Cohn, Delaire & Kaufman	Akroyd & Smithers International, Netherlands	38
Donaldson, Lufkin & Jenrette	Olayan, Saudi Arabia, and several German and Japanese banks	9*
Drexel Burnham Lambert	Groupe Bruxelles Lambert, Belgium Sofindel, Switzerland	22–27
Lazard Frères	Lazard Frères, France	25
Lepercq, de Neuflize	Paul Lepercq, France	90
Lehman Brothers	Banca Commerciale Italiana, Italy	10–15
Oppenheimer	Cables Investment Trust, United Kingdom	10
Reynolds Securities	Banque Arabe et Internationale d'Investissement, France, and several Arab nations	16†
Weeden	Nomura Securities, Japan	3
Weiss, Peck & Greer	Crown Agents for overseas governments and administrations, United Kingdom	20
White Weld Holdings	Crédit Suisse, Switzerland	40

*After Donaldson, Lufkin & Jenrette's merger with Pershing, foreign ownership in the new enterprise dropped to less than 5 percent.

†Reynolds' recent merger with Dean Witter decreased the foreign ownership in the new firm to less than 12 percent.

SOURCE: *Institutional Investor*, December 1977.

Street scene. He has purchased a significant slice of a major New York investment management firm, assumed control of one of the foremost dealers in U.S. government securities, and has bought out one of Wall Street's most respected institutional research firms. To add some geographical balance to his thrust into the American market, Lambert has also purchased a Los Angeles brokerage house. What prompted this sudden onslaught emanating from Belgium? Quite simply, Lambert believes that increased state management of the European economies portends escalating tax rates and rampant inflation. As a Belgian banker succinctly put it, "The Baron is less interested in Europe these days. He thinks the future is in the U.S."[44]

Much talk, of course, still revolves around the possible impact which the OPEC countries could have on the Big Board if they were to increase the flow of their funds into Wall Street. From 1974 through 1977, the United States imported 108 billion dollars in goods and services from the OPEC countries, predominately in the form of black gold. In turn, the United States sold 70 billion dollars to these nations during the same period, leaving a net deficit of 36 billion dollars. However, the OPEC nations channeled 38 billion dollars back into the United States in the form of treasury securities, stocks and bonds, private investments, and advance payments for military hardware.[45]

Most of this money has gone directly into rather conservative U.S. government issues and only a sprinkling thus far has been earmarked for the market. As is becoming a marked trend, the U.S. Treasury has borrowed heavily from foreign interests to help finance the large U.S. budgetary deficit. In 1977, for example, foreign representatives bought 31.5 billion of the 52.1 billion dollars in securities that the Treasury sold to finance the debt, with a fairly significant amount being sold to OPEC countries.[46] Currently, foreigners control an astounding 25 percent of all federal government securities, representing America's single largest creditor. Ironically, many American homeowners also owe a deep debt of gratitude to the Saudi Arabians. The largest single holder of the paper of the Federal National Mortgage Association (Fannie Mae) is Saudi Arabia, which has therefore supplied a large chunk of the mortgage money needed by Americans to purchase homes.[47]

A relatively modest 1.5 to 2 billion dollars has been invested in the U.S. stock market annually by the OPEC nations since the precipitous rise in oil prices began in late 1973.[48] There are signs, however, that some of the OPEC nations have now begun to take off the wraps and become much more serious about investing in the equity market. For example, the Saudis are now funneling hundreds of millions of dollars through the Saudi Arabian Monetary Agency (SAMA), which has already arranged private placements in such American corporate stalwarts as American Telephone & Telegraph, U.S. Steel, Dallas Power and Light, and Pacific Telephone and Telegraph.[49] The Saudis are constantly looking for portfolio investments in sound U.S. industries, with the exception of the religious-linked distaste for alcoholic beverage and entertainment companies. In addition, a vice president of the Morgan Guaranty Trust Company revealed to a Senate subcommittee in November 1978 that his firm had personally invested 900 million dollars on behalf of Abu Dhabi, 700 million dollars for Kuwait, and 600 million dollars for Saudi Arabia, a good share going into portfolio investments in U.S. airline and air freight industries.[50] If the OPEC nations ever do decide to become more actively involved in the major U.S. stock exchanges, the foreign share of the American equity market would certainly climb beyond the present 5 percent level. A handful of the Wall Street brokerage houses already have strong Middle Eastern links (see Table 5-2) and OPEC money could easily be channeled through these institutions.

Do the OPEC interests, in particular, and foreign investors, in general, represent a danger to the average American investor? Scenarios could certainly be concocted to show how foreigners could precipitate marked instability on the Big Board. For example, if the U.S. government were to take a stance on Middle Eastern affairs which was perceived by the OPEC nations as blatantly pro-Israeli, OPEC money might suddenly be withdrawn from the market as a form of reprisal. Indeed, even leaving OPEC out of the equation, the American market would certainly be damaged by any sudden exodus of foreign money from Wall Street because of events linked specifically to international occurrences and not to the fragility of U.S. economic conditions. Moreover, it would be extremely difficult for the U.S. government to legislate in advance against such an occurrence, because American-held portfolio investment and government securities purchases abroad are still almost three times greater than current foreign holdings in the United States.[51] Once again, possible repercussions abroad for U.S. investors would make the men and women on Capitol Hill very leery about passing restrictive legislation of this sort.

On the other hand, for emotional content, it is very easy to assemble a chorus of Cassandras to blare out "worst possible" scenarios. Undeniably, the clout of foreign investors on Wall Street has grown, as Figure 5-2 clearly illustrates. Nevertheless, overall foreign investment on the Big Board is still relatively modest, and judging from past experience, foreigners have often shown greater confidence in the market than their American counterparts. For example, in 1968 foreigners were net purchasers of 2.3 billion dollars worth of stock, more than all of the American mutual funds combined. During 1977's bear market period, foreigners were again net buyers of 2.7 billion dollars of stock, at a time when many of the mutual funds and individual American investors were net sellers.[52] Foreigners prefer to buy when the market is on the upswing, but they also have a tendency to toughen up and weather the storm when the Dow-

Jones industrial average periodically dips down into a valley. Moreover, once the American dollar does stabilize in the world currency markets, billions of dollars of additional foreign money can be expected to flow into Wall Street because of the diminished fear of losses attributable to currency fluctuations.

FIGURE 5-2
Foreign Purchase of Equities, 1967–1977

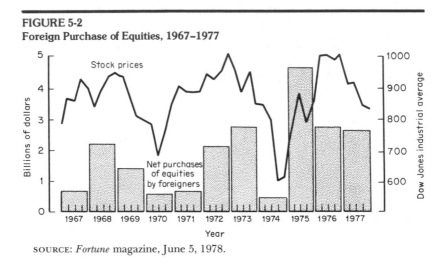

SOURCE: *Fortune* magazine, June 5, 1978.

Thus, using the worst possible scenario option, one might conclude that the average American investor could definitely be hurt if massive foreign investment in the stock market were suddenly to be withdrawn. In addition, the higher the percentage of U.S. equity holdings in the hands of foreign investors, the greater the risk that the market will be affected by political and economic perturbations abroad. Conversely, when one throws out the worst possible option and returns to the realm of future "probabilities" instead of remote "possibilities," it is likely that foreign investment will have a positive effect on the average U.S. investor. In essence, overseas investors often cast emotion aside and are willing to stick with the market even through troubled times, a phenomenon which over the months and the years certainly contributes to the Big Board's stability and benefits most domestic investors. But regardless of which scenario one chooses to embrace, the fact remains that Wall Street and the major financial centers in New York and California have been inundated with overseas money and that foreign investors and foreign banking institutions have dramatically increased their clout within the American market.[53]

SIX

The Foreign Appetite
for American Land
and Natural Resources:
How Serious Is the Problem?

The Foreign Surge and the
Reasons Behind It

Massive overseas purchases of U.S. farmland and American natural resources have precipitated the greatest public outcry against foreign investment activity in the United States. In the latter half of the 1970s, foreign investment in American real estate surged conspicuously upward as investors from abroad added appreciably to the estimated 4.9 million acres of U.S. land which they owned and the 62.8 million acres which they leased at the end of 1974.[1] Because of the laxity in reporting mechanisms in the United States, it is difficult to pin down the exact amount of foreign investment in this sphere. However, during the past few years, it is certain that billions of dollars annually have flowed into the United States from abroad for commercial and residential property development and for the purchase of farm and timber land and other terrain which is rich in natural resources.

Some of the foreign transactions or proposed deals in American real estate have received a great deal of national press attention. In a November 1978 broadcast, "60 Minutes" presented a segment on the foreign appetite for farmland. One congressman interviewed on the program estimated that as much as one-half of the rich agricultural land in California's Central Valley which is now being sold is going to foreign interests.

Another congressman prognosticated that intense foreign purchases in this sphere could conceivably give foreigners control of 30 percent of all U.S. farmland by 1988. The American press has also devoted an ample quantity of ink to the exploits of Arab and Iranian investors who have reportedly spent more than 150 million dollars during the past couple of years just for the acquisition of expensive homes in Beverly Hills.[2] In addition, the Deutsche Bank of Germany, the world's third largest banking institution after the Bank of America and Citibank with deposits topping 60 billion dollars, recently purchased an 80 percent stake in Houston's Pennzoil Place for 93 million dollars and then sold it off to the German public in $5,000 shares.[3] On behalf of a consortium of clients, the Deutsche Bank has also entered into serious negotiations to acquire one of the twin towers of the World Trade Center in New York City from the Port Authority of New York and New Jersey. Reportedly, the bank has been willing to ante up 500 million dollars for the towering structure. German investors have also joined with Playboy Enterprises to finance the construction of a 75 million dollar casino complex in Atlantic City. Indeed, top real estate people in that area estimate that perhaps one-half of the total investment in the New Jersey resort city over the next five years will come from foreign countries.[4] Many Hawaiian hotels are also owned by Japanese investors, Canadian newspapers have begun to refer to Florida as Canada's "Southern province" because of massive Canadian investment in that state, and some of the choicest oil and mineral rich land in Alaska is currently controlled by foreign interests.[5]

The so-called farmland dimension (which also includes land rich in timber and other resources) has undoubtedly sparked the most controversy among the American public. Foreigners purchased at least 2 billion dollars in farmland in 1977 and 1978 and in a series of columns linked directly to foreign farm acquisitions, Jack Anderson has estimated that 21 percent of all U.S. farm sales in 1977 involved overseas purchasers, many of them working through hard-to-trace "middleman" corporations. The public alarm over the foreign involvement in this sphere has prompted several bills to be introduced in farm state legislatures which would either severely restrict or prohibit altogether foreign ownership of farms.[6] In April 1978 the Missouri legislature actually passed a bill barring foreigners from acquiring more than five acres of agricultural land.[7]

At the least, American farmers complain that the foreigners are driving up the prices on farmland and are thus preventing young Americans from buying land. The higher prices also prompt an escalation in the taxes which farmers must pay. More ominously, however, some assert that "in a few decades of harvesting, foreign investment in U.S. farmland could eclipse American ownership. Then the nation's single greatest source of power would pass from the hands of American citizens."[8] Harold Dodd, the president of the Illinois Farmers Union, has offered this troublesome scenario: "Let's say the Arabs are buying huge portions of our land and a famine hits Arabia. Is there any question in your mind what they'll do with that food? Hell, they'd let our people go hungry and ship it to the motherland."[9] George Burrows, a member of the Nebraska State Senate who has introduced a bill to prohibit alien ownership of farmland in that state, carries the antiforeign ownership argument one step farther. He objects to foreign land purchases "because the people that own don't have to obey our laws. If we give alien ownership to parts of our nation, they're not subject to our laws when they live in other nations."[10] Burrows adds that the foreign owners "have no national heritage to care about. And when we turn it over to these people to own, it is political power, it's economic power, and they are one and the same thing."[11]

In spite of the hullabaloo which the foreign real estate investors have stirred up, including aspersions that they are threatening the sanctity of the family farm, overseas money continues to pour into the United States at unprecedented levels. Why has American turf become such a prized commodity for citizens of other nations? Undoubtedly, many of the general investment incentives outlined in Chapter Three also apply to the real estate sphere. Approximately two-thirds of the investors in land are from Europe, another one-quarter from Canada, and a sprinkling from Asia, the Middle East, and a few other areas of the world.[12] As mentioned in an earlier chapter, many of the European countries are small in comparison to the United States and land in these countries is pegged at ultra-premium prices. For example, Great Britain is the size of Oregon but has almost 30 times the population of that Western state. France stacks up with Texas in geographic size and West Germany is smaller than Montana. A national official of a U.S. farm and realty association recently visited a rural area several miles outside of Hamburg, Germany, and discovered that farmland in that region was selling for $16,000 an acre, the going rate in that part of Germany.[13] Japan, a nation of 120 million people, is also smaller than Montana and four-fifths of that island nation is virtually uninhabitable because of mountains. Thus what farmland does exist in between the major urban centers is literally priceless. In view of these conditions which prevail in most of Western Europe and in Japan, it is easy to understand why so many foreigners perceive that American farm prices are pegged at bargain basement rates. The foreigners are also aware that average farm prices have doubled during the past five years, and that the U.S. farm real estate value index has significantly outpaced the Dow Jones index over the past decade, thus representing a fairly good hedge against inflation. Equally important for many investors is the fact that the U.S. political system is stable and the capitalist tradition continues to prevail in the formulation of U.S. economic policies. As Jack A. Horn, the director of the Brussels-based European Investment Research Center, has surmised: "There is a trend today for the landed gentry and others to sell off their holdings and to reinvest in the United States for reasons of security against rising taxes, rent controls, and risk of nationalization."[14] An extreme but nonetheless germane illustration of the foreigners' consternation concerning events in their own homelands is offered by a Kansas City farm broker: "We had a group of Italians through here last week. One had been kidnapped by the Red Brigade, and they were thinking of moving here."[15]

On the Asian continent, Hong Kong investors have been very concerned because the British lease of Hong Kong will expire in 1997 and, ostensibly, 90 percent of the land which is now part of the British colony will revert back to the control of the Chinese. A great deal of Hong Kong money has recently made its way to San Francisco and even Taoist priests in the Asian colony have doled out more than a million dollars for 634 acres of land in Northern California's Napa County. This land will serve as a future site for a Chinese Temple.[16]

In summary, American land prices continue to be exceptional bargains when compared to prices in most other advanced industrial nations, even in terms of urban property. As a Japanese employee renting a home for $800 a month in a suburb of New York City pointed out, he would have had to pay twice as much for similar accommodations in Tokyo. He added, "I know New York prices seem high to New Yorkers, but to us housing here is so much cheaper it looks like a bargain."[17] Moreover, foreign investment in U.S. land is viewed as a hedge against worldwide inflation and as insurance against political and economic uncertainties in various parts of the globe. As long as the bargain basement remains open to the foreign buyer, the amount of land falling under foreign control will steadily increase and American reaction to this escalation in foreign land ownership will undoubtedly be accentuated.

Government Restrictions on Foreign Land Ownership

Historical examples Today, approximately one-half of the American states have statutes on the books which limit alien ownership of land in one way or another (see Appendix I for a list of these state land restrictions).[18] Indeed, American suspicions and apprehensions about alien land ownership seem to have deep roots. Prior to 1659, the colony in present-day Connecticut prohibited the sale of land to "outsiders" unless the town in the vicinity of where the property was located first gave its permission.[19] During the American Revolution, a widow was denied dowry rights to her husband's land because she had not joined with her spouse in accepting

U.S. citizenship.[20] Later, Congress also for a time specifically excluded English aristocracy from the ownership of American land.[21]

The Territorial Land Act of 1887 forbade alien landholdings in U.S. territories, except for immigrant farmers who had applied for U.S. citizenship. This law was prompted by fears that affluent investors from Great Britain and other parts of Europe would buy up huge chunks of land for farms and ranches and thus overly influence the economic development of those regions.[22] Several states in the Midwest followed the example of Congress and passed similarly restrictive legislation.

California and a few other Western states expressly excluded Oriental land ownership in the latter part of the nineteenth century and early decades of the twentieth. In effect, the California law denied ownership to "aliens ineligible for citizenship." At the time, Orientals were the only racial group specifically excluded from citizenship by federal immigration laws, thus it was quite clear which group the California legislation was designed to hinder.[23] Later on during the height of the Cold War, federal and some state legislation also prohibited land ownership by residents of the so-called Iron Curtain nations. Many of these aforementioned restrictions have now been removed or have fallen into complete disuse.

Contemporary state restrictions State laws which currently curtail alien access to land ownership are far from uniform, but Figure 6-1 and Table

---

FIGURE 6-1
State Restrictions on Alien Ownership of Land

Key
General prohibition
Major restrictions
Minor restrictions

SOURCE: U.S. Department of Commerce, *Foreign Direct Investment in the United States*, Vol. 8, 1976.

6-1 indicate what states do have limiting provisions of one type or another on their books. Land law in the United States is fundamentally state law and potential foreign investors must therefore be aware of state legislation before committing their funds to the purchase of real estate.[24]

Connecticut, Indiana, Kentucky, Minnesota, Mississippi, Missouri, Nebraska, New Hampshire, and Oklahoma generally prohibit or severely restrict foreign nationals who live abroad from owning property. Iowa, Minnesota, Missouri, Pennsylvania, South Carolina, and Wisconsin place specific acreage restrictions on foreign buyers. For example, Iowa and Wisconsin limit nonresident aliens to possession of no more than 640 acres, Minnesota restricts them to a measly 2 acres, Missouri to 5, and Nebraska prohibits foreign ownership altogether, unless the land is within incorporated municipalities or within three miles of municipal boundaries. At the opposite extreme, South Carolina has a rather meaningless statute on the books which restricts alien ownership of land to less than 500,000 acres. States also frequently limit the sale of state land to U.S. citizens and a state such as Hawaii also denies foreigners the right to purchase residential lots in specified development districts. Iowa and Minnesota also require nonresident aliens to file annual reports on their agricultural landholdings, and these two states, plus Nebraska, require corporations holding farmland to file yearly statements identifying the names of alien shareholders.

At least six states also place time limits on foreign ownership. Illinois, for one, limits the term of alien ownership of land to a maximum of six years. Several states also limit the right of an alien to inherit property or they specifically link inheritance privileges to the existence of reciprocity agreements with the affected alien's home country.[25]

Even in view of this confusion of state statutes, most experts agree that foreign investors can still purchase or lease land in a great majority of the states. As one such expert concluded: "There is little in present state law

TABLE 6-1 State Regulations Pertaining to Foreign Ownership of Farmland

Classification of state laws	Number of states
Restrictions on alien ownership of U.S. farmland	25
General prohibition or major restrictions on nonresident alien ownership of land	9
Restrictions on size of landholdings or duration of ownership	11
Restrictions on inherited land	9
Restrictions on acquisition of state property	4
Other minor restrictions on ownership	6
No restrictions on alien ownership of U.S. farmland	25
Restrictions on corporate ownership of U.S. farmland	13

SOURCE: U.S. General Accounting Office 1978 Report on Foreign Investment.

that effectively and validly excludes foreign investment in real estate." He adds that "the bark of state regulation is much worse than its bite. Except with regard to agriculture land, present laws prohibiting alien ownership of real estate have little more than nuisance value."[26]

As an example of the rather dubious quality of some of these state laws, certain states prohibit alien individuals from owning land but give a green light to alien corporations. Even those that do limit corporations often simply stipulate that the entities cannot be incorporated outside the borders of the United States. Thus if State A has just such a provision, a foreign group can take out papers of incorporation in State B and then buy land in State A in the name of the so-called domestic corporation. Likewise, state land in certain regions might legally have to be sold directly to U.S. citizens, but nothing stands in the way of these citizens either representing the interests of foreign buyers or turning around and selling the land to foreign investors. Similar loopholes exist in a host of other state statutes which on the surface seem to limit alien access to land.

The governors of the 50 states apparently have very mixed opinions about the present and potential impact of foreign investment in land in their respective states. A 1978 General Accounting Office survey of the statehouses found that only 4 percent of the governors perceived that foreign investment activity in their states was a current problem, 20 percent surmised that it might be a problem in the future, 36 percent concluded it was not an actual or a potential problem area, and 22 percent either did not respond or had no opinion on the subject. The survey also determined that ten states were at the time considering additional constraints on foreign ownership of land.[27]

Federal restrictions The Trading with the Enemy Act and the Foreign Assets Control Regulations are the two federal laws which are the most germane when considering federal restrictions on foreign investment in real property. The former act stipulates that property belonging to nationals of enemy countries may be seized by federal authorities and even auctioned off. Using authority granted by the Trading with the Enemy Act, federal officials confiscated land belonging to Japanese and German nationals during World War II. On the other hand, the Foreign Assets Control Regulations permit nationals of "listed" nations to hold title to American land, but these nationals are blocked from transacting any property-related business and U.S. citizens are forbidden to deal with these alien owners. In order to enter into discussions involving the future status of the property, special permission must first be granted by the Department of the Treasury.[28]

As of mid-1979, nationals of Cambodia, the People's Republic of China, North Korea, and Vietnam were on the "blocked" list and citizens of Cuba and Rhodesia were also subject to very similar restrictions. Potentially, the Foreign Assets Control Regulations remain a very important weapon in the arsenal of the federal government because if certain foreign investment activity were deemed to be injurious to American interests, the President could invoke this provision and thereby block foreign assets. Such an action, however, would have to be precipitated by very serious international conditions and could not be relied upon in nonemergency situations.

In response to growing public criticism directed at foreign ownership of farmland, President Carter signed a congressional bill in October 1978 which establishes a nationwide system for the monitoring of foreign purchases and divestitures of farms and other rural land. President Carter strongly emphasized that this new law was not intended in any way to dissuade foreign investment in the real estate sphere. However, the foreigners, who are often publicity shy, are now required to report their current land holdings and any future purchases, leases, or sales to the Department of Agriculture. These reports will then be made available for public scrutiny within ten days of receipt by Agriculture officials, and failure to comply with the new law could result in civil penalties ranging up to 25 percent of the value of the land held by the offending aliens. This law is expressly intended to determine how much rural land is actually controlled by foreign investors so that the government can ascertain whether major restrictions on such investment would be in the best interests of the United States. In a corollary provision, the 1978 law also orders the Secretary of Agriculture to evaluate the impact of foreign investment activity on family farms and rural communities.[29]

A few relatively minor limitations are also placed by the government on the lease by foreign nationals of federal land to be used for the extraction of coal, oil, oil shale, metallic substances, and a host of other natural resources. However, corporations are often permitted to lease such land from the federal authorities, and foreigners can usually own a piece of these corporate entities.[30] In addition, the U.S. Farm Home Administration has recently proposed new guidelines which would make it much easier for foreign owners of agricultural land to receive loan assistance from the U.S. government. The Farm Home Administration has suggested that business and industrial loans be made available to foreign firms operating in the United States which have a work force composed of at least 85 percent "rural" Americans. Under existing law, only firms with at least 51 percent American ownership are eligible for such loans.[31] Furthermore, foreign investors, through obvious loopholes in federal legislation, have been able to avoid paying capital gains taxes when they sell their U.S. property, a substantial benefit which is not available to American investors.[32] And finally, treaties negotiated by the U.S. government with other nations may contain most-favored-nation and reciprocal agreement clauses which effectively limit what state and federal authorities can do in trying to regulate foreign investment in real estate.[33]

Thus a patchwork quilt of restrictions, nonrestrictions, and even a few incentives face the potential foreign investor in American land. Some members of Congress, however, would prefer to see a more restrictive government policy toward such investment activity. H.R. 1213, for example, which has been dubbed the Foreign Investment Control Act, would establish a National Investment Control Commission with power to prohibit or restrict foreign ownership and control of resources deemed as essential to the national or economic security of the United States. Another proposed measure, H.R. 13183, would prohibit nonresident aliens from purchasing U.S. agricultural land altogether.

The precedent for measures involving restrictions on, and disclosure of, alien land purchases is to be found in the laws of two North American neighbors of the United States. Ownership or control of Mexican land is subject to that nation's foreign investment regulations, and aliens are barred from owning coastal, border, and certain other types of land in the country. In Canada, the provinces of Alberta, Ontario, and Nova Scotia require foreign owners to register their land purchases, and Ontario also tacks on a 20 percent transfer tax. Whether the Congress or the state legislatures would go along with such a special foreign investor land tax is highly unlikely for the time being, but remains an option available for future consideration.

Foreign Investment in Farmland and Other Natural Resources

At the turn of the twentieth century, the father of Alfred Zuckerman settled on agricultural land in California's fertile San Joaquin River Delta region. In 1937, the Zuckerman family purchased a 5,200 acre island on the river and began to grow potatoes, onions, asparagus, and a few other crops. Because of the need to pay inheritance taxes upon the death of his father, Alfred Zuckerman sold the family farm for 5.8 million dollars in the spring of 1978 to a corporation based in the principality of Liechtenstein and owned by a group of investors from Italy. Zuckerman frankly admitted that he had never met the investors in person and had no idea who they were. Zuckerman also lamented the fact that his property was among the last of the big family-owned farms in that region.[34]

The foreign takeover of the Zuckerman homestead is apparently just one of many fairly similar episodes occurring all over the United States. Separate studies conducted by Jack Anderson and Gerald Jackson of the San Francisco-based Amrex Corporation indicate that perhaps 20 percent or more of recent purchases of American farmland have been made by foreign buyers. Jackson has also estimated that up to 40 to 50 percent of recent transactions in the Mississippi Delta, parts of the Midwest, and California's Central Valley have involved foreign funds.[35]

Some of these transactions have caught the attention of the press and have been given some notoriety. The seemingly ubiquitous Ghaith Pharaon has recently purchased an interest in 32,000 acres of potentially rich mineral land in Louisiana, and he has made a tender offer to buy up to 950,000 shares in the OKC Corporation, a Dallas-based petroleum, cement products, and real estate company.[36] Crown Prince Franz Josef II of Liechtenstein owns a 10,000 acre spread in the Red River Valley of Texas; the Flicks, heirs to the Mercedes-Benz fortune, have a large farm-ranch combination in Kansas; and the Buitonis, celebrated Italian pasta makers, have recently acquired 12,000 acres of Illinois farmland for 17.5 million dollars.[37]

According to the Commerce Department 1976 study, foreign petroleum companies at that time accounted for 93 percent of the 63 million acres leased by foreign interests. In that year, 30 foreign-owned companies were operating in the U.S. petroleum industry and their cumulative investment in the petroleum sector had grown from 18 percent in 1962 to 23 percent in 1970 to 27 percent in 1974. British Petroleum (BP) controls more than 50 percent of the rich Prudhoe Bay oil field in Alaska and has a 49 percent interest in the famed Alyeska pipeline. BP and Standard Oil of Ohio (SOHIO) also have a combined interest in another 175,000 acres of potentially oil-rich land in Alaska, and BP is currently in the process of acquiring a controlling interest in SOHIO itself and many of its retail service stations (see Table 6-2 for a look at foreign firms having a particular interest in oil and other natural resources which are currently operating in the United States). It should be noted in reference to Alaska oil that U.S. law does stipulate that the entire production of the North Slope oil must be marketed in the United States unless the President expressly approves foreign sales and the Congress does not overturn this White House recommendation.[38]

In spite of the appearance of frenzied foreign activity in the purchasing of farms and other land rich in natural resources, official U.S. government studies almost invariably conclude that the foreign ownership in this sphere is still quite minimal. For example, even though foreigners control more than 2 million acres of timberland, the U.S. Department of Agriculture has pointed out that foreign interests represent only 0.33 percent of commercial timber operations in the United States.[39] Foreign ownership of farmland has also been consistently pegged by government sources at less than 1 percent.[40] The 1978 General Accounting Office study which

TABLE 6-2 A Sampling of Foreign Firms Engaged in the Extraction of America's Natural Resources

Country of origin	Foreign firm	U.S. affiliate	State location	Resource extraction
Belgium	Bunge Group	Bunge	La.	Soybean oil, grain
	Petrofina	American Petrofina	N.Y.	Petroleum
Bermuda	Coastal Caribbean Oils and Minerals	Coastal Petroleum	Fla.	Oil exploration
Canada	Algoma Steel	Cannelton Coal	W.Va.	Coal
	Aquitaine	Aquitaine Pennsylvania	Pa.	Coal
	Beaudry Lumber	Beaudry Lumber	Maine	Lumber
	British Columbia Packers	Nelbro Packing	Alaska	Seafood
	Canada Development	Texasgulf	Several	Minerals
	Canso Oil & Gas	United Canso Oil & Gas	Several	Petroleum exploration
	Colonial Oil & Gas	Colonia Oil & Gas	Calif.	Petroleum
	Consolidated Mining & Smelting	Cominco American	Mont., Neb., Wash.	Chemicals; metals, phosphate; nitrogen
	Denison Mines	Denison Mines	Colo.	Uranium, yttrium
	Distillers Corp. Seagrams	Texas Pacific Coal & Oil	Tex.	Coal, oil
	Dome Petroleum	Dome Petroleum	Alaska	Petroleum
	Domtar Ltd.	Sifto Salt Division	La.	Salt mining
	Ferrox Iron	Ferrox Iron	N.Y.	Minerals
	Francana Oil & Gas	Francana Exploration	Mont., Wyo.	Petroleum
	Home Oil	Home Petroleum	Kan., Alaska	Petroleum
	Hudson Bay Mining & Smelting	Inspiration Consolidated Copper	N.J.	Copper
	Husky Oil	Husky Oil	Wyo.	Petroleum
	International Nickel of Canada	International Nickel	Ky., N.C., N.Y.	Nickel mining
	Irving Pulp & Paper	Irving Pulp & Paper	Maine	Lumber

TABLE 6-2 A Sampling of Foreign Firms Engaged in the Extraction of America's Natural Resources (Continued)

Country of origin	Foreign firm	U.S. affiliate	State location	Resource extraction
	MacMillan Bloedel	Delta Industries	Miss.	Plywood, lumber
		Blanchard Lumber	Oreg.	Lumber
	Maine Timber Holdings	Maine Timber Holdings	Maine	Lumber
	McIntyre Porcupine Mines	McIntyre Mines	Ariz.	Gold concentrates
	Noranda Mines	Noranda Aluminum	Miss., Mo.	Aluminum
	Pan Canadian Petroleum	Pan Canadian Petroleum	Tex.	Petroleum, gas
	Petrol Oil & Gas	Petro Oil & Gas	Tex.	Petroleum
	Pominex	Pominex	Ohio	Petroleum
	Ranger Oil	Ranger Oil	Kan., N.Dak., Wyo.	Petroleum
	Royalite Oil	Royalite Oil	Several	Petroleum exploration
	Tricentral Canada	High Crest Oils	Several	Petroleum exploration
	Wainco Oil	Wainco	Tex., N.Mex.	Petroleum
France	Compagnie Générale de Géophysique	Georex	Tex.	Petroleum and mineral exploration
	Elf-Erap	Elf Petroleum	Calif.	Petroleum exploration
	Gardinier Group	Gardinier	Fla.	Phosphates
		Arkla Chemical	Ark.	Cement
	Société de Mines et de Produits Chimiques	Reactive Metals	Ohio	Metals
	Société Nationale des Pétroles d'Acquitaine	Acquitaine Oil	Tex.	Petroleum
	Union Minière	Jersey Minière Zinc	Tenn.	Zinc refining
	Usinor	Hawley Coal Mining	W.Va.	Coal mining

Country	Company	Project	Location	Activity
Germany	Kuehl Lange	Carbona Mining	W.Va.	Coal mining
	Salzdetfurth	Chemsalt	Utah	Potash, sodium
	Hugo Stinnes	Ruhrkohle-Stinnes	W.Va.	Coal mining
	VIAG	Hatco Mining	Mass.	Mining
Japan	Alaska Pulp	Alaska Lumber & Pulp	Alaska	Lumber, pulp
		Wrangell Lumber	Alaska	Lumber
		Harbor Seafoods	Alaska	Seafood
	Alaska Shokai	JAD, Alaska Shoji	Alaska	Seafood
	Iwakura Gumi	South Central Timber Development	Alaska	Lumber
	Kanematsu-Goshu	Tuscaloosa Resource	Alaska	Coal
	Kyokuyo	Whitney-Fidalgo Seafoods	Alaska	Seafood
Netherlands	Deli Maatschappi	Viking Drilling	Several	Oil well drilling
		Triple Five Oil	Several	Petroleum exploration
	Royal Dutch Petroleum	Shell Oil	Tex.	Petroleum
Norway	Det Norsk Objeselshap	DNO-USA	La., Okla., Tex.	Petroleum
United Kingdom	American Associates	Cumberland Gap	Ky.	Lumber, chips
	Bowater	East Highlands	Ala.	Lumber
	British Petroleum	BP Exploration	Alaska, Calif.	Petroleum
		Standard Oil (Ohio)	Ohio	Petroleum, gas
	Burmah Oil	Burmah Castrol Oils	Calif.	Petroleum
	Consolidated Gold Fields	American Limestone	Tenn.	Limestone
	Rio Tinto-Zinc	United States Borax & Chemical	Calif.	Borax, potash
		The Pyrites	Del.	Cobalt

SOURCE: U.S. Department of Commerce, *Foreign Direct Investors in the United States*, March 1976.

surveyed foreign investment in 25 counties in California, Georgia, Kansas, Missouri, and Oklahoma, also found that such investment activity was actually quite miniscule, ranging from zero in five Oklahoma counties to 1.5 percent of total acreage in eleven Georgia counties.[41] Officials in Iowa, the first state to require disclosure of foreign purchases, have concluded that only 7,000 acres of that state's farmland is owned by foreign investors, about 0.2 percent of the total farm acreage in that Midwestern state. Minnesota's foreign-controlled land accounts for less than 0.1 percent of that state's total acreage.

As a result of these studies which have been conducted at the national and state levels, studies which have often been supported by strong empirical evidence, one must conclude that the great publicity given to certain foreign transactions in the agricultural sphere has certainly distorted the significance of the overall impact of foreign investment in this important sector. In effect, foreign ownership of agricultural land is still relatively small when put within the context of the total agriculture-related acreage in the United States.

One must add the caveat, however, that the pace of foreign activity in this sector has certainly quickened, with foreign-originated transactions perhaps representing 7 percent or more of the total land sales in the United States in 1977.[42] Government officials also frankly admit that the monitoring of foreign purchases in the past has been abysmally inadequate. As Milton Berger, the director of the Commerce Department's Office on Foreign Investment in the United States, has observed: "What we are seeing may only be the tip of the iceberg. You can't hide the purchase of a factory, but little is known about sales of farmland."[43] Commerce Department reports on land purchases have almost exclusively been based on voluntary disclosures of acquisitions by alien individuals or corporations of 200 or more acres. Oftentimes, it is virtually impossible to determine who the true beneficiary of the land transaction actually is. Foreign buyers often shield their identities by channeling money through holding companies in Liechtenstein, Luxembourg, the Netherlands Antilles, the British Virgin Islands, or other island spots in the Caribbean.[44] Moreover, lawyers, banks, trusts, and corporations in the United States often serve as conduits and purchase real estate on behalf of foreign buyers. Consequently, a transaction arranged through a domestic intermediary would not even have to be reported to U.S. monitoring agencies.

Eastdil Realty of New York claims that it arranged the sale of 200,000 acres of Western land to foreign buyers in 1976 and another 400,000 acres in 1977.[45] A large California real estate firm has disclosed that it has arranged hundreds of millions of dollars of Western farm sales for foreign interests in the past few years, and has had serious inquiries from

European bank consortiums and other groups which plan to spend literally billions of dollars for future purchases of U.S. agricultural land.[46] A Clovis, New Mexico, real estate agent contends that 60 to 70 percent of his serious inquiries now come from foreign nationals, and several other agents in relatively isolated parts of the United States concede that overseas investors have been in constant touch with their offices in the hopes of buying choice rural land.[47] To top it all off, the chief executive officer of the New York-based Amivest Corporation, which invests for European institutions, claims that his problem is not in finding the foreign money, but rather in finding enough U.S. choice land for the foreigners to buy.[48]

Unless most of the aforementioned examples are simply "hype" jobs, foreigners are indeed scurrying about the countryside seeking out quality U.S. agricultural land.[49] Hopefully, the new 1978 law, which will require the disclosure of farmland holdings by foreign nationals, will clear up this muddled picture somewhat and provide a good indication of the impact which foreign interests are having on the farming, timber, mineral, and other natural resources spheres. There is no guarantee, of course, that this new law will smoke out the ultimate beneficiaries of the land purchases, for the names on the title deed do not necessarily correspond with the names of those people or groups who actually put up the money. Why are some of these overseas investors so publicity shy that they want to avoid having their names placed on the title deed? Undoubtedly, some are hesitant because they have qualms about how local American communities near their landholdings would react to their investment activities. Furthermore, an appreciable number strongly desire to avoid public disclosure so that pertinent authorities in the home country will not discover that they have taken money out of their own domestic economies in order to invest in the United States.

Some of these foreign investments are also motivated by the search for a secure source of raw materials, and the United States still does offer a veritable cornucopia of many of these resources. A great many foreign investors, however, are simply looking for a safe and attractive haven for their funds. Surveys strongly suggest, for example, that crops and other resources found on foreign-owned land are generally earmarked for the exact same purposes as those spelled out by U.S. owners.[50] Perhaps an executive of Oppenheimer Industries of Kansas City has placed the apparent foreign thirst for agricultural land in the proper perspective:

> There is a lot of old wealth in Europe and these people know from experience that after wars and conflicts have ended, retention of farmland has enabled them to retain a net worth and get back on their feet. They're looking now at American farm properties because they feel this is the last place in the world where land will be confiscated.[51]

Foreign Activity in Commercial, Recreational, and Residential Properties

The bill signed into law by President Carter in the autumn of 1978 does not provide for the monitoring of foreign investment in commercial, recreational, or residential properties. Although attracting less publicity than that accorded to the farmland episode, foreigners have indeed been quite active in these spheres and have spent a great deal of money on projects within major metropolitan core city areas. As illustrations, Iran's Bank Omran pledged a half billion dollars for the Canal Place project in downtown New Orleans, and several million more have been funneled into the purchase of an office building on New York's Fifth Avenue. The Canadian development firm Olympia and York has acquired seven New York City office buildings for 350 million dollars, and a consortium headed by Middle Eastern investors has offered 50 million dollars to buy the Barclay, Biltmore, and Roosevelt Hotels in the Big Apple from the bankrupt Penn Central Transportation Company.[52] Another firm from north of the border, Daon Development of Vancouver, is constructing a 38-story high rise office complex in downtown San Francisco known as the 444 Market Street Project. The Deutsche Bank spent well over 100 million dollars to purchase the Pennzoil Plaza and Shell Towers in Houston and has offered 500 million dollars for one tower of New York City's World Trade Center. The German bank offered its Houston properties to German citizens in $5,000 shares and sold out within 24 hours.[53] Money from a host of foreign nations is also a pivotal force in the resurrection of Atlantic City, and Sheik Hamzi Bedria of Prudential International Commodities has announced plans to spend up to 40 million dollars of Middle Eastern oil money to start up two new industries in Harlem and the South Bronx.[54] In view of all of these transactions, one might be prompted to observe that foreigners are spearheading the way toward urban renewal in several major U.S. cities.

A good share of the development money in recent months has emanated from Canada. Cadillac Fairview Corporation, Canada's biggest real estate developer, is building office towers in San Francisco and Denver, three California industrial parks, three Florida housing projects, and several shopping centers scattered across the United States. The chairman of Cadillac Fairview, A. E. Diamond, has openly admitted that "the U.S. is where our main thrust will be" and that his company plans to acquire about 1 billion dollars of U.S. properties in the next seven years.[55] Other Canadian giants such as Olympia and York, Genstar, and Daon have dramatically increased their own development activities in the Lower 48. These companies perceive very limited growth opportunities for their industry in Canada and fully expect government restrictions to increase at both the national and provincial levels.[56] Some of the Canadian provinces already have exorbitant "antispeculation" tax rates which may run as high as 75 percent.[57] Moreover, the United States offers attractive opportunities for Canadian penetration. As Cadillac Fairview's chairman has surmised: "What better place to go than a country ten times as large as you are, one that speaks the same language, has the same basis for law? Besides, we can be very competitive there."[58]

Much of the foreign money for commercial, residential, and recreational projects has been concentrated in the so-called Sunbelt region. An estimated 450 million dollars of Canadian money has streamed into Florida, a state which has long been an attractive vacation oasis for Canadians trying to flee the northland's grueling winters. However, certain realtors in Miami have estimated that in spite of the influx of Canadian investment funds, 25 percent of the property in the Miami area is now being sold to investors from Latin America, although the realtors have not specified whether these investors intend to live permanently in the United States.[59] The Kuwaiti Investment Company has spent many millions for the purchase and renovation of Kiaweh Island off the coast of South Carolina. The same Kuwaiti enterprise has also invested substantially in a downtown complex in Atlanta which includes the Atlanta Hilton, and Ghaith Pharaon has offered nearly 31 million dollars to secure a majority interest in the Hyatt International hotel chain with facilities in most of the major U.S. cities.[60] Pharaon's fellow countryman Adnan Khashoggi, has also purchased development sites in Houston and Salt Lake City. Houston's Coldwell Banker real estate group has stated that its sales to foreigners of property in the Houston area has jumped from 5 percent of its overall business half a decade ago to 20 percent in recent months.[61] An estimated 300 million dollars in foreign investment capital is now going annually into Texas real estate.[62]

In California, Daryoush Mahboubi-Fardi is financing a 20 million dollar complex of elegant stores in Beverly Hills to complement the hundreds of millions which Middle Eastern investors have recently placed in an elegant residential section of the city now referred to as the "Persian Gulf."[63] Farther north, the owner of one of San Francisco's largest residential realty firms has stated that 60 percent of his company's sales over the past two years have been to buyers who have funds from some foreign country or are foreign citizens themselves.[64] Asian buyers, predominately from Hong Kong and Taiwan, have also been scooping up properties in San Francisco's commercially oriented Montgomery Street district. Far out from California's shores and nestled in the Pacific, Hawaii has also experienced a great influx of foreign money. Foreign investment, mainly from Japan, has gone into several beachfront hotels, although the land under the hotels often remains in the hands of Hawaiian or mainland American owners.

Even though foreign investors have been active in most spheres of real estate activity, many seem to prefer joint ventures with American partners in commercial or other types of real property which have produced a good investment record in past years. Furthermore, the overseas investors are often willing to take a lower rate of return than most domestic investors. They usually have longer time horizons and seek to preserve capital first and then think about income second. Mahmood Jafroodi, director of the Bank Omran which was once part of the Shah of Iran's Pahlavi Foundation, once amplified on what he considered to be a "good" return on Iranian investments in the United States: "In the U.S., anything that could return to us more than what we would earn if we left our money in a savings account or a certificate of deposit, or purchased corporate bonds, would be a 'good' return."[65]

Large sums of foreign capital are apparently available for the right type of commercial, recreational, and residential property projects, and there is little doubt that foreign investment in the overall real estate sector will continue to accelerate.[66] As Jafroodi of the Omran Bank has asserted in reference to foreign investment in the United States:

> I have a firm belief that it is going to increase. Looking from the outside into the U.S., and comparing it with what is available worldwide, the gap that has existed that distinguishes the U.S. from the rest of the world is increasing—it's not narrowing. Although you, looking from within, may think that you're not reaching certain goals or standards—that you may be falling behind what is expected—in relative terms, the U.S. is increasingly attractive.
>
> So, obviously, investment will flow into the U.S. Take a country like Japan. Everything that could possibly be done has already been done in that small country, and the surplus funds of foreign currency are on the upslope. Even those countries have to find their way into the U.S. more.[67]

The First Showdown

The most acute public reaction to foreign investment activity in the United States has thus far occurred within the domain of land ownership, particularly agricultural property. The U.S. government has been sensitive to this public concern and has instituted a program which will monitor overseas purchases of farms and other resource-rich properties. Although restrictions on foreign activity in this sphere are now minimal, it is highly probable that it is within the farm sector that the first U.S. showdown with foreign investors will take place. Indeed, if the estimates of annual foreign purchases of farmland which have been made by Jack Anderson and Gerald Jackson are correct, alien investors are now acquiring control over an alarmingly high percentage of America's food-producing land, a phenomenon which some claim will make U.S. food policy much more vulnerable to overseas demands. Thus, the first major limitations on foreign investment activity in the United States will most likely be imposed within the realm of rural land ownership. Some state legislatures are already very close to formulating such a policy, and Congress may well endorse such a restrictive program by the end of the 1980s, if not before.

SEVEN

The Geographic Distribution of Foreign Investment: A Region-by-Region Survey

The Emerging Importance of the States in the Foreign Investment Process

Foreign investors have often been perplexed by the significant taxing and regulatory powers which the U.S. federal system assigns to state governments. There are, of course, a few other advanced industrial societies in the world which have adopted federalist frameworks dividing governmental responsibilities among national and regional levels. The list of federal nations includes West Germany, Switzerland, Austria, Canada, and Australia. However, a much larger group of developed nations have unitary systems wherein the national governments establish the major regulations for the nation as a whole. Consequently, a potential outside investor desiring to learn about regulatory practices in Great Britain would first look to London, and in France first to Paris. In sharp contrast, the foreign investor wanting to understand the regulatory climate in the United States would have to keep fully abreast of federal statutes emanating from Washington, as well as pertinent legislative and administrative decisions of the state and even the county and the city in which the investment is earmarked.

Moreover, even though foreign direct investment does have a definite impact on the U.S. economy as a whole, its most profound influence will be felt in the localities and the regions where the investment activity is concentrated.[1] Moreover, as the Conference Board has pointed out, some foreign investors initially perceive the U.S. market as being too vast for small and medium-sized overseas firms to compete in successfully, but later recognize that the United States actually consists of a series of regional markets within the larger national market.[2] Furthermore, these regional markets are often quite distinctive and manifest a fairly broad range of business and cultural characteristics.

In the past few years, many state governments have come to realize the potential bonanza which foreign investment could represent for their respective state economies and have thus been out hustling for overseas money. For state officials, foreign investment capital represents an opportunity to expand their employment roles, raise their tax base, and diversify their statewide economic structure. Prior to 1970, only three or four states had offices overseas and these facilities were used primarily to drum up business for port authorities and to seek out export possibilities for local industries. At the beginning of 1977, 23 states, Puerto Rico, and 11 port authorities had established promotion offices in Western Europe, 7 states had similar facilities in Japan, 2 in Hong Kong, and 1 in São Paulo, Brazil.[3] Several other states currently have plans to open in Europe and in Asia either individual state offices or multistate offices through regional economic commissions. The National Association of State Development Agencies (NASDA) has also established a special international division to help facilitate the growing state interest in attracting foreign investment.

Some of the states have already reaped significant economic benefits from their international activities. Virginia, for example, opened a promotion office in Brussels in 1969 and within five years was able to attract more than 60 foreign firms to Virginia cities and towns. These firms invested over 450 million dollars in the economy, and generated more than 31,000 new manufacturing and other related jobs for Virginia residents.[4]

The Bank of America has estimated that 14,000 distinct industrial organizations exist at the state and local government levels to assist in the hunt for foreign investors.[5] Indeed, state and local government delegations and civic groups are literally criss-crossing the globe in search of foreign money. The volume of such overseas activity has increased to the point where U.S. Foreign Service officers in each of the major overseas nations are having to work at a frenzied pace, and many foreign businesses and trade organizations have undoubtedly wearied of the constant barrage of American delegations. Nevertheless, the onslaught continues, spurred on by the occasional success story which results from these overseas missions. A European chemical producer, for example, has admitted that it decided to locate in South Carolina because of the personal visit to the firm by the governor of that state. A European manufacturer of optical equipment also stated that it had established a facility in New York because of the personal interest shown by a delegation from the Empire State.[6] Several other foreign firms have also asserted that the personal interest shown by local or state envoys was a critical factor in their ultimate decision to locate in one region of the United States instead of another.

State level restrictions and incentives Specific state restrictions on foreign investment activity have been discussed in previous chapters. To recapitulate, the most severe state restrictions on foreign-owned enterprises are in the realm of banking and insurance, although selected states also frown on nonresident alien ownership of real estate. Several states also place certain limitations on foreign involvement in fishing, mining, and the alcoholic beverage industries, as well as individual alien participation in medicine and law.

State legislation pertaining to business activities in general has increased 250 percent over the past 15 years, but most states have been careful not to discriminate against foreign firms.[7] A great number of state laws conform with the Model Business Corporation Act prepared in 1946 and substantially revised in 1969 by a special committee of the American Bar Association. In the Model Act, the term "foreign corporation" is used to refer both to alien firms and to corporations formed under the laws of a different state. In effect, foreign-based corporations are normally entitled within a given state to the same privileges and restrictions placed on domestic firms incorporated elsewhere in the United States.

With the possible exception of agricultural land, state governments have definitely been more inclined in recent years to entice foreign investment than to restrict it (see Appendix II for a detailed list of state incentive programs). In 1959, Luther Hodges, then Governor of North Carolina, sent the first state industrial mission to Europe in the quest for foreign investment funds. Later, as Secretary of Commerce, Hodges pushed for the creation of the Invest in U.S.A. program and openly encouraged the states to seek overseas money in order to spur on state industrial development. Invest in U.S.A. has worked closely with pertinent state agencies from the beginning and continues to draw praise from most state officials even though the budget of this Commerce Department office has been pared down substantially. In 1972, 27 states participated in the Invest in America seminars sponsored jointly by the Commerce Department and NASDA and conducted in West Germany and Sweden. Similar conferences held a year later in Japan were attended by 36 states, and 35 returned when the program headed back to Europe in 1974. In all, 48 different states, Puerto Rico, and the Virgin Islands have participated in these overseas projects.

More than half of the states now maintain permanent overseas offices, primarily within the European Economic Community and in Japan.[8] A handful also have facilities in Canada, and state agencies from Arizona, Colorado, Florida, Maryland, New York, and West Virginia have advertised extensively in Canada since the Parti Québécois came to power in Quebec in late 1976.[9]

When contemplating the establishment of businesses in the United States, foreign investors are primarily concerned with the following considerations: (1) taxes and financing; (2) resource availability; (3) labor characteristics (wage rates, supply of workers, and union or nonunion affiliations); (4) local and regional services and supply sources; (5) market accessibility; (6) technical and educational facilities; and (7) community quality of life and local acceptance of foreign ownership.

In an attempt to satisfy as many of these conditions as possible, and in a better fashion than competing states, many state governments have now begun to offer incentive packages to potential foreign investors, packages which often include tax breaks, low-interest loans, special mortgage arrangements, and state-subsidized educational and vocational training. Twenty-three states currently offer tax exemptions or moratoriums on land and capital improvements, up from fourteen in 1968. Twenty-eight also provide tax breaks on the purchase of equipment. In order to entice Volkswagen to the rolling hills of Pennsylvania, the state government in Harrisburg offered the German auto giant more than 60 million dollars in low-interest loans plus several other plums costing additional millions (see the case study of the Volkswagen transaction in the next chapter).

The state of Michigan cuts taxes sharply for new plant construction or for the renovation of old ones. New plants can receive a 50 percent reduction on property taxes for 12 years; in addition the owners will be able to write off capital investment in the plant against state taxes in a single year instead of over a longer period of time.[10] Many other states also offer incentive packages that come close to the Pennsylvania and Michigan plans, and more than 30 states have already contacted Datsun, Toyota, Mazda, and Honda about setting up assembly plants in their locales.[11]

Through global junkets, state-sponsored tours of local sites for potential investors, and incentive packages, literally hundreds of millions of dollars are being spent by state governments to attract foreign investors to America's shores. In an era when some Americans seem to have second thoughts about the dramatic escalation in foreign investment activity in the United States, most state development agencies have shown little hesitancy toward seeking overseas money to foster industrial growth and greater employment opportunities within state boundaries. Although not all states have been mesmerized by the foreign investment gambit, a huge percentage of the most populated states is risking a lot of money on the premise that foreign capital will be a partial panacea for their unemployment woes. Michigan, for example, has even gone so far as to place advertisements in European trade magazines which lead off with the title, "FOR SALE, ONE STATE." Not to be outdone, the New York Commerce Department spent $400,000 in the spring of 1978 for the placement of ads in European, Asian, and Canadian newspapers and magazines. These ads asserted that "no other state in America offers better financial incentives than New York." As of June 1978, New York authorities claimed to have received 1,319 "serious" inquiries as a result of these ads.[12]

The state competition has become so intense that Washington and many of the state capitals may now be on an inevitable collision course. In September 1978 a top U.S. Treasury official asserted that the incentive programs put together by state and local governments in order to lure overseas money are definitely hurting U.S. international trade relationships. Washington is currently advocating at the GATT conference in Geneva an end to "unfair" government subsidies for private businesses, and U.S. representatives have been openly embarrassed by the millions of dollars of incentives which state government agencies are now offering in order to entice some of the world's largest multinational conglomerates to their regions. According to the Treasury official, the federal government is now investigating ways to "head off" these state and local efforts, an indication that a major federal-state confrontation may be in the offing.[13]

The Geographical Distribution of Foreign Investment

In general, foreign investment in the manufacturing sphere has been concentrated in the Northeast, Southeast, and along the Pacific Coast. Of the 2,053 foreign-owned facilities surveyed by the Department of Commerce in the mid-1970s, 710 (34.6 percent) were located in the East, 641 (31.2 percent) in the South, 415 (20.2 percent) in the Midwest, 214 (10.4 percent) in the West, and 73 (3.6 percent) in Puerto Rico and the Virgin Islands.[14] New York led the parade with 222 foreign industries, followed by New Jersey (178), Pennsylvania (125), and California (103). At the opposite end of the spectrum, the Rocky Mountain region had attracted only 49 (2.4 percent) foreign-controlled facilities, and New Mexico (1), Nevada (2), Montana (3), and South Dakota (3) trailed the list of the 50 states in terms of the number of foreign manufacturing plants within their boundaries. Of course, this list only goes up until the end of 1975 and does not indicate the size of the facilities. Table 7-1 sheds some additional light on this subject by indicating the number of employees hired by the foreign firms on a state-by-state basis. Surveys have also shown that almost all of these employees of foreign-owned industries are American citizens.[15]

TABLE 7-1   Foreign-Owned Manufacturing Plants on a State-by-State Basis, 1974

State	Foreign-owned plants	Percent of all plants with 20+ employees	Number of employees	Wages and salaries, $ millions
Ala.	20	1.23	11,519	101
Alaska	30	33.33	5,440	61
Ariz.	6	1.01	6,290	38
Ark.	14	1.33	10,565	74
Calif.	103	0.92	104,373	1,155
Colo.	17	2.04	11,538	127
Conn.	44	1.97	20,299	206
Del.	14	5.76	4,177	65
D.C.	0	0.00	1,338	16
Fla.	55	1.90	25,326	217
Ga.	68	2.55	22,200	197
Hawaii	8	3.39	13,095	91
Idaho	9	2.57	1,773	13
Ill.	92	1.25	71,380	822
Ind.	47	1.54	24,034	248
Iowa	8	0.68	7,139	80
Kan.	27	2.82	5,598	62
Ky.	34	2.70	13,627	135
La.	35	3.09	19,102	223
Maine	19	3.21	20,299	206
Md.	41	2.85	17,610	177
Mass.	74	1.78	21,015	220
Mich.	87	1.73	37,307	436
Minn.	8	0.41	13,025	154
Miss.	18	1.69	4,765	35
Mo.	30	1.21	13,729	156
Mont.	3	1.46	710	7
Neb.	8	1.34	2,178	22
Nev.	2	1.83	1,398	14
N.H.	22	3.89	7,044	64
N.J.	178	3.01	79,388	969
N. Mex.	1	0.44	1,790	18
N.Y.	222	1.71	146,642	1,747
N.C.	90	2.37	41,736	371
N. Dak.	5	4.27	1,143	14
Ohio	51	0.79	44,297	427
Okla.	9	1.00	6,493	66
Oreg.	7	0.48	5,012	56
Pa.	125	1.55	56,448	552
P.R.	67	—	10,289	62
R.I.	16	1.77	2,940	31
S.C.	71	4.93	23,318	223
S. Dak.	3	1.99	306	3
Tenn.	19	0.83	21,713	186
Tex.	82	1.71	50,130	613
Utah	6	1.40	2,719	24

TABLE 7-1   Foreign-Owned Manufacturing Plants on a State-by-State Basis, 1974   *(Continued)*

State	Foreign-owned plants	Percent of all plants with 20+ employees	Number of employees	Wages and salaries, $ millions
Vt.	10	3.65	3,235	29
Va.	58	3.28	21,107	201
V.I.	6	—	—	—
Wash.	17	1.16	11,206	132
W. Va.	13	2.14	9,419	112
Wis.	49	1.71	29,702	263
Wyo.	5	6.41	1,506	16
Total	2,053	1.80	1,083,431	11,442

SOURCE: U.S. Department of Commerce, *Foreign Direct Investment in the United States*, Vols. 1 and 3, 1976.

In other foreign investment spheres, the geographic distribution is somewhat different. Banking activity, for example, is heavily concentrated in New York, California, and Illinois. On the other hand, approximately one-half of the foreign land ownership is in the Rocky Mountain, Far West, and Southwest regions, and another one-quarter is in the Southeast.[16]

The South   In spite of the impressive incentive packages offered by the highly industrialized states of Pennsylvania, Michigan, and other northern tier states, foreign investors have shown a special affinity for the Sunbelt region of the Southeast, and for good reason. Fantus Company, the industrial consultancy division of Dun and Bradstreet, recently evaluated the "business climate" in each of the 50 states on the basis of taxes, labor laws, unemployment costs, welfare costs, and state indebtedness. Seven of the eight top-rated states turned out to be in the South; specifically, Texas, Alabama, Virginia, South Carolina, North Carolina, Florida, and Arkansas.[17]

The Southern states have among the lowest wage rates in the United States, an attractive feature to prospective foreign investors. For example, the average wage in mid-1978 in North Carolina was $3.51 per hour, in South Carolina $3.55, and in Georgia $3.88. In comparison, the average wage in Michigan was $6.15 and in the United States as a whole, $5. Foreign firms have also had the tendency to be extremely wary of American unionism. In this respect, the Southern states have been very accommodating because of their right-to-work laws and the overall scarcity of organized unions. Combine these features with the growing Southern market, the proximity to East Coast ports, the respectable energy situation, the relatively low land and construction costs, the attractive climate, and a vigorous promotion program which one European source has called "a blend of Southern charm and Northern hucksterism," and one begins to understand why foreign investors have flocked into the region.[18]

In 1971, Georgia opened for the first time a special division in its Department of Community Development to promote foreign investment in that Atlantic Coast state. The state now has permanent foreign offices in Brussels, Tokyo, Toronto, and São Paulo, and has sponsored trade and investment missions to most regions of the world, including the first state foray into Eastern Europe.[19] By 1973, Georgia had reported 140 million dollars in capital investment from foreign sources. Governor Jimmy Carter, for example, was instrumental in convincing YKK, Incorporated, a Japanese firm, to construct a plant in Macon, Georgia. YKK is the world's largest zipper maker and has worldwide sales in excess of 1.5 billion dollars. By mid-1978, businesses from at least 23 countries had poured 1 billion dollars into facilities on Georgia soil. Eighty-four foreign-owned manufacturing plants were situated in 27 Georgia cities with the largest facility being the 500 million dollar Columbia Nitrogen fertilizer and chemical plant in Augusta. This plant is Dutch-owned. Coats and Clark, Incorporated, the famous yarn and thread maker from Scotland, has six plants in the state and provides more than 4,000 of the 22,000 jobs created in Georgia by foreign investors.

Officials from South Carolina estimate that 35 percent of all new industrial development in that state now comes from abroad.[20] South Carolinians continue to hustle for foreign capital, and Spartanburg is perhaps the most international city in the entire United States (see the case study of this South Carolina community in the next chapter). The South Carolina development office offers potential foreign investors free special surveys on land, markets, and natural resources, and pledges to recruit and train workers at no cost to the investor. The state will also arrange financing and negotiate building contracts on behalf of the foreign investor, and provides free English lessons for the children and spouses of foreign personnel. Frequently, state officials will usher a prospective investor into South Carolina by private aircraft and then show him the sites in a chauffeured limousine.[21] These promotional strategies have apparently been eminently successful because hundreds of millions of dollars of overseas money has recently found its way to the shores of South Carolina.

Frankly, the South, which has so often been stereotyped by many Americans as the most parochial region in the United States, has possibly been the most aggressive in seeking foreign investment. A governor from Tennessee has hosted the United Nations ambassadors from a hundred different nations, a Georgia head of state has made at least seven trips abroad to drum up overseas investment, and seven Southeastern states have joined with Japan in the formation of the Southeast United States-

Japan Association to facilitate economic cooperation. These incidents typify what is currently going on south of the Mason-Dixon line. Moreover, another original Confederate state, Texas, has been referred to by foreign sources as the land of "America's Arabs" and a London-based magazine has singled it out as a great area for foreign investment, insisting that "the smell of money, fresh, new and in the making permeates the Texas air."[22] The inherent attractive features found in most Southern states, combined with the vigorous state agency promotion programs, should continue to make the South a fertile area for the implantation of overseas capital.

The East   The large Eastern industrial states such as New York, Pennsylvania, and New Jersey have attracted well over a billion dollars of foreign capital in the past half decade. A 1978 survey conducted by New York City's Office of Economic Development and New York University's Graduate School of Business Administration helps to illustrate the "foreign" presence just within the Big Apple. Eight hundred and thirty-nine of approximately two thousand foreign-owned businesses in New York City responded to the survey. These firms accounted for nearly 50,000 jobs and paid in excess of 100 million dollars annually just for the leasing of premises within the city. Almost one-third of the firms were from Japan, with another 35 to 40 percent from Great Britain, West Germany, France, Italy, and South Korea combined.[23]

New York and the New England states which border on Canada have also been the recipients of a large infusion of Canadian money since late 1976. Certainly, part of this phenomenon is attributable to "flight capital" fleeing the country because of the uncertainty associated with the Quebec situation and the future of the Canadian Confederation. On the other hand, Canadian firms are naturally attracted to the larger market and the lower wage and production costs to be found south of the border. For example, the minimum wage in Quebec is $3.65 per hour, far above comparable figures in the American states. Quite frankly, the business climate has recently been much better in the United States than in Canada and some of the American border states have benefited substantially from this situation.

The Midwest   Although attracting a wide variety of foreign-owned enterprises, such as Honda and British Petroleum in Ohio, the Midwest stands out as an area of heavy overseas investment in agricultural land and in the grain and food-processing industries. The Northern Trust and Continental Illinois banking establishments in Chicago and Oppenheimer Industries in Kansas City have been instrumental forces in arranging the purchase of prime Midwest farmland for foreign buyers. In its 1976 annual report, for example, Northern Trust states that it was managing 460,000 acres of land in 35 states, mostly for overseas owners.[24] In response to the avid overseas interest in American farmland, Midwestern legislatures have been among the first to pass bills which closely monitor or strictly limit foreign investment activity in the farming sector. In particular, Missouri, Iowa, and Minnesota have taken very forceful action in this sphere.

Foreigners have also shown a keen interest in the Midwest grain exporting business. In the 1974–1975 marketing year, 46 percent of all U.S. grain exports was handled by firms having foreign owners, and the Commerce Department has predicted even greater foreign activity in the grain industry in the future.[25] Aside from the traditional profit motives, foreigners have been especially interested in this economic sector in order to obtain reliable supplies of grain for their overseas clients. On the whole, Commerce officials have not been unduly alarmed by the rising foreign involvement in this key sector, contending that foreign capital "contributes to a high level of grain exports, and tends to strengthen farm income and the U.S. balance of payments."[26]

The West Among the Western states, California stands out as the chief magnet for foreign investment. In particular, Japanese and other Asian investors have been attracted to the Pacific Coast state, with 400 offices, agencies, and plants of Japanese firms located in the Los Angeles region alone. Interestingly enough, a Japanese language television station has recently begun operations in the Southern California area to service a growing demand for Japanese-produced programs. Governor Jerry Brown traveled to Tokyo in 1977 to discuss trade and investment opportunities with Japanese officials and has suggested that Asian capital may be a key element in California's future economic expansion. The California Governor has periodically insisted that the Golden State must develop its own "foreign policy," and Brown's international trade coordinator has publicly supported California's entry into what he refers to as Japan's "coprosperity sphere." The trade representative speaks of California as being the third largest market in the Pacific region after Japan and the rest of the United States. He has also asserted that capital investment from Japan and other foreign nations would help make California's economic development less dependent on Eastern U.S. funding.[27]

California's Pacific Coast neighbors, Oregon and Washington, have also been recipients of increased foreign capital over the past few years and many of the Sunbelt states in the Southwest have garnered a growing share of overseas investment money. All of the West has also been a prime area for farm, timber, ranch, and mineral land purchases by foreign investors. In Alaska, Japanese investors have significant interests in that state's forest products and fish processing industries. Moreover, British

Petroleum has led the foreign investment parade into Alaska's all-important oil sector, controlling a large share of the North Slope fields and having close to a half interest in the Alyeska Pipeline.[28] One-third of all job opportunities for Alaskans in manufacturing plants with more than 20 employees are currently provided by foreign-owned firms.

The major investing country in Hawaii is once again Japan, with the foreign investment concentrated in the tourism and real estate sectors. In February 1975 Japanese investors owned 16 hotels in Hawaii, representing 5.5 percent of the state's total hotels and 17 percent of the total room capacity. On Waikiki, 25 percent of the hotel units were Japanese-owned at that time.[29] Public concern over the possible impact of foreign investment prompted the state and federal governments to investigate the situation. In general, the government surveys concluded that foreign investment in Hawaii was actually a minimal force in the state's overall economic picture and did not adversely affect Hawaiian interests.[30]

Conclusion

Without a doubt, state governments have in recent years been much more actively involved in international affairs and have established major programs costing millions of dollars of taxpayers' money to attract foreign investment. If Commerce Department computations are correct, it seems that the taxpayers' money in this case has usually been spent rather propitiously, at least in terms of the creation of new jobs and an expansion in tax revenues. Using case studies from Pennsylvania and Georgia, the Department of Commerce has calculated that in 1976, $1 of state funding was needed to attract $667 in direct foreign investment. Thus, $60 in state funds would be necessary to entice $40,000 in foreign capital, which in turn is estimated to create one new industrial job. Because of the added jobs and the increasing tax revenues generated from the expansion in the state's economy, Commerce Department officials conclude that the state funds earmarked for foreign investment purposes represent a real bargain.[31] Of course, inflation and keener competition among the states have driven up the cost figures over the past few years, but most state governments still insist that their foreign investment incentive programs represent state money well spent. However, growing concern in Washington over the escalating costs of the incentive packages offered to foreign firms may lead in the future to a reassessment of some facets of state-level overseas activities. But for the moment, at least, state and local governments continue to be among the most ardent supporters of large-scale overseas investment in the United States and are engaged in what amounts to cutthroat competition to attract this investment from abroad.

EIGHT

The "Art" of Attracting Foreign Investment: A Presentation of Three Case Studies

Introduction

Although foreign investment activity in the United States has recently generated some negative publicity, the accelerating flow of overseas money into the country is big business for various American groups and organizations. State and local government agencies spend millions of dollars annually to attract foreign investment because they believe that the additional jobs and higher tax receipts which result will in the long run be of great benefit to their constituencies. Local chambers of commerce and other civic groups have also anted up significant amounts of money because they recognize that local businesses will attract more customers if new foreign-owned manufacturing facilities are established within the community. Moreover, big U.S. banks, brokerage houses, and consulting firms take in millions of dollars in fees for handling and investing vast sums of money for overseas clients. Real estate brokers and agents can also earn substantial commissions by arranging the sale of agricultural, commercial, and other types of property to foreign buyers.

    This chapter will present three case studies of efforts made by American groups to attract significant amounts of foreign investment money. The first case study looks at the campaign which Pennsylvania officials waged to beat out numerous other state competitors and finally convince

Volkswagen to construct a 300 million dollar automobile assembly plant near the small town of New Stanton. The second case examines the eminently successful program of the Chamber of Commerce of Spartanburg, South Carolina, which has enticed more than 40 foreign firms to invest upwards of 600 million dollars in facilities adjacent to this modest-sized Southern community. Finally, the third case study chronicles the San Francisco-based Amrex Corporation's success in handling more than 50 million dollars in annual sales of Western agricultural land to foreign investors. This section also discusses Amrex's ambitious new project to internationalize the American real estate business and in the process to attract billions of dollars of additional foreign capital into the U.S. market.

The VW—New Stanton Connection

In what has been called one of the greatest "industrial-governmental courtships" of all time, Volkswagenwerk AG of West Germany signed an agreement in late 1976 with the State of Pennsylvania to construct and operate an automobile assembly plant in that state.[1] Governor Milton Shapp and the Pennsylvania Industrial Development Authority had thus won out over at least a dozen other serious state competitors in attracting the eighth largest automaker in the world. In the process, this major multinational firm agreed to build a 300 million dollar facility which would eventually employ 4,500 workers and produce 200,000 VW Rabbits a year. Moreover, the VW experiment now underway on American soil will have a major influence on whether the large Japanese and other European automakers will finally decide to invest hundreds of millions of dollars in order to establish similar assembly plants in the United States.

Volkswagen's decision to assemble cars in the United States was prompted by the ominous decline in its share of the American car market. In 1971, VW sold 570,000 cars in the U.S., close to 6 percent of all American car sales that year. In 1976, VW's sales had plummeted to 238,000 units and a 2 percent share of the market, and the German company had slipped from the top imported car company to number three behind Datsun and Toyota.[2] The big problem for VW was the drop in the value of the dollar vis-à-vis the German mark, causing a sharp increase in the price of its cars on the American continent. In April 1976 Volkswagen's supervisory board agreed unanimously to begin to produce Rabbits in the United States by late 1977, thus committing their robust marks to the acquisition of an American property site, the construction of a huge assembly facility, and an increasingly larger purchase of American-made automobile parts.

Intensive bidding soon broke out among the American states for the proposed facility of VW, which ironically, is 40 percent owned by the West German federal government and the Land government of Lower Saxony.

Eventually, the competition narrowed down to two sites—Brook Park, Ohio, and New Stanton, Pennsylvania. In May 1976 VW officials expressed a strong preference for the New Stanton location and Governor Milton Shapp announced confidently in June that the final pact would be signed with VW within 30 days. However, some groups in Pennsylvania were leery about providing VW with a multimillion dollar incentive package and the process of passing the required legislation in the state capital of Harrisburg dragged on a bit. Perhaps in an effort to speed up this process, VW announced in early July that it had postponed its decision on a U.S. plant and soon after asked Ohio industrial development representatives to reopen talks. A vice president of Volkswagen of America, VW's traditional importer and marketer in the United States, coyly remarked that "we still prefer New Stanton. However, there have been delays in those negotiations, so we are beginning talks with Ohio again."[3] Governor James A. Rhodes and his Ohio compatriots tried once again to convince VW to select Brook Park, a suburb of Cleveland, as its U.S. location. Reportedly, Ohio offered a 5 million dollar grant for the site acquisition, millions more for improved transportation routes to the site, training funds to provide a competent work force for VW operations, and possible tax abatements.[4]

The Ohio package was impressive, but actually was relatively insignificant in comparison to the ultimate Pennsylvania deal which must rank as the largest state subsidy to a foreign investor in history. In mid-July, after some fast-paced scurrying around in Harrisburg, representatives of the state of Pennsylvania and VW signed a provisional agreement in Germany for the New Stanton project. On September 15, 1976, Governor Shapp and VW officials initialed the formal agreement finalizing the transaction.[5]

The VW site three miles down Route 119 from New Stanton was originally selected by Chrysler Corporation for the location of an assembly plant, but work on the building was never completed. The Pennsylvania incentive package which had finally won over VW officials included a 40 million dollar loan from the state's Industrial Development Authority, channeled through the regional development agency, to purchase the site from Chrysler. In turn, the development agency has leased the facility to VW for 30 years with the German company paying interest on the original state loan of 1.75 percent annually for the first 20 years, and the principal and interest at an 8 percent rate for the last 10 years of the agreement, highly propitious terms for VW, to say the least. The state also threw in a 30 million dollar public bond issue for the construction of a railroad spur to the plant and for the renovation of nearby roadways, including the completion of a four-lane highway to the plant. The pot was further sweetened with a 4 million dollar commitment by the state to train workers for VW, and an additional 6 million dollar loan was kicked in by two

Pennsylvania employee pension funds for plant renovation projects. Last but not least, VW was given a five year break on local property taxes, being required to pay only 10 percent of the customary taxes during the first two years after production commenced, and 50 percent of customary taxes for the following three years. As for VW, its initial commitment to the project was 50 million dollars in start-up money.

The VW operation has now revved up in New Stanton and the Rabbits have already begun to hop off the Pennsylvania assembly line. Not everyone, however, has been overjoyed by the VW-Pennsylvania transaction. New Stanton is a town of 3,000 people located within a 40-minute drive of Pittsburgh. Although having been described by one source as an "unlovely little town," New Stanton is nestled in the verdant, undulating hills of southwestern Pennsylvania, a favorite vacation area for many Easterners.[6] Residents of the area worry that the quality of life will rapidly deteriorate; and, frankly, the predominately white populace has expressed certain concerns about an influx of minority groups into the region from Pittsburgh and other urban centers. When asked about the impact of the VW plant on community life, the mayor of New Stanton observed: "Well us, you can say we're just not benefiting that much from it. There's very, very few blacks around here and people worry about it. I always tell them, hey, they've got to live too, but what can you do?"[7] On its part, the National Association for the Advancement of Colored People (NAACP) and a coalition of other black organizations have labeled VW's performance in hiring blacks as unsatisfactory because fewer than 10 percent of the initial job openings at the plant went to blacks. These black groups have demanded that 25 percent of the jobs go to blacks and that VW provide shuttle buses to bring black workers from Pittsburgh.[8] The director of Pennsylvania's Human Relations Commission also publicly observed that VW was not in compliance with affirmative action requirements.[9] For its part, VW insists that it has hired the best qualified personnel and has not discriminated in terms of race or sex. It also adds that the percentage of minorities working at the plant coincides fairly closely with the percentage of minority groups in the general vicinity of New Stanton. However, Volkswagen has pledged to look more closely at its hiring practices.

The general populace in and around New Stanton fears that the small town, rural atmosphere which once typified that section of Pennsylvania is now a thing of the past. To a certain extent, their fears have been warranted. Hundreds of people have moved into the area and real estate prices have escalated dramatically. The town has also attracted its first dentist and two banks have now constructed facilities to compete head-on with the one Mellon bank which had served the area for decades. Moreover, businesses have complained that the tax breaks offered to VW will mean a higher tax liability for local firms and for homeowners. Small businesses also fear that VW's higher wage package will lead to an exodus of their present employees. In essence, this southwestern Pennsylvania region is in the midst of a major transition because of the VW plant, and a significant number of the local residents are not overly pleased with this change.

Nevertheless, VW will directly provide close to 5,000 new jobs, and perhaps an additional 30,000 jobs will be created in automobile-related industries; and this is the main reason why the Pennsylvania state government put together the incentive package in the first place. VW insists that its extensive surveys show the U.S. workers are more productive and stay on the job longer than their German counterparts, helping to solidify a previous decision to hire Americans to fill almost all management and assembly line positions.[10] The German company may well have had some second thoughts about its strategy when a wildcat strike broke out only six months after production had begun, but the United Autoworkers leadership stepped in quickly to end the strike action within a week.[11] Volkswagen also claims that it has already provided business for more than 1,800 Pennsylvania firms.[12] In addition, VW has recently purchased from American Motors a metal stamping plant in West Virginia. Although the engines and a large share of the parts for the Rabbits are still produced in Germany, VW hopes to manufacture eventually anywhere from 70 to 85 percent of the parts in the United States and Mexico, thus insulating itself against further fluctuations in the value of the dollar and the mark.[13]

Furthermore, in an effort to regain at least a 5 percent share of the total American car market within five years, the chairman of VW in Germany has intimated that the firm might even construct a second U.S. assembly plant, preferably in the West.[14]

If Volvo finally decides to open its assembly plant in Chesapeake, Virginia, and if the major Japanese and other European auto firms follow suit, the VW experiment will have paved the way for a literal four wheel invasion of the United States.[15] Likewise, one must wonder whether the approximately 100 million dollar incentive package pieced together by the state of Pennsylvania will be a precursor for bitter and ultraexpensive competition among the states in bidding for the favor of major foreign companies in the future.

The International Charisma of a Small Southern City—The Case of Spartanburg

A national magazine recently singled out Spartanburg, South Carolina, as one of the top ten U.S. "job meccas" for the 1980s. This moderately sized

Southern community was labeled as one of the handful of growth towns in the United States "where the living seems easy, and often is."[16]

Nestled in the foothills at the base of the Blue Ridge Mountains, 190 miles northeast of Atlanta, Spartanburg sports a rather modest population of 50,000. Until a few years ago, Spartanburg typified the Billy Carteresque "good old boy" rural life-style of so many small Southern enclaves. The pace of life was generally slow and meandering and the economic vitality of the city swayed with the ups and downs of the Southern-based textile industry.

In order to diversify its economic base and provide steady employment opportunities for its citizens, Spartanburg officials began a concerted campaign in the early 1960s to attract industries to the region. Spartanburg's promotional efforts were rather unique, however, because the prime target area was not the rest of the United States, but rather Europe.

The executive vice president of the greater Spartanburg Chamber of Commerce, Richard Tukey, has been the chief architect of this European strategy. A cigar-chomping, transplanted New Yorker with physical dimensions rivaling Orson Welles's, Tukey first made a careful study of European firms which could best take advantage of the assets which Spartanburg had to offer. Once this initial research was completed, Tukey prepared slides, films, and booklets extolling Spartanburg's virtues; and then he took his show on the road to Europe. The "quality of life" benefits accruing from a small city atmosphere, a pleasant climate, and Southern conviviality were, of course, high on Tukey's list of incentives. In dollars and cents terms, Tukey could also assure European executives that state and local funds would be available to provide vocational training for the working force of transplanted industries. He also strongly emphasized that South Carolina is a right-to-work state and that unions are a rare species in that part of the South. The wage rates in the area have also been comparatively low. Moreover, public funds were available to provide roads, sewers, and other conveniences for the foreign-owned industries. In addition, low-cost financing, tax abatements, cheap electricity, adequate raw materials, and a good transportation network were other prominent features on Tukey's list. And finally, the Chamber of Commerce representative could point out with pride that land costs in the region were very cheap. For example, he could adequately demonstrate that land tailor-made for industrial purposes which would cost $120,000 or more an acre in Switzerland and parts of West Germany, would cost only $3,000 an acre in Spartanburg.

Tukey also pledged that city officials would work closely with the foreign firms and attempt to eliminate or at least mitigate much of the red tape associated with setting up subsidiaries in foreign lands. To a large extent, this pledge has been fulfilled. As one foreign executive has stated, "you can get everything from building permits to bank credit lines in five days. You can be in business six months earlier here than in Germany."[17] The sales pitch, initially aimed at European textile firms, began to pay rich dividends; and for its size, Spartanburg may now have emerged as America's most international city. To date, more than 40 European and Japanese firms have either individually or jointly set up operations in the vicinity of Spartanburg. Approximately 1,500 Europeans live in the city, but as Spartanburg officials had always intended, a huge percentage of the thousands of jobs created by the inflow of foreign businesses has gone to U.S. citizens from the South Carolina area.

Hoechst, the German giant, has set up a 300 million dollar fiber plant in Spartanburg, and Michelin, France's leading tire maker, has recently opened up a truck tire plant which cost an estimated 100 million dollars. Between these two foreign multinationals, 3,500 new jobs have been created for local residents; and by itself, the Hoechst plant pays more taxes than 30 of South Carolina's 46 counties.[18] However, Hoechst officials believe that they are getting a bargain because they estimate that local labor costs are nearly 25 percent lower than in European fiber plants and that units per hour efficiency rates are somewhat higher in the United States than in Europe.[19] In addition, European firms have racked up impressive savings on fringe benefits costs, for in Europe workers are often assured of virtual "cradle to grave" security.

Spartanburg's population has increased by almost one-quarter since 1960, but its unemployment rate has consistently been well under the national average. In addition, noticeable life-style changes have occurred in the small South Carolina community since the influx of foreign firms. In effect, the international, cosmopolitan tastes of the foreign executives have blended in rather well with the traditional Southern ambience. The Europeans, for example, have been a pivotal force in the establishment of the Spartanburg Symphony Orchestra and the Spartanburg Arts Council. The city now has French and Swiss consuls, an Alliance Française, German-American, Italian-American, Swiss-American, and Indo-American associations, an International Festival Society, and a French cooking school. Bastille Day, Oktoberfest, and other traditional European holidays are given almost as much fanfare in Spartanburg as the Fourth of July. The counters of delicatessens in the city also abound in such European specialties as Kartoffelsalat, bratwurst, Wurzburg headcheese, snails, frogs legs, baguettes, and couscous. On the other hand, southern fried chicken and grits and gravy have made their way onto the tables of many of the 1,500 European residents.

South Carolina state officials currently estimate that 35 percent of all new industrial development activities in that state are financed by overseas interests, and foreign factories already operating in the state have assets close to 2 billion dollars.[20] Spartanburg has attracted a significant chunk of the foreign money, and the city fathers have succeeded in expanding the tax revenues and diversifying the city's economic base. Perhaps even more important in the long run, residents of the area have generally been pleased with the transition taking place in Spartanburg since the early 1960s. Even though a few of the spouses of the foreign executives need to return to Europe every few months to "recalibrate" themselves, a vast majority of the foreigners have adapted very nicely to the Southern milieu and they thoroughly enjoy the so-called Spartan gemütlichkeit. The Chamber of Commerce has set up free English language lessons for the spouses and attempts to provide personal assistance to the foreigners during their initial exposure to the new life-style. For their part, the foreigners have not been clannish, and they have sent their children to local public schools. They have also been quite pleased by the cost of living in the Spartanburg area. As a Swiss national pointed out, one could buy a home in Spartanburg for from one to two times one's annual income, whereas a similar home in Switzerland would cost five to ten times one's annual salary.[21]

The small city in South Carolina's interior region has already been given the nickname of "Euroville," and Tukey and his associates continue to seek out foreign firms which would fit in well with the community's development plans.[22] Spartanburg has shown that an aggressive promotion program can bring impressive results in the foreign investment sphere. The question that now remains to be answered is how many other American cities will enter the competition to attract foreign funds and what will be the short- and long-range effects on the life of their communities. For Spartanburg, at least, the overall impact of the invasion of foreign capital has thus far been very positive.[23]

Amrex—A Major Step Toward the "Internationalization" of the American Real Estate Market

Gerald Jackson is the descendant of a Zurich family which immigrated to the United States in 1878 and purchased a farm in California's lush San Joaquin Valley. As a child, Jackson grew up on this farm and was greatly saddened when the family property was recently sold as a result of what Jackson calls California's unfair tax system toward agricultural land.[24]

Jackson's major field of study in college was the relatively new discipline of open space planning, and he was soon involved in agricultural real estate sales and in planned unit developments in the San Joaquin Valley region. A decade ago, a real estate company mentioned to Jackson that a family from Lugano, Switzerland, was looking for agricultural property and wondered if Jackson could accommodate them. Jackson arranged for a meeting between these foreign investors and a northern California real estate broker, and a deal was finally consummated. From that time on, Jackson has been involved in numerous transactions resulting in the purchase of hundreds of millions of dollars of U.S. agricultural land by overseas investors.

Jackson is currently the president of the American Real Estate Exchange (Amrex), an organization which he believes will revolutionize the real estate profession and make American land much more readily accessible to foreign buyers. Quite simply, Amrex is destined to become, if Jackson has gauged correctly, the real estate equivalent of the New York Stock Exchange.[25]

The new real estate Big Board is headquartered in San Francisco, has six regional centers in the United States, and plans in the near future to have major permanent facilities in Toronto, London, Zurich, Hong Kong, and the Middle East. Jackson contends that the American real estate industry is extremely fragmented and localized, and has been hampered by a "horse-and-buggy" communications system. He firmly believes that the future of the profession is highly dependent on how well it can adapt to space age technological changes in the communications industry. Jackson further explains that American real estate has been an "imperfect" marketplace because of the lack of meaningful communication among potential buyers. He offers Atlanta as an illustration of the major flaw in current real estate practices. For several years, Atlanta was plagued by a large excess of downtown office space, causing some downtown owners to take a financial beating. The problem, Jackson asserts, was that a lot of outside investment money poured into Georgia's capital without sufficient knowledge of the intricacies and the idiosyncrasies of the Atlanta market, precipitating massive overbuilding in the downtown corridor. In effect, money sources tend to be concentrated in a few major financial centers, whereas the real estate profession is highly decentralized. Thus New York money may be available for investment purposes all over the United States, but real estate markets in the nation are very localized and only a few local brokers and agents really have a feel for the "turf" in each community. Therefore, in the Atlanta case, money poured in from various parts of the United States and the world, but these outside investors had only a marginal understanding of the particular characteristics of the Atlanta real estate market.

Jackson envisions that Amrex will take advantage of advanced communication's techniques and begin the process of "centralizing" and "perfecting" the real estate business in the United States. In September 1978 Jackson took a major step in this direction by opening a permanent trading floor in San Francisco. The main trading area has 10,000 square feet, and 25 offices are available for the traders and floor specialists trained in specific real estate areas such as multitenant housing, triple leasebacks, and so forth. A trader, in effect, is viewed as the "interface" between property owners and potential buyers. On the trading floor, computers belch out five-foot paper strips showing properties available and properties desired. These strips are then placed on a large board and the traders attempt to match up potential buyers and sellers. If preliminary interest is expressed on the trading floor among those with representative accounts, then the buyers and sellers, or their designated agents, are matched up directly through the use of WATS lines or other means of communication.

As a starting point, ten traders from the West, ten from the rest of the United States, and five from other nations will be allowed to transact business in the Exchange. To qualify for trader status, the individual or organization must guarantee to buy or sell at least 10 million dollars in property annually and provide a minimum of $30,000 in commissions to the Exchange. At its inception, the American Real Estate Exchange reportedly had an inventory of 4 billion dollars in properties.

Preview sessions using the basic Amrex approach were held in Zurich in March 1977, in San Francisco in September 1978, and in a few other major cities. The Zurich session lasted for two days and brought together major owners and buyers of real property from all over the world. Part of the first day activities featured keynote speeches on the American and European "mentalities" vis-à-vis real estate transactions. The rest of the time was spent arranging deals on some 1.7 billion dollars worth of property on hand during the session.

Jackson readily admits that he was somewhat disappointed that only 25 percent of the Zurich participants were there as potential buyers, and he attempted to rectify this situation in his 1978 "Market Day" held in the Bay Area city. Approximately 2 billion dollars worth of property was on the bidding block for that day, and buyers came from the United States, Canada, Europe, and Asia, often prepared to make cash down payments of 40 to 50 percent of the property's total selling price. Members associated with Amrex paid $275 for the privilege of attending the Market Day and nonmembers doled out $350. Participation was also strictly limited to principals or to those empowered to negotiate directly on behalf of the principals. The minimum value of listed properties was 1 million dollars and any deal consummated directly or indirectly as a result of the Market Day provided Amrex with a commission of 0.5 percent on the first million dollars of the sale and another 0.25 percent on the remaining portion of the transaction. Thus a 2 million dollar deal would bring a $7,500 commission to Amrex, $3,750 coming from the buyer and an equal amount from the seller.

The Market Day and Exchange procedures are also designed in such a way as to safeguard the confidentiality of the listed properties. A potential buyer or his agent thumbs through a book giving a brief description of the available properties. A description of a typical property would read something like this: "Class A, 14 story hi-rise office building, in Northwest. Ninety-four percent occupancy, under 8 years old. Price, 10 million. Good market in major metropolitan area. AC-76." If interested in the property, the potential buyer writes down the code number, AC-76, on a slip of paper and gives it to a runner. Eventually, the potential buyer and seller, or their representatives, are paged and brought together in a tête-à-tête conference. The seller then has the option of revealing as much specific information about the property as he deems necessary, depending on how serious he considers the buyer's interest to be. Jackson summarizes the Market Day approach by contending that "we compress into one source, and in this case into one day, the months of hit-and-miss, word-of-mouth selling that is usual in dealing with sensitive properties."[26]

Jackson staunchly asserts that billions of dollars of overseas money is currently available for investments in American real estate and he believes that Amrex will pave the way for this money to flow into the United States. Ever since 1968, Jackson has been working on a computer system hooked up with a satellite which will make it almost as easy for an investor in London or Hong Kong to find out about American property as an investor living in the same area where the property is located. In his cluttered office situated in a rather inconspicuous building in San Francisco's Fillmore district, Jackson has one of the terminals which will eventually be linked up with other terminals in major cities all over the world. The main computer located in San Francisco has been programmed to show available properties, as well as up-to-the-minute fluctuations in world currencies, changes in government regulations, and other pertinent data. A potential investor in London, for example, could type the appropriate code into the terminal and find out instantaneously about commercial properties available in any region of the United States. One-line descriptions are given for each property, such as "S.F. Bay Area, K-Mart, 84,000 S. Ft.—3201." If the British investor desires to have more information about the K-Mart property, he simply types in the code 3201 and is provided with a full page narrative of the property. This description is fairly complete, but key identifying information about the property is, of course, omitted. Once having scrutinized the one-page narrative and still having an avid interest in the property, the potential investor can then contact Amrex officials who will arrange for direct communications between the principal and the London buyer.

Although some people in the real estate profession believe that Jackson has greatly overstated his case and is simply a shrewd promoter, Jackson has nonetheless established a framework which should facilitate greater foreign investment activity in American real estate.[27] Through the novel Exchange concept and the Market Day format, steps have indeed been taken to centralize the real estate industry and internationalize the American real estate marketplace. In fact, because of the greater liquidity which he anticipates will occur in the real estate domain, Jackson is even contemplating the establishment of a futures market for real property. Through its extensive communications system, Amrex may well help to "perfect" the current real estate business and assist investors everywhere in gaining a much more complete overview of what is going on in local real estate markets. Moreover, Jackson has joined with McGraw-Hill to work toward the establishment of the largest centralized real estate information data bank in the world. One day, perhaps, European, Asian, and other overseas investors will view transactions in American agricultural, commercial, residential, and recreational property with the same confidence and alacrity that they view deals in their own home markets. If this "internationalization" process does occur, the foreign impact on all phases of the U.S. real estate industry will increase dramatically.

NINE

The Challenge
of Foreign Investment
in the United States:
The Issue in Perspective

The American Market Under Siege?

Is an overseas financial invasion of unprecedented proportions now under way in the United States and, if so, is the onslaught expected to continue in the foreseeable future? As this study has documented, the answers to both parts of the question are yes. Foreign holdings in U.S. securities and direct investment in American industries climbed to an all-time high of 311 billion dollars at the end of 1977, up from 175 billion dollars just five years earlier and not far behind the 381 billion dollars of similar investments made by U.S. citizens abroad. Wall Street has become particularly attractive to the overseas investor. As a Securities Industry Association report released in late 1978 points out, foreign investors played virtually no role in the American stock market prior to the 1970s. Today, however, they are buyers and sellers of several billion dollars worth of stock annually and have emerged as a major force on Wall Street.

In what ranks as the biggest ever foreign takeover transaction in the United States to date, Unilever of the Netherlands doled out 482 million dollars to purchase National Starch and Chemical in August 1978. In addition to the spectacular price tag, this deal is noteworthy because Unilever may have paved the way for overseas companies to have an easier time in acquiring American firms in the future. Prior to the Unilever transaction, foreign firms were impeded somewhat in acquiring existing U.S. companies because they could not offer shareholders of the targeted company the foreign firm's stock as an inducement for selling, something which American firms engineering a takeover bid do quite frequently. Consequently, the foreign companies have at times been at a distinct disadvantage vis-à-vis their American competitors and have often had to pay more money up front as compensation for not offering a stock swap. However, Lazard Frères came up with a novel arrangement on behalf of Unilever which may well set a precedent for future transactions involving overseas bidders. In effect, Lazard set up a U.S. company whose sole purpose is to hold National Starch stock. This new company then proceeded to offer an exchange of its preferred stock for shares of National Starch Stock. The Internal Revenue Service has ruled that the arrangement is legal and that the exchange of stock is tantamount to a preferred share swap which is essentially tax-free, thus providing another major inducement for shareholders to be very receptive to the overtures of foreign companies.[1]

Billions of dollars of additional foreign capital have recently flowed into the United States for the purchase of agricultural land, residential property, and small businesses. In fact, foreign investment has become a major route through which aliens may achieve permanent residency in the United States. A provision in the U.S. immigration laws makes it easier for a foreigner to attain resident alien status in the United States if he is willing to make at least a $40,000 investment in a business in which he will be the principal manager and which will employ at least one American citizen. Thousands of aliens have recently purchased such enterprises in order to take advantage of this provision and thereby gain the privilege of residing permanently in the United States. A *Los Angeles Times* survey has estimated that over the past three years, a staggering one-third to one-half of all business ownership transfers in six Western states, including California, have involved foreign buyers, mainly from the Orient and the Middle East.[2]

The rationale for the rapid expansion in foreign investment activity in the United States has already been well documented. Overseas investors believe that in the wake of the dollar's dismal performance against most of the world's other major currencies, they can make bargain basement purchases in the world's largest and most integrated market. For the Japanese, who as consumers are used to paying 7 cents each for every cherry, $7 for each apple, and $170 for a pound of fresh mushrooms, the price tags on American commercial and industrial products appear to be exceedingly low. To a large extent, the same holds true for the residents of Europe and the Middle East. These astute investors recognize that labor unit rates and other pertinent production costs are now very competitive in the United States. Residents of the Netherlands, for example, have emerged as the most prolific investors in the United States, and as a Dutch government official has observed, there is a "far more favorable cost structure in American industry. It has become more attractive to industry to produce goods here because the costs and social charges have become much higher in Europe."[3]

The foreign love affair with American real estate is also quite understandable. Very few nations in the world come even close to having the expansive geographic dimensions of the United States and only a handful have a lower population density than that of the U.S.A. As an illustration of this point, Japan, West Germany, and Great Britain are each appreciably smaller than the state of California, but have a combined population which is greater than that of the entire United States. Land is at a premium in these countries and it should therefore not be surprising that a wealthy West German industrialist is willing to buy hundreds or even thousands of acres of prime U.S. agricultural land at from one-third to one-tenth the price he would have to pay in his own home country.

Moreover, the stability of the U.S. political system and the American affinity for capitalism should not be underestimated as factors which help entice the flow of money from abroad. Many foreign investors fear that their own countries are moving steadily to the left and are in danger of major political and economic upheavals. In contrast, the moderate, consensus-oriented American political system is viewed by many outsiders as a literal Rock of Gibraltar and thus as a safe haven for their money. Furthermore, most large investors from other Western advanced industrial nations believe that the capitalist socioeconomic ethic will endure much longer in the United States than anywhere else in the world. As a German investor bluntly put it: "the last capitalist will die in the United States."[4]

The OPEC Specter

Investment by the OPEC nations in U.S. securities has mounted significantly in the past few years and billions of dollars of additional oil revenues are available for investment activities in the American market. Moreover, Middle Eastern members of the OPEC cartel have retained some of the most influential firms and individuals in the United States to guide their investment pursuits. In addition to major banking institutions such as Morgan Guaranty, prominent individuals such as former Texas Governor John Connally, ex-CIA Director Richard Helms, former Secretary of State William P. Rogers, and retired Senator J. William Fulbright have been retained by OPEC nations to safeguard and to enhance their interests in the United States.[5]

However, in spite of the flood of publicity which has been accorded to the exploits of Ghaith Pharaon and Adnan Khashoggi, and the frenetic buying activity of Middle Easterners in Beverly Hills, one must conclude that on an overall basis, OPEC investment in the United States has remained at a very modest level. Most of the money from the Middle East has been earmarked for the purchase of conservative U.S. Treasury notes and for portfolio investments on Wall Street. In the important domain of direct investment in U.S. enterprises, which is tantamount to having a controlling voice in the firms' policies, OPEC's share of the total overseas investment in the United States is less than 1 percent. Western European, Canadian, Japanese, and Latin American investors all continue to have a much greater impact on the U.S. market in the direct investment sphere than their Middle Eastern counterparts.

In order to diversify their international investment activity, the OPEC countries have spread their money among the Western advanced industrial nations and have not actually concentrated their funds in the United States. Moreover, it is difficult to perceive how the OPEC nations could nefariously use their U.S. investments as a retaliatory weapon against American support of Israel. Certainly, the Middle Eastern countries could cause some havoc on Wall Street by a sudden and unexpected withdrawal of their investment money. On the other hand, the federal government has a wide variety of laws and statutes at its disposal to mitigate any concerted OPEC effort to disrupt the U.S. economy from within. Frankly, there is no credible evidence available to indicate that the OPEC investors have even seriously considered such an option. On the whole, these investors have traditionally been friends of the United States and share the view of their colleagues from other nations that the U.S. provides a safe and attractive sanctuary for their money. Moreover, if the situation in the Middle East were suddenly to worsen and if the United States were to find itself once again on opposite sides from the Arab countries, OPEC efforts to attack the stability of the dollar overseas, and ultimately, to reinstitute the oil embargo, would be much more effective strategies than any attempt to shake up the U.S. economic structure from within.

In summary, the U.S. government certainly needs to develop better methods to monitor OPEC and other overseas investment activity in the United States. In particular, Washington must ensure that OPEC investments in existing U.S. enterprises are not used as a means to prevent these enterprises from doing further business with Israel. Nevertheless, the U.S. administration has been justified in concluding that OPEC investments in the United States are not presently a threat to American economic and political independence.[6] However, the recent Arab threat to withdraw funds from Canada after Prime Minister Joe Clark suggested that the Canadian Embassy in Israel be moved from Tel Aviv to Jerusalem has undoubtedly triggered some second thoughts among American officials.

The American Response to the Foreign Investment Challenge

Transforming a molehill into a mountain? It is farfetched to depict foreign investment in the United States as a sinister force threatening America's economic integrity. Money has poured into the United States from abroad because of the secure and attractive investment opportunities which the American market so bountifully offers. In an increasingly interdependent world, the American public must not succumb to xenophobic impulses which might prompt them to demand that the American open door be slammed shut in the faces of overseas investors. The United States itself has too much invested abroad and too many interests and concerns in other parts of the world to ever again resort to the Fortress America posture of the post-World War I era. Strategically, politically, and economically, the United States is no longer impervious to what transpires elsewhere in an increasingly interdependent global community of nations.

Furthermore, in relative terms, the massive upsurge in foreign investment activity in the United States still does not have the impact on the American economy which overseas investment has had on the economies of many other nations. For example, foreigners may have controlled 132 billion dollars in U.S. assets at the end of 1977, but this figure is comparatively small when stacked up alongside the 3.3 trillion dollars worth of total assets in the United States. Therefore, even though the United States will soon become the number one host country in the world for foreign investment, the vastness of the American market makes this investment process much less pronounced than similar activity occurring in Canada, France, Belgium, or scores of other nations with much smaller economic bases.

The U.S. government also has a variety of weapons at its command which may be used to guard against foreign investment excesses or irregularities in specific economic sectors. In the event of an emergency situation, the President of the United States can always invoke the Trading with the Enemy Act or the Foreign Assets Control Regulations which would effectively freeze foreign-controlled assets held in the United States. Profit remittance controls, equity requirements, local content stipulations, and other such maneuvers can also be implemented in order to protect U.S. economic interests.[7] Existing restrictions on foreign involvement in banking, transportation, communications, energy, defense, and resource-related industries can also be tightened even further if gross improprieties are uncovered. In effect, the United States and the state governments have adequate authority to combat most emergency situations involving foreign investment activity.

The future thrust of U.S. policy On the other hand, even though foreign investment activity does not presently imperil U.S. interests and the U.S. government does have measures at its disposal to cope with future contingencies, America's traditional open door policy must nevertheless be modified. It is absolutely imperative, however, that these modifications be based on empirical evidence and not on innuendo.[8] To say the least, much of the controversy swirling around the farmland issue has been fomented by conjecture and hearsay, and government leaders at the national and regional levels should not be stampeded into rash actions because of the emotional outcry of some of their constituents. In the past, Washington has been extremely derelict in monitoring foreign investment activity and in gathering sound empirical data from which sensible policies can be formulated. Hopefully, this regrettable situation is now being rectified. In 1978, Congress passed two laws which will permit federal agencies to keep a close tab on foreign investments in the banking and agricultural land sectors. Although the reporting mechanism is particularly questionable in the new farming bill, government officials will at least be able to clear up some of the uncertainty currently enshrouding this very provocative issue. For example, a U.S. Senate Agriculture Committee study has recently asserted that between January 1, 1977, and June 30, 1978, foreigners purchased 826,000 acres of U.S. agricultural land, a much more conservative estimate than those of Jack Anderson and Gerald Jackson. Unfortunately, the United States has not yet taken steps to require disclosure of the true beneficiaries of the land purchases and it is therefore nearly impossible to determine how much land is actually controlled by foreign interests.

The Commerce Department must also be granted the authority and adequate funds to closely monitor foreign takeovers of U.S. businesses, particularly small and medium-sized firms. In this respect, one should remember that foreign investment in nineteenth century America was largely in the form of debt financing, whereas a large chunk of recent overseas investment has been in the form of equity holdings. This equity investment usually endows foreigners with a controlling interest in existing U.S. enterprises and thus may have a much more significant long-term impact on the American business community and on American society as a whole than did foreign investment during the 1800s.

Moreover, Commerce and the Department of Housing and Urban Development should work together to keep constant track of investments by nonresident aliens in commercial and residential properties. In order to protect individual foreign investors, information gathered by the monitoring agencies could in certain specific cases be kept confidential and only aggregate data on a regional or sectoral basis need be made available to the general public.

Once the empirical data have been gathered and digested, U.S. policy-makers can then decide, on a rational basis, whether further regulation of foreign investment activity is necessary. It is probable, however, that additional limitations on foreign acquisitions of choice agricultural land will be considered in the national legislative bodies and in many state legislatures. The United States is the major breadbasket of the world and certainly the great bulk of agricultural land should remain under direct American ownership. Moreover, there is adequate precedence in the laws of Japan, France, Iran, Mexico, and certain provinces in Canada to ensure that moderate U.S. restrictions would not result in major retaliatory moves against American investors in other parts of the world. Many nations already restrict agrarian land ownership to residents and the leaders of these countries would not react harshly to similar limitations imposed on American agricultural land by the U.S. government. It would be preferable, of course, for the United States and the state governments to get together and attempt to agree on common policy denominators in this controversial farmland sphere.

The U.S. government should also strongly consider the creation of a modified version of Canada's Foreign Investment Review Agency (FIRA). As discussed previously, this organization screens all new investment proposals made by overseas interests, as well as many of the new projects considered by foreign firms already operating in Canada. Once this screening process is completed, FIRA then recommends to the Canadian Cabinet the acceptance or the rejection of the proposal, based on its assessment of how the proposed investment activity will affect Canadian economic interests.

The envisioned U.S. counterpart to FIRA could likewise screen both new proposals emanating from abroad and the expansionary plans of foreign enterprises already situated in the U.S. market. However, the authority to disapprove such transactions, except perhaps on strictly antitrust or national security grounds, should initially be denied the new U.S. agency. In effect, this organization would become the information clearinghouse for major foreign investment activity in the United States and would fulfill a vital monitoring function. In addition, it would have responsibility for investigating complaints linked to alleged incidents of technology drain, product "dumping," excess profit remittances, and unfair treatment of U.S. employees.

Without interfering with the basic principles of American federalism, the United States and the 50 state governments must also reach an acceptable compromise on incentive programs aimed at attracting private and government-owned foreign firms to American soil. The competition among the states and in North America in general has greatly intensified, and hundreds of millions of dollars in grants, loans, and tax abatements are now being offered to entice foreign firms. For example, Pennsylvania put up close to 100 million dollars to entice Volkswagen away from an Ohio site, and Ohio was once again a loser when Ford, a domestic company, accepted 68 million dollars in grants from the Ottawa and Ontario governments to build a new engine plant on Canadian soil right across the river from Detroit.[9] New jobs, a broader tax base, better technology, and improved management skills may all result from the state efforts to attract foreign firms to their areas of jurisdiction, but the competition seems to be getting out of hand, at the expense of local taxpayers.

An integral part of a potential federal-state government compromise may well be a joint program to offer major incentives for foreign investment in economically depressed, high unemployment regions of the United States. Even though France and Canada are selective in permitting foreign investment activity, they both offer impressive incentive packages to overseas firms willing to set up facilities in depressed areas. Several other Western governments also have similar policies. Specifically, Washington and the state capitals should design a program which would entice overseas investment into certain designated regions within each state. Moreover, selected geographic areas covering one or more states which have traditionally been plagued by endemic unemployment and widespread poverty should be singled out for foreign investment activity. Overseas investors would not be forced to set up facilities in these demarcated areas, but special grants and other enticing benefits would be made available to them by Washington and the pertinent state governments.

Many foreign enterprises are also in the habit of buying U.S. raw materials and shipping them overseas before transforming them into finished products. The Japanese, for example, have long preferred to purchase U.S. raw timber instead of finished lumber. The U.S. government should thus implement an incentive program which would encourage these foreign firms to set up U.S. facilities and turn these raw materials into finished or semifinished products while still on American soil. Such a policy would create thousands of new jobs for American workers and would lay to rest the notion that some foreign corporate giants simply perceive the United States as a "resource colony" ripe for exploitation.

In conclusion, a veritable flood of foreign-controlled money has recently inundated the American marketplace, a financial onslaught which is gathering greater momentum with each passing year. However, this investment from abroad does not for the time being endanger the interests of farmers, businessmen, Wall Street investors, nor the American public in general. U.S. authorities must nonetheless be vigilant and begin to effectively monitor foreign investment on a sectoral and geographical basis. Moreover, if empirical evidence justifies it, certain restrictions should be imposed on foreign involvement in the agricultural sphere, restrictions which have already been sanctioned by parliaments in several other Western nations. In addition, federal and state-level incentive programs which are geared to attract foreign investment need to be restructured and emphasis placed on encouraging overseas investment in economically depressed regions of the United States. Capital gains loopholes in U.S. tax laws which currently work to the advantage of overseas investors should also be eliminated immediately.

In general, the precipitous drop in the value of the dollar vis-à-vis many other major currencies has helped to pave the way for the financial invasion of the United States. Furthermore, attractive investment opportunities provided by the world's largest integrated market, as well as the stability and vitality of the U.S. economic system, have also helped to engender an avid foreign interest in the United States. The foreign investors have thus far been willing to play the game by American rules; and as long as this remains the case, overseas money should generally be welcomed to America's shores.[10] However, the traditional open door to overseas investors should be replaced by a turnstile system which will continue to allow foreign entry into the United States, but at the same time will keep close tabs on the comings and goings of foreign capital.

Without a doubt, the American business community is now facing a formidable foreign challenge within America's own borders, a challenge which has no parallel in U.S. history. Optimally, the pervasive overseas interest and activity in the U.S. market will spur American industries on to greater innovation and competitiveness, with the American consumer emerging as the ultimate winner.

State Restrictions on Alien Ownership of Real Estate

The following list of state laws which restrict alien ownership of property was compiled by the U.S. General Accounting Office and released in June 1978 as part of a publication entitled *Foreign Ownership of U.S. Land— Much Concern, Little Data.*

ALABAMA

No restrictions. (Ala. Const., art. I, sec. 34; Ala. Code, title 47, sec. 1.)

ALASKA

No restrictions on alien ownership of farmland.

Mining rights in state-owned lands may be acquired only by adult citizens (or their guardians or trustees), adult aliens who have declared their intention to become U.S. citizens, adult aliens whose home country grants reciprocal treatment, associations of the above persons, and qualified corporations. To be qualified, a corporation must be organized under the laws of a state or territory of the United States, and no more than 50 percent of its stock may be owned or controlled by aliens who could not own directly. (Alaska Stats., sec. 38.05.190.)

ARIZONA

Aliens "eligible for citizenship" have the same rights as citizens. Aliens not "eligible for citizenship" have only rights provided by federal treaties. (Ariz. Rev. Stats. Ann., secs. 33–1201 through 33–1207.)

Sale, lease, and sublease of state lands is limited to citizens, aliens who have declared their intention to become U.S. citizens, and corporations qualified to do business in the state. No person may purchase more than 640 acres of grazing land or more than 160 acres of land susceptible of immediate use for agricultural purposes. (Ariz. Const. art. X, sec. 11; Ariz. Rev. Stats. Ann., sec. 37–240.)

ARKANSAS

No restrictions.

CALIFORNIA

No restrictions. (Calif. Civil Code, sec. 671.)

COLORADO

No restrictions.

CONNECTICUT

Aliens resident in the United States may purchase, hold, inherit, or transmit real estate. Citizens of France may also own real estate, even though not residents in the United States. The spouse and lineal descendants of an alien owner may inherit and hold the real estate of the alien. Nonresident aliens may own real estate for the purposes of mining or quarrying activities. (Conn. Gen. Stats. Rev., secs. 47–57 and 47–58.)

DELAWARE

No restrictions.

FLORIDA

No restrictions.

GEORGIA

Aliens have equal rights with citizens, so long as their government is at peace with the United States. (Ga. Code Ann., sec. 79–303.)

HAWAII

No restrictions on alien ownership of farmland.

Persons seeking to purchase certain residential lots must be citizens or aliens who have declared their intent to become U.S. citizens and have resided in the state for five years or more. (Hawaii Rev. Stats., sec. 206–9.)

IDAHO

State lands may be sold only to citizens and to those who have declared their intention to become citizens. (Idaho Code, sec. 58–313.)

ILLINOIS

Aliens have full rights to acquire and hold land, either by purchase or inheritance or otherwise, but must dispose of it within six years. (Ill. Rev. Stats., c. 6, secs. 1 and 2.)

INDIANA

All aliens residing in Indiana who have declared their intention to become U.S. citizens may acquire and hold real estate in the same manner as citizens of the state. All other aliens may only take and hold land by devise and descent and must dispose of it within five years. Any alien, whether or not residing in Indiana may take real estate as security for a loan and may, in the same manner as a citizen of the state, take and hold title to real estate in collection of a debt. (Burns Ind. Stats. Ann., secs. 32–1–7–1 and 32–1–7–2.)

All aliens must dispose of land in excess of 320 acres within five years of acquisition. (Burns Ind. Stats. Ann., sec. 32–1–8–2.)

IOWA

Aliens resident in Iowa have the same rights as citizens. Nonresident aliens may acquire and hold property within city or town limits and also may acquire and hold up to 640 acres outside of municipal limits. (Iowa Const., art. 1, sec. 22; Iowa Code sec. 567.1.)

The right of an alien who resides outside the United States to inherit property depends on the existence of a reciprocal right for U.S. citizens to inherit in the alien's home country. (Iowa Code, sec. 567.8.)

Corporations incorporated outside the United States and all other corporations in which half or more of the stock is owned by nonresident aliens may enforce a lien or judgment for any debt or liability and may be a purchaser at a sale of real estate by virtue of such lien, liability, or judgment if all real estate acquired by such method is sold within ten years after the title was perfected in said corporation. In all other instances the above corporations are prohibited from acquiring title to or holding real estate. (Iowa Code, secs. 491.67, 567.1, and 567.2.)

Aliens, corporations, and limited partnerships are required to register land holdings and make certain annual disclosures. (Iowa Code, c. 172A and section 567.9.)

KANSAS

Aliens may own property. Aliens eligible for citizenship may inherit in the same manner as citizens. Other aliens may inherit only as provided in a treaty between the United States and the country of the alien's citizenship. (Kans. Stats. Ann., sec. 59–511.)

There are substantial restrictions on corporations owning farm land. (Kans. Stats. Ann., sec. 17–5901.)

All corporations are required to report annually to the secretary of state.

KENTUCKY

An alien, not an enemy, who has declared the intention to become a citizen of the United States may acquire or inherit land as if he or she were a citizen. If the alien has not become a citizen within eight years of acquisition, the property may escheat to the state. (Ky. Rev. Stats. Ann. 381.290 and 381.300.)

An alien who is a resident of the state may take and hold lands for a residence, or for a business, trade, or manufacture, for not more than 20 years. (Ky. Rev. Stats. Ann. 381.320.)

Special rules apply for the alien wife or child of a U.S. citizen. (Ky. Rev. Stats. Ann. 381.310.)

Aliens who reside in the state but who have not declared their intention to become citizens and nonresident aliens are only entitled to inherit property, but they must dispose of it within eight years. (Ky. Rev. Stats. Ann. 381.300 and 381.330.)

No corporation may hold any property, except that property "proper and necessary for carrying on its legitimate business," for longer than five years. (Ky. Rev. Stats. Ann. 271A.705(1).)

LOUISIANA

No restrictions.

MAINE

No restrictions.

MARYLAND

All aliens, except enemy aliens, have the same rights as citizens. (Ann. Code of Md., Real Property, sec. 14–101.)

MASSACHUSETTS

No restrictions. (Chap. 184 sec. 1.)

MICHIGAN

No restrictions.

MINNESOTA

Only U.S. citizens or permanent resident aliens can acquire any future interest in agricultural land (with some exceptions). The legislation does not affect the rights of aliens to inherit land, or the rights of citizens of a foreign country to hold land in cases where their rights are secured by treaty. The legislation permits aliens to retain title to any agricultural land acquired before May 27, 1977.

Corporations (with certain exceptions) are prohibited from farming or acquiring real estate used for farming or real estate capable of being used for farming. (Minn. Stat. sec. 500.24.)

Nonresident aliens, corporations, and other business entities must report annually on their agricultural landholdings to the state Department of Agriculture.

MISSISSIPPI

Resident aliens are treated on the same basis as citizens. Nonresident aliens may not acquire or hold land, except that they may hold a lien on land and take title to the land by foreclosing on the lien but must dispose of it within 20 years. Citizens of Syria and Lebanon may inherit land, despite the fact that they are not residents. (Miss. Code. Ann., sec. 89–1–23.)

MISSOURI

On May 5, 1978, Missouri passed a law which prohibits nonresident aliens from acquiring more than five acres of agricultural land in Missouri for the purpose of farming. The law does not affect agricultural land that nonresident aliens already own, as long as the land is held by the present owner. Nonresident aliens may acquire and hold other types of real estate as if they were U.S. citizens and residents.

Corporations not engaged in farming before September 28, 1975, are prohibited from farming. As of this same date corporations are prohibited from acquiring an interest in any title to agricultural land in Missouri subject to certain exceptions.

Corporations are required to report annually.

MONTANA

The right of an alien to inherit real estate is dependent on the existence of a reciprocal right for U.S. citizens to inherit real estate in the country where the alien resides. (Rev. Codes of Mont. sec. 91A–2–111.)

NEBRASKA

Aliens may hold real estate within city or village limits and within three miles of those limits. They may also hold leases in other lands for up to five years. Other alien land ownership is prohibited. (Nebr. Rev. Stats., secs. 76–402 and 76–414.)

Resident aliens may acquire property by inheritance, but must sell it within five years. An alien not resident in the United States may inherit only if reciprocal inheritance rights are afforded U.S. citizens in the nation of the alien's residence and must dispose of it in five years. (Nebr. Rev. Stats., secs. 76–405, 76–402, and 4–107.)

Corporations organized outside Nebraska may hold land within city or village limits and within three miles of those limits. They may also hold land necessary for their business as common carriers or public utilities, or for manufacturing plants, petroleum service stations, or bulk stations. Subject to the above exceptions, no corporation (whether organized in Nebraska, another state, or in a foreign country) may hold land if a majority of its directors are aliens, if its executive officers or managers are aliens, or if a majority of its stock is owned by aliens. (Nebr. Rev.

Stats. secs. 76–402 through 76–414.) Corporations must make annual reports of land holdings. (Laws, 1975, L.B. 203.)

NEVADA

No restrictions.

NEW HAMPSHIRE

An alien resident in the state has the same rights as a citizen. A nonresident alien may not hold real estate. (N.H. Rev. Stats. Ann., sec. 477.20.)

NEW JERSEY

"Alien friends" have the same rights as citizens with respect to real estate. (N.J. Stats. Ann., sec. 46:3–18.)

NEW MEXICO

No restrictions. (N.M. Stats. Ann., sec. 70–1–24.)

NEW YORK

No restrictions. (McKinneys Consolidated Laws of N.Y. Ann., Real Property sec. 10.)

NORTH CAROLINA

Aliens may hold real estate on the same basis as citizens. (N.C. Gen. Stats. sec. 64–1.)

The right of a nonresident alien to inherit real estate depends on the existence of a reciprocal right for U.S. citizens to inherit real estate in the alien's home country. (N.C. Gen. Stats., sec. 64–3.)

NORTH DAKOTA

No restrictions on alien ownership of farmland.

Corporations are prohibited from engaging in farming or agriculture. (N.D. Century Code 10–06–01.)

OHIO

No restrictions.

OKLAHOMA

No alien may hold land unless he or she is a *bona fide* resident of the state. If an alien who is not a resident of the state acquires land (e.g., by inheritance) or if a resident alien leaves the state, he or she must dispose of the land within five years. (Okla. Const. art. 22, sec. 1; Okla. Stats. Ann. Title 60 secs. 121 through 123.)

Aliens may inherit land and may acquire title to land by foreclosing a lien in their favor, but if not residents of Oklahoma, they must dispose of it within five years. (Okla. Const. art. 22, sec. 1. Okla. Stats., Ann. Title 60 sec. 123, Title 84 sec. 229.)

No corporations may hold land outside of municipal limits except to the extent necessary for other business purposes. (Okla. Const., art. 22, sec. 2; Okla. Stats., Ann. Title 18 sec. 1.20.) Corporations may not engage in farming or ranching, except in special circumstances. (Okla. Stats. Ann. Title 18 sec. 951.)

OREGON

Aliens may not buy state land nor establish mineral claims on public lands unless they have declared their intention to become citizens. (Oreg. Rev. Stats. secs. 273.255, 517.010, and 517.044.)

In 1977 a law was passed requiring all corporations that own or lease farmland in the state to report certain data to the state Corporation Commission.

PENNSYLVANIA

Aliens may purchase and hold real estate up to 5,000 acres or a net annual income of $20,000. Certain other statutes give special exceptions. (Pa. Stats. 68, secs. 21 through 32.)

RHODE ISLAND

No restrictions.

SOUTH CAROLINA

No alien nor alien-controlled corporation may own more than 500,000 acres of land. (Code of Laws of South Carolina 27–13–30.)

SOUTH DAKOTA

No restrictions on alien ownership of farmland.

Corporate ownership of farm land is restricted. (South Dakota Constitution, article XVII, sec. 7, and South Dakota Compiled Laws chapter 47–9A.)

Every corporation engaged in farming must file annually with the secretary of state.

TENNESSEE

No restrictions.

TEXAS

No restrictions on alien ownership of farmland.

A corporation may acquire land only if it is necessary and proper for its business. It must convey away all excess land within 15 years of acquisition. A corporation may not have real estate holding as one of its purposes, except a "town lot" corporation, operating in or near a city. (Vernon's Ann. Tex. Stats., arts. 1302–4.01 through 1302–4.04.)

UTAH

No restrictions.

VIRGINIA

Any nonenemy alien may acquire and hold land on the same basis as a citizen. (Va. Code. Ann., sec. 55–1.)

VERMONT

No restrictions.

WASHINGTON

No restrictions. (Wash. Rev. Code, sec. 64.16.005.)

WEST VIRGINIA

No restrictions on alien ownership of farmland.

Corporations which acquire more than 10,000 acres of land in the state must obtain a license. A tax at the rate of 5 cents for each acre in excess of 10,000 is charged for the license. (W. Va. Code Ann., sec. 11–12–75.)

WISCONSIN

Resident aliens have the same rights as citizens. Aliens resident outside the United States may not acquire or hold more than 640 acres, except by inheritance. (Wis. Const., art. 1, sec. 15; Wis. Stats., secs. 710.01 and 710.02.)

Certain corporations are restricted from owning farm land. (Wis. Code, sec. 182.001.) In addition, no corporation in which more than 20 percent of the stock is held by nonresident aliens may acquire or hold more than 640 acres. (Wis. Stats., sec. 710.02.)

WYOMING

Resident aliens have the same rights as citizens. (Wyo. Const. art. 1, sec. 29; Wyo. Stats. Ann., sec. 34–151.)

A nonresident alien may inherit property only if a reciprocal right exists for a U.S. citizen to inherit in the nation of the alien's citizenship. (Wyo. Stats. Ann., sec. 2–43.1.)

State Programs Which Provided Incentives, Special Services, and General Assistance to Attract Domestic and Foreign Industries, 1977

TABLE A-1

STATES	| Data on communities in comparable form. Such as an Audit.	Site studies	Conduct or assemble research studies on state and areas	Climate	Civil characteristics	Financing	Labor	Legislation and taxes	Markets	Data on plant location factors for individual communities	Assist in design or layout of new plants	Own or share in ownership of industrial sites	Financial assistance to new or expanding plants	Raw materials
Alabama	√	√	√	√	√	√	√	√	√	√	√		√	√
Alaska	√		√	√	√	√	√	√	√	√			√	√
Arizona	√	√	√	√	√	√	√	√	√	√	√		√	√
Arkansas	√	√	√	√	√	√	√	√	√	√	√		√	√
California			√	√	√	√	√	√	√	√			√	√
Colorado	√	√	√	√	√	√	√	√	√	√				√
Connecticut	√	√	√	√	√	√	√	√	√	√	√	√	√	√
Delaware		√	√	√	√	√	√	√	√	√			√	√
Florida	√	√	√	√	√	√	√	√	√	√			√	√
Georgia	√	√	√	√	√	√	√	√	√	√	√		√	√
Hawaii			√	√	√	√	√	√	√	√			√	√
Idaho	√	√	√	√	√	√	√	√	√	√			√	√
Illinois	√	√	√	√	√	√	√	√	√	√			√	√
Indiana	√	√	√	√	√	√	√	√	√	√	√		√	√
Iowa	√	√	√	√	√	√	√	√	√	√			√	√
Kansas	√	√	√	√	√	√	√	√	√	√				√
Kentucky		√	√	√	√	√	√	√	√	√			√	
Louisiana	√	√	√	√	√	√	√	√	√	√			√	√
Maine	√	√	√	√	√	√	√	√	√	√			√	√
Maryland	√	√	√	√	√	√	√	√	√	√			√	√
Massachusetts	√	√	√	√	√	√	√	√	√	√			√	√
Michigan	√	√	√	√	√	√	√	√	√	√				√
Minnesota	√	√	√	√	√	√	√	√	√	√		√	√	√
Mississippi		√	√	√	√	√	√	√	√	√	√		√	√
Missouri	√	√	√	√	√	√	√	√	√	√			√	√
Montana	√	√	√	√	√	√	√	√	√	√			√	√
Nebraska	√	√	√	√	√	√	√	√	√	√			√	√
Nevada		√	√	√	√	√	√	√	√	√	√			
New Hampshire	√	√	√	√	√	√	√	√	√	√		√	√	√
New Jersey	√	√	√	√	√	√	√	√	√	√			√	
New Mexico	√	√	√	√	√	√	√	√	√	√				√
New York	√	√	√	√	√	√	√	√	√	√			√	√
North Carolina	√	√	√	√	√	√	√	√	√	√			√	√
North Dakota	√	√	√	√	√	√	√	√	√	√			√	√
Ohio		√	√	√	√	√	√	√	√	√			√	√
Oklahoma	√	√	√	√	√	√	√	√	√	√	√	√	√	√
Oregon	√	√	√	√	√	√	√	√	√	√				√
Pennsylvania	√	√	√	√	√	√	√	√	√	√			√	√
Rhode Island		√	√	√	√	√	√	√	√	√		√	√	√
South Carolina	√	√	√	√	√	√	√	√	√	√			√	√
South Dakota	√	√	√	√	√	√	√	√	√	√			√	√
Tennessee	√	√	√	√	√	√	√	√	√	√			√	√
Texas	√	√	√	√	√	√	√	√	√	√			√	√
Utah	√	√	√	√	√	√	√	√	√	√			√	√
Vermont	√	√	√	√	√	√	√	√	√	√			√	√
Virginia	√	√	√	√	√	√	√	√	√	√			√	√
Washington	√	√	√	√	√	√	√	√	√	√				√
West Virginia	√	√		√	√	√	√	√	√	√			√	√
Wisconsin	√	√	√	√	√	√	√	√	√	√	√		√	√
Wyoming	√	√	√	√	√	√	√	√	√	√			√	√
Puerto Rico	√	√	√	√	√	√	√	√	√	√	√	√	√	√
Virgin Islands				√	√	√	√	√						√

SOURCE: National Association of State Development Agencies.

								II. STATES PROVIDING FINANCIAL ASSISTANCE FOR INDUSTRY						
Power and fuels	Water and waste	Transportation	State, city or county incentive for establishing industrial plants in area of high unemployment	State, city or county loan guarantees for equipment, machinery	State, city or county loan guarantees for building construction	State, city or county loans for equipment, machinery	State, city or county loans for building construction	State, city or county general obligation bond financing	State, city or county revenue bond financing	Privately sponsored development credit corporation	State sponsored industrial development authority	State financing aid for existing plant expansions	State matching funds for city and/or county industrial financing program	State loan guarantees for building construction
√	√	√						√	√	√	√	√		
√	√	√				√	√		√		√	√		
√	√	√		√	√			√	√	√	√			√
√	√	√	√						√					
√	√	√							√					
√	√	√	√	√	√	√	√	√		√	√	√	√	√
√	√	√						√	√		√	√		
√	√	√							√	√	√			
√	√	√							√					
√	√	√			√	√	√	√	√			√		
√	√	√												
√	√	√				√			√	√	√	√		
√	√	√		√	√				√	√	√	√		
√	√	√						√	√	√				
√	√	√				√	√	√	√	√	√	√		
√	√	√						√	√					
√	√	√		√	√				√			√	√	√
√	√	√	√	√	√			√	√	√	√	√	√	√
√	√	√	√	√		√	√		√	√	√	√		√
√	√	√							√					
√	√	√	√			√	√		√	√	√	√		
√	√	√	√	√	√			√	√	√	√	√		√
√	√	√	√	√				√	√	√		√		
√	√	√							√	√				
√	√	√	√	√					√	√				
√	√	√							√					
√	√	√		√	√				√	√	√	√		√
√	√	√	√						√	√	√			
√	√	√							√		√			
√	√	√	√	√	√	√	√	√	√	√	√	√		√
√	√	√					√		√					
√	√	√		√	√			√	√	√	√	√		
√	√	√	√	√			√	√	√	√	√	√	√	
√	√	√	√				√	√	√	√	√	√		√
√	√	√							√					
√	√	√	√				√		√	√	√	√	√	
√	√	√		√	√				√	√	√	√		√
√	√	√			√	√			√	√	√	√		
√	√	√							√		√			
√	√	√		√	√			√	√	√				√
√	√	√			√	√	√		√	√		√	√	
√	√	√	√	√	√	√	√		√	√	√	√		√
√	√	√	√					√	√	√				
√	√	√				√	√		√	√	√	√		
√	√	√					√		√					
√	√	√							√					
√	√	√	√			√	√			√	√	√		
√	√	√	√											

TABLE A-2

III. TAX INCENTIVES FOR INDUSTRIES AND OTHER PERTINENT LAWS

STATE	Accelerated depreciation of industrial equipment	Corporate income tax exemption	Excise tax exemption	Tax incentive for compliance with pollution control laws	Inventory tax exemption on goods in transit (freeport)	Personal income tax exemption	Sales use tax exemption on new equipment	Tax exemption or moratorium on land, capital improvements	Tax exemption or moratorium on equipment, machinery	Tax exemption on raw materials used in manufacturing	Tax credits for use of specified state products	Tax stabilization agreements for specified industries	Tax exemption to encourage research and development	State right to work law	State minimum wage law	State fair employment practices code	Statewide uniform property tax evaluation law
Alabama			√	√	√		√	√	√	√				√			√
Alaska															√	√	
Arizona	√			√	√	√				√					√	√	√
Arkansas					√		√			√				√	√	√	√
California	√			√			√			√				√	√	√	√
Colorado					√					√					√	√	
Connecticut		√	√	√	√	√	√	√	√	√					√	√	
Delaware					√		√		√	√					√	√	
Florida				√	√	√				√	√			√			√
Georgia	√			√			√			√				√	√	√	√
Hawaii	√		√		√		√		√						√	√	√
Idaho	√			√	√		√			√					√		√
Illinois	√				√	√				√					√	√	√
Indiana	√			√			√			√					√	√	√
Iowa																	
Kansas					√			√	√	√				√		√	√
Kentucky	√				√		√	√	√	√				√	√	√	√
Louisiana				√	√				√		√						√
Maine	√				√		√			√					√	√	
Maryland				√			√	√	√	√			√		√	√	√
Massachusetts		√	√	√	√	√	√			√			√		√	√	√
Michigan		√		√	√	√	√	√	√	√					√	√	√
Minnesota		√		√	√				√	√	√	√	√		√	√	√
Mississippi	√				√	√	√	√	√	√				√			
Missouri		√		√	√		√			√						√	√
Montana				√	√			√	√								√
Nebraska					√					√				√	√	√	√
Nevada		√			√	√								√	√	√	√
New Hampshire				√	√	√	√			√					√	√	√
New Jersey	√			√	√	√				√			√		√	√	√
New Mexico			√	√	√				√						√	√	√
New York		√		√	√	√	√	√	√	√			√		√	√	√
North Carolina				√			√			√				√	√	√	√
North Dakota		√	√		√			√	√	√				√	√	√	√
Ohio				√	√					√					√	√	√
Oklahoma	√	√		√	√	√	√	√	√	√					√	√	√
Oregon		√		√	√	√				√					√	√	√
Pennsylvania		√		√	√	√		√	√	√			√		√	√	√
Rhode Island				√	√	√	√	√	√	√		√			√	√	
South Carolina	√			√	√		√	√	√	√			√	√	√		√
South Dakota		√	√	√	√	√		√		√				√	√	√	√
Tennessee				√	√	√	√	√	√	√	√			√	√		√
Texas		√			√	√		√						√	√		
Utah					√												
Vermont						√							√		√	√	√
Virginia	√			√			√			√				√			
Washington					√					√					√	√	√
West Virginia		√	√	√			√			√					√	√	√
Wisconsin	√			√	√		√		√	√					√	√	√
Wyoming		√	√	√	√	√				√				√	√	√	√
Puerto Rico	√	√	√		√	√	√	√	√	√			√		√	√	√
Virgin Islands	√	√	√		√	√	√	√	√	√			√		√	√	√

SOURCE: National Association of State Development Agencies.

IV. SPECIAL SERVICES TO ENCOURAGE INDUSTRIAL DEVELOPMENT

Statewide air pollution control law	Statewide water pollution control law	Statewide industrial noise abatement law	State, cities or counties provide free land for industry	State, city and/or county finance speculative building	State, city or county owned industrial park sites	State funds for city and/or county development-related public works projects	State funds for city and/or county master plans	State funds for city and/or county recreational projects	State program to promote research and development	State program to increase export of products	University R and D facilities available to industry	State and/or University conduct feasibility studies to attract or assist new industry	State recruiting, screening of industrial employees	State supported training of industrial employees	State supported training of hard-core unemployed	State incentive to industry to train hard-core unemployed	State help in bidding on Federal procurement contracts	State science and/or technology advisory council
√	√		√			√		√	√	√	√		√	√	√	√		√
√	√			√	√	√	√	√	√	√	√	√	√	√	√	√	√	√
√	√			√	√						√	√	√	√	√			√
√	√				√	√	√	√	√		√	√	√	√				√
√	√		√		√	√			√		√	√	√	√	√	√		
√	√			√	√	√	√	√			√	√	√	√	√			√
√	√		√	√	√	√	√	√		√	√	√	√	√	√	√	√	√
√	√					√	√				√	√	√	√	√		√	√
√	√		\	\	√	√		√	√	√	√	√	√	√	\	\		√
√	√		√	√	√	√	√	√	√	√	√	√	√	√			√	√
√	√						√	√	√	√	√	√	√	√				√
√	√			√		√	√	√	√		√	√	√	√			√	√
√	√	√		√	√	√	√	√	√	√	√	√	√	√			√	√
√	√	√	√		√	√	√	√	√	√	√	√	√	√	√	√	√	√
																		√
√	√			√	√				√	√	√	√	√	√			√	√
√	√					√	√		√	√	√	√	√	√	√		√	√
√	√		√	√	√				√	√	√	√	√	√	√			√
√	√	√	√	√	√				√		√	√	√	√	√			√
√	√	√		√	√	√	√		√	√	√	√	√	√	√	√	√	√
√	√			√	√	√	√	√	√	√	√	√	√	√	√		√	√
√	√		√	√	√		√	√	√	√	√	√	√	√	√	√	√	√
√	√				√						√	√	√	√				√
√	√		√	√	√	√	\		\	√	√	√	√	√	√	√	√	√
√	√			√	√						√	√	√	√		√		
√	√			√	√	√	√	√	√	√	√	√	√	√			√	√
√	√	√		√	√	√	√	√	√	\	√	√	√	√	√	√	√	√
√	√		√	√	√	√	√		\	√	√	√	\	√	√	\	√	√
√	√	√		√	√	√	√	√	√	√	√	√	√	√	√	√	√	√
√	√	√	√	√	√				√	√	√	√	√	√			√	√
√	√			√	√	√	√	√	√	√	√	√	√	√		√		√
√	√		√	√	√	√	√	√	√	√	√	√	√	√	√	√	√	√
√	√			√	√	√	√	√	√	√	√	√	√	√			√	√
√	√			√	√		√	√	√	√	√	√	√	√	√	√		√
√	√			√	√	√	√	√	√	√	√	√	√	√			√	√
√	√		√	√	√	√	√	√	√	√	√	√	√	√	√	√		√
√	√		√		√	\	\		√	√	√	√	√	√	√	\	√	√
√	√			√	√			√		√	√	√	√	√			√	√
√	√		√	√	√	√	√	√	√	√	√	√	√	√			√	√
√	√			√	√				√	√	√	√	√	√			√	√
√	√	√		√	√	√	√	√	√	√	√	√	√	√			√	√
√	√			√	√	√			√	√	√	√	√	√		√	√	√
√	√	√			√			√		√	√	√	√	√	√	√		√
√	√				√	√				√	√	√	√	√				
√	√			√	√	√	√	√	√	√	√	√	√	√				√
√	√	√		√	√	√	√			√	√	√	√	√			√	√
√	√	√	√	√	√	√	√	√	√	√	√	√	√	√		√	√	√
√	√				√	√	√		√	√	√	√	√	√			√	√

Chapter 1

[1]U.S. Department of Commerce, *Foreign Direct Investment in the United States,* Vol. 3, April 1976, p. A-7, and *Department of the Treasury News,* January 20, 1975, p. 3.

[2]A comprehensive study conducted by the Commerce Department on foreign investment asserts that "the United States remains a large, growing, and highly sophisticated market that will continue to be attractive and profitable to foreign multinationals and from which they can glean processes, strategies, and know-how applicable to their operations at home and elsewhere around the globe," (ibid., Vol. 3, p. A-10)

Another part of the same study concludes that "there are reasons for expecting the flow of foreign direct investment in the United States to continue at high levels over the next five years," (ibid., Vol. 1, p. 111).

[3]Miller delivered this speech at the National Press Club in Washington, D.C., on June 7, 1978.

[4]*Business Week,* August 14, 1978, p. 28.

[5]*The New York Times,* May 14, 1978, pp. 1 and 40. European Investment Research Center, a Brussels-based holding company, estimates that Europeans spent 800 million dollars for U.S. farmland in 1977 alone.

[6]Christopher H. Stern, "Invasion of the American Heartland," *Saturday Review,* October 15, 1977, p. 22. Stern states that in a few decades "foreign investment in U.S. farmland could eclipse American ownership," meaning that "American agriculture, the nation's single greatest source of power, would pass from the hands of American citizens."

[7]See *Newsweek,* May 22, 1978, p. 55.

[8]U.S. Department of Commerce, *Foreign Direct Investment,* Vol. 3, p. A-1.

[9]For this study, Commerce prepared a comprehensive questionnaire in 1974 covering the ownership and operation of foreign-owned U.S. firms. Approximately 7,200 replies to the questionnaire were received prior to the publication of the final report in 1976. On an annual basis, Commerce has also begun to monitor investment activity in the form of acquisitions, mergers, and equity increases.

[10]Ibid., Vol. 1, p. 233. The study points out that a number of foreign-owned companies rank among the three or four largest U.S. producers of individual products, such as agricultural chemicals, building and construction supplies, and phonograph records. However, this is not an indication that the foreign company's share of the overall market is substantial (ibid., Vol. 3, p. A-8).

[11]Ibid., p. 234.

[12]Ibid., p. 237.

[13]Ibid.

[14]Ibid., p. 236.

[15]Ibid., p. xi.

[16]Ibid., p. 240.

[17]Ibid., pp. 242–243.

[18]Ibid., p. 233, and Bank of America, *Survey of Foreign Investment*, 1978.

[19]U.S. Department of Commerce, *Foreign Direct Investment*, Vol. 3, p. A-8.

[20]Ibid., p. A-9. Reinvested earnings by foreign firms were estimated at 1.2 billion dollars in 1975 and 1.6 billion in 1976 (Ida May Mantel, "Foreign Direct Investment in the United States, 1976," *Survey of Current Business,* October 1977, p. 31).

[21]*The New York Times,* January 8, 1978, XII, pp. 40, 52.

[22]J.J. Servan-Schreiber, *The American Challenge* (New York: Avon, 1968), p. 3.

[23]Ibid., pp. 11, 101, 277.

[24]Ibid., p. 278.

[25]U.S. Department of Commerce, *Foreign Direct Investment in the United States,* December 1977, p. 6.

[26]William J. Storck, "New Incentives Are Spurring Growth of Foreign Investment in U.S. Chemicals," *Chemical and Engineering News,* February 27, 1978, p. 14.

[27]See Alfred Britain III's article, "The Role of Foreign Investment in the U.S.," *Nation's Business,* March 1977, p. 54.

Chapter 2

[1]See Raymond Vernon, "Multinational Business and National Economic Goals," in *Transnational Relations and World Politics,* Robert O. Keohane and Joseph S. Nye, eds, (Cambridge, Mass.: Harvard, 1972), p. 344.

[2]Hugh Stephenson, *The Coming Clash: The Impact of Multinational Corporations on National States* (New York: Saturday Review Press, 1972), p. 10.

[3]Ibid., pp. 161–162. For a view of the World Auto Council, consult Burton B. Bendiner, "A Labor Response to Multinationals: Coordination of Bargaining Goals," *Monthly Labor Review,* July 1978, pp. 9–13.

[4]Philip Colebrook, *Going International: A Handbook of British Direct Investment Overseas* (London: McGraw-Hill, 1972), p. 5.

[5]Ibid., pp. 24 and 27.

[6]Charles Kindleberger documented these cases and his findings are discussed in Don Wallace, ed., *International Control of Investment, The Dusseldorf Conference on Multinational Corporations* (New York: Praeger, 1974), pp. 62–63.

[7]See the U.S. Department of Commerce, *Foreign Direct Investment,* Vol. 1, p. 9.

[8]Servan-Schreiber, *The American Challenge,* p. 46.

[9]Ibid., p. 41.

[10]Ibid., p. 47.

[11]U.S. Department of Commerce, *Statistical Abstract of the United States, 1977,* p. 855.

Charles P. Kindleberger has written an article on pre-1950 U.S. direct investment in France in which he estimates that U.S. investment was 12 million dollars in 1900, 35 million in 1914, 250 million in 1929, 250 million in 1936, and 450 million in 1950. He also indicates that the book value of U.S. direct investment doubled from 1952 until 1956 and tripled by 1961. See Kindleberger, "Origins of United States Direct Investment in France," *Business History Review,* 48 (no. 3, 1974): 382–413.

[12]U.S. Department of Commerce, *Foreign Direct Investment,* Vol. 1, pp. 172–173.

[13]See ibid., Vol. 9, pp. N-6–N-15.

[14]The largest subsidies have gone to the steel, shipbuilding, and textile industries. The OECD pledge was signed in June 1978, as a result of intense U.S. pressure on the European allies. See "Europe's Subsidy Spree," *Dun's Review,* August 1978, pp. 57–59.

[15]See "American Business in Europe: A Seminar on the Next 10 Years," *European Community,* November–December 1976, pp. 25–29.

[16]In a report released in February 1978, which was based on 1972 data, Statistics Canada stated that 66 of Canada's 100 largest firms are foreign-owned, 74 of the next 100 foreign-controlled, as well as 207 of the following 300. See *Canadian News Facts,* February 16–28, 1978, p. 1909. For a look at Canadian reaction to foreign investment, consult Abraham Rotstein, "Canada: The New Nationalism" *Foreign Affairs,* 55 (October 1976): 97–118.

[17]Stephenson, *The Coming Clash,* p. 145.

[18]For example, see the arguments discussed in R. P. Bowles et al., ed., *Canada and the U.S.: Continental Partners or Wary Neighbors?* (Scarborough: Prentice-Hall of Canada, 1973), pp. 20–73.

[19]See Melville H. Watkins, "The Canadian Experience with Foreign Direct Investment," *Law and Contemporary Problems,* 34 (Winter 1969): 126–134.

[20]See U.S. Department of Commerce, *Foreign Direct Investment,* Vol. 9, p. N-60. A "take-over" of a Canadian firm is defined as the purchase of at least 5 percent of the voting shares of a publicly traded company and at least 20 percent of a privately held enterprise.

[21]*FIRA News Release,* January 26, 1978. Criteria for ascertaining "significant benefit" include: (1) the effect of the proposed investment on the level and nature of economic activity in Canada, including employment; (2) the degree and significance of participation by Canadians in the business enterprise and in any industry or industries in Canada of which it forms a part; (3) the effect of the proposed investment on productivity, industrial efficiency, technological development, product innovation, and product variety within Canada; (4) the effect of the proposed investment on competition within any industry or industries in Canada; and (5) the compatibility of the investment with national industrial and economic policies, including those enunciated by the provinces (U.S. Department of Commerce, *Foreign Direct Investment,* Vol. 9, p. N-60).

[22]If the Canadian government does not respond to the application within 60 days, the investment is automatically approved. What usually occurs, however, is that FIRA will demand additional information from the applicant and several more weeks will pass before the application is finally approved or rejected.

[23]See Isaiah A. Litvak and Christopher J. Maule, "Interest-Group Tactics and the Politics of Foreign Investment: The Time–Reader's Digest Case Study," *Canadian Journal of Political Science,* 7 (December 1974): 616–629.

[24]See Garth Stevenson, "Foreign Direct Investment and the Provinces: A Study of Elite Attitudes," *Canadian Journal of Political Science,* 7 (December 1974): 630–647. Stevenson's data indicated that provincial legislators in many of the provinces would support federal initiatives in the direction of greater economic nationalism, particularly in Ontario and the

West. However, these legislators were united in their desire to protect provincial government autonomy from any encroachment on the part of federal authorities.

Once again, it must be remembered that governmental authority in the Canadian federal system is much more decentralized than in the American system. For more information on this topic, see Earl H. Fry, *Canadian Government and Politics in Comparative Perspective* (Washington, D.C.: University Press of America, 1978).

[25]See Rotstein, "Canada," p. 100. This reference to Murder, Inc., originally appeared in a *Barron's* article.

[26]*FIRA News Release,* January 26, 1978. Early 1978 figures again showed an upward trend in terms of submitted investment proposals.

[27]"Regional Economic Development—A Canadian Priority," *Foreign Investment Review,* Winter 1977/78, pp. 13–15.

[28]*Canadian Press Comment,* August 16, 1978.

[29]*Quebec Update,* August 28, 1978. It is estimated that American and other foreign-owned industries in Canada show a 50 percent higher productivity rate than indigenous-owned enterprises in the nation.

[30]A Gallup Poll issued in the summer of 1978 indicated that 52 percent of the Canadian people would like their government to begin to buy back control of Canada's principal industries from the United States and other foreign investors.

In terms of government intervention in the functioning of the economy, rather severe wage and price controls were instituted by the Trudeau government from October 1975 through April 1978, and Ottawa continues to oversee wage and price increases in the nation. A government investment company has also been organized and there are several state-owned corporations in Canada.

Provincial governments have also been very active in this sphere with several invoking their own program of price controls. The Alberta government also purchased its own airline and the Saskatchewan government has begun the nationalization of its key potash industry which provides a good share of the world's supply of that commodity.

[31]As Fred C. Bergsten et al. point out in *American Multinationals and American Interests* (Washington, D.C.: Brookings, 1978), p. 4: "Claims are made that foreign direct investment creates jobs and that it exports jobs, that it helps the balance of payments and that it hurts it, that it promotes U.S. foreign policy, that it subverts U.S. foreign policy, that it fosters economic development, and that it depresses economic development. These differences reflect value judgments, the bases for which were formed long before multinational corporations became a central issue."

[32]For an overview of the neorevisionist argument, see Gabriel Kolko, *The Roots of American Foreign Policy* (Boston: Beacon Press, 1969), and Gar Alperovitz, *Cold War Essays* (Garden City, N.Y.: Doubleday, 1970).

[33]As illustrations of the far right point of view toward these groups and their international activities, see Gary Allen, "America, 1977," *American Opinion,* July–August 1977, pp. 1–20, and William P. Hoar, "The New World Order," *American Opinion,* April 1977, pp. 13–20, 99–104.

[34]The "international corporation" is depicted as having "no country to which it owes more loyalty than any other, nor any country where it feels completely at home. It equalizes the return on its invested capital in every country, after adjusting for risk which is free of the myopia that says home investment is automatically risk-free and all foreign investments are risky. It is willing to speculate against the currency of the head office because it regards holdings of cash anywhere as subject to exchange risks which should be hedged." Quoted in Charles P. Kindleberger, *American Business Abroad* (New Haven: Yale, 1969), p. 182.

[35]See Richard J. Barnet and Ronald E. Muller, *Global Reach: The Power of the Multinational Corporations* (New York: Simon & Schuster, 1974), p. 26.

[36]Ibid., p. 380.

[37]Raymond Vernon closely examines the sovereignty-at-bay thesis in his book, *Sovereignty At Bay: The Multinational Spread of U.S. Enterprises* (New York: Basic Books, 1971).

Another source even goes so far as to insist that the activities of multinational corporations are a potential threat to democratic government: "Transnational relations and other multinational processes seriously threaten democratic control of foreign policy, particularly in advanced industrial societies. The intermeshing of decision making across national frontiers and the growing multinationalization of formerly domestic issues are inherently incompatible with the traditional framework of democratic control. The threat is all the more serious because it is sustained not by enemies of democracy but unknowingly by people who consider themselves to be acting within Western democratic traditions and because it results in part from the very forces of internationalism, interdependence, and economic advancement that have come to be regarded as indispensable." Quoted in Karl Kaiser, "Transnational Relations as a Threat to the Democratic Process," in *Transnational Relations and World Politics,* Robert O. Keohane and Joseph S. Nye, eds. (Cambridge, Mass.: Harvard, 1972), p. 356.

Bergsten et al., *American Multinationals,* p. 450, also discusses the various perspectives of foreign direct investment.

[38]Ibid., pp. 449 and 492. After scrutinizing nine instances of U.S. investment abroad, another study concluded that "our case analyses indicate that virtually all of the U.S. exports of capital equipment would have been lost if the U.S. firms had not invested abroad," (Robert B. Stobaugh, *Nine Investments Abroad and Their Impact at Home, Case Studies on Multinational Enterprises and the U.S. Economy* (Cambridge, Mass.: Harvard, 1976), p. 199.

[39]Kindleberger has defined pure nationalism as the "uneasiness that many people instinctively have when they contemplate the fact that the activities of institutions within their economy and politics are 'controlled' from outside the political unit" (*American Business Abroad,* p. 5). However, he does not believe that within the present context of international investment, such nationalist suspicions are justified.

[40]See the American Enterprise Institute, *Criminalization of Payments to Influence Foreign Governments* (Washington, D.C.: American Enterprise Institute for Public Policy Research, 1977).

[41]A juxtaposition of international investor and national government interests is presented in W. B. Reddaway, *Effects of U. K. Direct Investment Overseas* (Cambridge: Cambridge, 1967), pp. 23–24.

However, as Raymond Vernon points out in his book, *Storm Over the Multinationals: The Real Issues* (Cambridge, Mass.: Harvard, 1977), p. 212, national leaders often blame multinational enterprises for "the emptiness, the corruption, the inequities, and the ugliness that so often accompany the industrializing process." Consequently, Vernon emphasizes that these conditions which often plague the developing nations are symptoms of the overall industrialization process and not necessarily the fault of the multinationals.

[42]The "extraterritorial" dimensions of international investment and the problems which such investment represent for national governments are discussed in Isaiah A. Litvak and Christopher J. Maule, eds., *Foreign Investment: The Experience of Host Countries* (New York: Praeger, 1970), pp. 22–27.

[43]The charter is discussed in James Greene, *The Search for Common Ground: A Survey of Efforts to Develop Codes of Behavior in International Investment* (New York: Conference Board, 1971), p. 2.

[44]Ibid.

[45]Ibid.

[46]Ibid., p. 3.

[47]See U.S. Department of Commerce, *Foreign Direct Investment,* Vol. 9, Section "N." This section of the nine-volume Commerce study looks at the foreign investment climate in Belgium, France, Germany, Italy, the Netherlands, Switzerland, the United Kingdom, Canada, and Japan.

[48]These nations are Peru, Bolivia, Chile, Ecuador, Colombia, and Venezuela.

[49]*The Wall Street Journal,* May 4, 1978, p. 10.

[50]Quoted in Kindleberger, *American Business Abroad,* pp. 180–181. The declaration was prompted by Canadian irritation over the U.S. government's Voluntary Credit Restraint Program in 1965, which had an adverse effect on certain types of corporate investment in Canada.

[51]C. Fred Bergsten has predicted an increase in economic nationalism in Bergsten et al., *American Multinationals,* p. 386. Another dimension of the nation-state–multinational corporation dichotomy is discussed in Detlev F. Vagts, "Coercion and Foreign Investment Arrangements," *American Journal of International Law,* 72 (January 1978): 17–36.

For a look at the international regulation of investment activity, see George Modelski, "The United Nations and Regulation of Transnational Corporations," *Journal of Contemporary Business,* 6 (Autumn 1977): 73–98.

Chapter 3

[1]In particular, a great deal of attention has been accorded to the activities of financier Ghaith Pharaon, the Kuwaiti development of Kiaweh Island off the coast of South Carolina, and the Arab investment in Beverly Hills. A book which stresses the "Arab" dimension of foreign investment in the United States is Kenneth C. Crowe, *America for Sale* (Garden City, N.Y.: Doubleday, 1978).

[2]Sales of the 200 largest foreign industrial corporations reached 228 billion dollars in 1969 and 611 billion dollars in 1974, as compared to U.S. sales of 368 billion dollars and 678 billion dollars respectively. In percentages, the foreign industrial sales went up 111 percent from 1964 to 1969, and 168 percent from 1969 to 1974. In 1969, only 50 foreign industrial firms had sales greater than or equal to the sales of the one-hundredth largest U.S. corporation, with only 6 foreign firms having sales equal to or better than America's twenty-fifth largest industrial company. By 1974, 99 foreign firms were on par with or were surpassing the sales of America's one-hundredth largest firm, and 26 had sales figures exceeding those of the twenty-fifth largest company in the United States.

See U.S. Department of Commerce, *Foreign Direct Investment,* Vol. 5, pp. G-30 and G-32. This section of the Commerce report was prepared by Arthur D. Little, Inc.

[3]Ibid.

[4]Prior to making investments in the United States, many foreign-based multinationals have already learned a great deal about the American business community through the exporting and the marketing of their products in the United States. Moreover, some of the key people in these other nations have been trained in America's most prestigious business schools. It is quite true, for example, that there are more American-trained Ph.D.'s in the present Saudi Arabian cabinet than in the U.S. cabinet.

[5]*Business Week,* November 14, 1977, p. 63 and *The Wall Street Journal,* February 9, 1979, p. 40. Recent Japanese investment setbacks in Brazil and Southeast Asia will probably make the United States an even more attractive site for Japanese investment funds.

[6]*Economist,* December 17, 1977, pp. 11–12. In this editorial, the *Economist* called for greater foreign activity in the United States in order to help alleviate the anemic U.S. trade deficit, bolster confidence on Wall Street, and lower the U.S. unemployment rate.

[7]Germans were especially attracted to the American market because production costs in the U.S. are now lower than in Germany. For a view of German investment abroad, see the following newspapers: *Kieler Nachrichten,* July 12, 1978; *Handelsblatt,* August 23, 1978; and *Die Welt,* May 22, 1978.

[8]*The New York Times,* January 16, 1978, IV, p. 1.

⁹*OECD Observer,* March 1978, pp. 20–21.

¹⁰*Fortune,* February 13, 1978, p. 80.

¹¹*Business Week,* November 14, 1977, p. 63. The Bank of America, among other major banking institutions, has produced a short but fairly comprehensive booklet aimed specifically at the foreign investment audience. This booklet is entitled *Direct Investment in the United States from Abroad.*

¹²U.S. Department of Commerce, *Foreign Direct Investment,* Vol. 5, p. G-4. Some of these executives were concerned, however, with the slower rate of economic growth in the world in general and in Europe in particular, with the inherent weaknesses in the international monetary system, with the leveraged corporate and banking debt rampant in all of the industrialized nations, and with the uncertainty associated with how the OPEC nations would finally decide to use their monetary surpluses.

In a second study conducted by the New York-based Conference Board in 1976, most of the executives interviewed expected production costs abroad to continue to rise at a rate faster than in the United States (James R. Basche, Jr., *Foreign Production Costs: A Survey of Recent Trends and Their Effects on Business Policy* [New York: Conference Board, 1976], p. 26).

In another Conference Board report, a Dutch executive observed that the United States "has had the lowest cost increase. The devaluation (of the dollar) has made it practically impossible to export from the EEC to the United States except for certain very specialized products. So we increased our local production activities in the United States."

The chairman of a Swiss firm which was then constructing a plant in the United States commented that "production in Switzerland is further handicapped by the high value of the Swiss franc. This makes our products more expensive in the export markets and attracts lower priced competition in the Swiss home market. As almost all our raw materials are imported, the effect of the high Swiss franc is basically limited to the added value. As a result, new production capacities will be built abroad rather than in Switzerland."

A Canadian executive predicted that the United States would be more attractive than Canada for investors in the manufacturing sphere: "New investment in plant and equipment will most likely occur in the United States unless significant cost savings can be obtained in Canada by fully integrating existing 'nonintegrated' operations. We expect that the United States will still be the low-cost producers with respect to Canada over the next five years." See James R. Basche, Jr., *Production Cost Trends and Outlook: A Study of International Business Experience* (New York: Conference Board, 1977), pp. 30–31, 38.

In a fourth survey involving firms from five different nations which had decided to invest in the United States, 24 executives stated that they had decided to invest because of U.S. government restrictions pertaining to imports. Of these 24, 10 stated that these restrictions emanated from "Buy American" provisions, 7 from tariffs, 3 from safety restrictions, and 2 each from state and local governments and from quota policies respectively.

Executives from four additional firms contended that they had set up facilities in the United States because of strong consumer demand for their products. Four others mentioned a need for a different product line in the U.S. market and eight cited the cost advantages of U.S. production as the motivating force for setting up plants in the United States. See John D. Daniels, *Recent Foreign Direct Manufacturing Investment in the United States: An Interview Study of the Decision Process* (New York: Praeger, 1971), pp. 52–53.

¹³U.S. Department of Commerce, *Foreign Direct Investment,* Vol. 5, p. G-18.

¹⁴Ibid., pp. G-17 and G-18.

¹⁵A study of the methods of financing foreign direct investment in the United States was completed for the U.S. Department of Commerce by Booz, Allen, and Hamilton, Inc. Acquisitions of U.S. firms were made through obtaining either a controlling or minority interest in the voting shares of common stock or through an increase in the percentage of ownership of an already partially owned U.S. subsidiary.

The study concluded that the major types of financial vehicles used by foreign investors to complete their transactions in the United States included (1) initial capitalization (providing capital for a new company), (2) the acquisition of a certain number of shares of common stock through cash for stock, debt for stock, a "stock swap," or assets for stock, and (3) the purchase of certain assets of a company such as a single plant, rather than the entire company. See ibid., pp. H-11–H-13.

In the survey discussed in Daniels, *Manufacturing Investment,* pp. 96–97, 21 of the 40 foreign firms interviewed expressed a strong preference for 100 percent ownership of their U.S. subsidiaries because they did not want to share profits nor risk minority stockholder problems. Of the 40, 25 entered the U.S. market by buying into existing U.S. firms and 18 accepted geographical sites on the basis of where the company was already located.

[16]U.S. Department of Commerce, *Foreign Direct Investment,* Vol. 5, pp. H-18 and H-19. The cash for stock route was preferred by both parties with the U.S. owners wanting cash for retirement purposes. The British company accepted these terms because of (1) its policy to fund fixed investment through Eurodollars and working capital in the United States through U.S. banks, (2) its close contacts with the London banks which put up the Eurodollars, and (3) the greater flexibility provided by Eurodollar banks over U.S. banks in extending lines of credit.

[17]Felix G. Rohatyn, who has consummated many deals for foreign investors as an executive for Lazard Frères, a Wall Street firm, asserts that foreign buyers, "usually want companies with good track records, and good management, management that will stay in place. They don't want to get into a fight so they usually prefer to pay a higher price." See *The New York Times,* January 16, 1978, IV, p. 1.

[18]Hamilton's remarks are recorded in his *Report on Manufactures,* December 5, 1791.

[19]One should also keep in mind that overseas investment had permitted the establishment and the development of the American colonies in the first place. As an example, the voyage of the *Mayflower* was promoted by the Massachusetts Bay Company and financed by a group of London speculators who had acquired the right to certain northern territories from the previously established Virginia Company. Thus, in the quest for valuable raw materials and increased trade opportunities, the European development of the New World commenced.

[20]U.S. Congress, House, Committee on Foreign Affairs, *Direct Foreign Investment in the United States,* July 7, 1974, p. 2.

[21]Jay Laurence Lenrow, "Foreign Direct Investment in the United States: Possible Restrictions at Home and a New Climate for American Investment Abroad," *American University Law Review,* 26 (Fall 1976): 113.

[22]U.S. Department of Commerce, *Foreign Direct Investment,* Vol. 8, p. L-8. This section of the Commerce study was prepared by T. L. Anderson of Montana State University and is entitled "A Survey of Alien Land Investment in the United States, Colonial Times to Present."

[23]It should be stressed, however, that many foreign investors took a financial beating in the United States. Widespread defaults on canal bonds in the 1830s and railroad bonds in the 1870s particularly took a toll on foreign money interests.

[24]Foreign money has generally always been welcomed in the United States. As late as 1950, European direct investment in the United States was 500 million dollars greater than U.S. investment in Europe. In fact, it was not until the mid-1960s that overall American investment in Europe finally surpassed European investment in the United States.

[25]As enunciated in U.S. Department of Commerce, Domestic and International Business Administration, *Informal Survey of Legal Provisions Affecting Foreign Investment in the United States,* May 1977, p. 1, the following position has been adopted by the U.S. government vis-à-vis foreign investment:

> The basic general policy of the United States is to admit and treat foreign capital on a basis of equality with domestic capital.

In examining possible variations from this general policy, it should be borne in mind that a substantial portion of the jurisdiction over doing business in the United States belongs to the several states. Therefore, the law and practice both of the States and of the Federal Government need to be taken into account.

This Department of Commerce report also points out that the investment picture is further clouded because in addition to the jurisdictional network of the federal and state governments, there are separate statutes and administrative regulations applicable to the District of Columbia, the Commonwealth of Puerto Rico, Guam, the Virgin Islands, and American Samoa.

[26]Permits for the use of scarce materials in the United States are only required during what are considered "emergency" periods.

[27]The equal protection provision as applied to foreign investors is discussed in John R. Liebman and Beth Levine, "Foreign Investors and Equal Protection," *Mercer Law Review,* 27 (Spring 1976): 615–628.

[28]See U.S. Department of Commerce, Domestic and International Business Administration, *Informal Survey.*

[29]The Bureau of Economic Analysis within the Commerce Department currently keeps track of foreign direct investment on a quarterly basis.

[30]U.S. Department of Commerce, Domestic and International Business Administration, *Informal Survey,* p. 2.

[31]Conference Board, *Foreign Investment in the United States: Policy, Problems and Obstacles* (New York: Conference Board, 1974), p. 25.

[32]Quoted in Daniels, *Recent Foreign Direct Manufacturing Investment,* p. 204.

[33]This issue is discussed in Colebrook, *Going International,* p. 75. For related material, see Sidney E. Rolfe and Walter Damm, eds., *The Multinational Corporation in the World Economy* (New York: Praeger, 1970), pp. 52–71.

The Swiss-based Nestlé Company, for one, has expressed great consternation about U.S. antitrust laws because the firm prefers to buy existing concerns in the United States and has experienced some difficulties with the Justice Department (see *Fortune,* February 13, 1978, pp. 89–90).

[34]See U.S. Department of Commerce, *Foreign Direct Investment,* Vol. 7, appendix K, and Lenrow, "Foreign Direct Investment," pp. 109–153.

Most of the restrictions discussed in this section of the chapter are also examined in these two sources and in Jeffrey S. Arpan, "Regulation of Foreign Direct Investment in the United States: Quo Vasit, Quo Vadit?" *Journal of Contemporary Business,* 6 (Autumn 1977): 99–119.

[35]The Natural Resources Act of 1887 stipulates that public land may be transferred or leased only to citizens or persons who intend to naturalize, partnerships consisting of citizens or individuals who intend to naturalize, or corporations organized under U.S. law. Corporations involved in the use of public land may be wholly owned by aliens only if their country of origin allows U.S. citizens to own land within its jurisdiction.

Although no state specifically restricts foreign activity in mining, some state regulations pertaining to foreign ownership of land in general may effectively preclude aliens from mining activities on nonfederal land. See Chapter Six for a list of these state restrictions.

[36]Just such a claim is made by Crowe in *America for Sale,* p. 4.

[37]U.S. Department of Commerce, *Foreign Direct Investment,* Vol. 6, p. J-6.

[38]For additional information on the taxation issue, consult Simon G. Sturm, "Taxation of the Foreign Investor in the United States," *Taxes,* August 1977, pp. 542–565.

The U.S. Department of the Treasury has recently proposed guidelines which would tax foreign governments on income which they earn from operating businesses in the United States. In effect, income derived from financial instruments (stocks, bonds, interest-bearing bank deposits, etc.) would still be tax exempt, but income accruing from commercial activities, such as the ownership of a hotel, would be taxable. See *The Wall Street Journal,* August 14, 1978, p. 3.

[39]U.S. Department of Commerce, *Foreign Direct Investment,* Vol. 7, p. K-249.

[40]Ibid., p. K-247.

[41]Cawthorne was quoted in Vernon Louviere, "A Tiny Federal Office That Produces Big Results," *Nation's Business,* January 1978, p. 68.

[42]Ibid., p. 67.

[43]Ibid.

[44]In a letter sent out on July 14, 1978, to the International Divisions of State Industrial Development Agencies, Thomas J. Pierpoint of the Invest in U.S.A. program announced that the mission to Japan was designed "to promote U.S. exports and facilitate reverse investment to the United States by Japan." Mr. Pierpoint also asked each state agency to forward "twenty sets of the three best pieces of literature of each state designed to attract industry." This literature would then be distributed to interested Japanese businesses on request.

[45]Even during its halcyon days from 1967 until 1974, Invest in U.S.A. managed to operate with a staff of eight and an annual budget of $300,000.

[46]Invest in U.S.A. has published a brochure which simplifies for foreign investors the visa requirements of the U.S. government. Before an amendment to the Immigration and Nationality Act eased the situation somewhat in 1970, the admission of foreign management and technical personnel to the United States was a very arduous process tied up in a great deal of red tape.

[47]Quoted in Daniels, *Manufacturing Investment,* p. 77.

[48]Ibid., p. 98.

[49]Even some of the restrictions on the books are mitigated or voided altogether by U.S. treaties with other governments. Commencing with the Treaty of Unity and Commerce with France in 1778, the United States has concluded 130 bilateral treaties with other nations containing reciprocal arrangements for the protection of foreign investors.

Chapter 4

[1]The statistics on foreign investment in the manufacturing sector were compiled by the New York-based Conference Board. Also consult *The Wall Street Journal,* October 10, 1978, p. 1.

[2]Ibid.

[3]*Economist,* December 17, 1977, pp. 11–12.

[4]U.S. Department of Commerce, *Foreign Direct Investment,* Vol. 1, p. 234. As an illustration, the Department of Commerce announced that during the first half of 1977, acquisitions, mergers, and equity increases represented 49 percent of the total transactions in the foreign investment sector, and 68 percent of the reported investment values, percentages which correspond fairly closely with foreign investment transactions during the previous five years. See *U.S. Department of Commerce News,* April 18, 1978.

[5]David Bauer of the Conference Board pointed this out in *The Wall Street Journal,* January 25, 1978, p. 2.

[6]Darrell Delamaide, "Hans Across the Sea: West German Industry Has Launched a U.S. Invasion," *Barron's,* April 10, 1978, p. 9.

[7]These prognostications were made in U.S. Department of Commerce, *Foreign Direct Investment,* Vol. 5, p. G-5.

[8]Delamaide, "Hans Across the Sea," p. 16. The author of this article concludes on page 17 that "the invasion is likely to continue to hold significant implications for stockholders on both sides of the Atlantic."

[9]William J. Storck, "New Incentives Are Spurring Growth of Foreign Investment in U.S. Chemicals," *Chemical and Engineering News,* February 27, 1978, p. 14.

[10]Delamaide, "Hans Across the Sea," p. 16.

[11]Storck, "New Incentives," p. 16.

[12]See ibid., pp. 12–16, for further details on foreign activities in the chemical sphere. Henkel, for example, has expressed a strong interest in expanding its activities in the U.S. specialty chemicals business (see *Business Week,* May 15, 1978, pp. 114–115). For a look at Nestlé's activities, consult *Fortune,* February 13, 1978, pp. 80–90.

[13]U.S. Department of Commerce, *Foreign Direct Investment,* Vol. 1, p. 67.

[14]Delamaide, "Hans Across the Sea," p. 16.

[15]Ibid.

[16]Ibid.

[17]*The Wall Street Journal,* October 10, 1978, p. 1.

[18]*Business Week,* August 14, 1978, p. 28.

[19]*Science,* May 5, 1978, p. 512.

[20]Ibid. Also see *Economist,* February 25, 1978, pp. 98–100; *Forbes,* October 16, 1978, pp. 104–109, and November 13, 1978, pp. 70–76.

[21]*The Wall Street Journal,* October 13, 1978, p. 8.

[22]Ibid., p. 1. The wildcat protesters also demanded the right to turn down overtime work, a provision in the UAW's contract with the large automakers in Detroit.

[23]*Business Week,* August 15, 1977, pp. 34–35.

[24]U.S. Department of Commerce, *Foreign Direct Investment,* Vol. 3, p. 93.

[25]*Business Week,* April 24, 1978, pp. 118 and 120.

[26]Stobaugh, *Nine Investments Abroad,* p. 216.

[27]U.S. Department of Commerce, *Foreign Direct Investment,* Vol. 1, p. 207. The NSF study also indicated that U.S. companies are more likely than the foreign-managed firms to channel greater amounts of research and development funding into specific product development areas.

[28]Ibid., Vol. 5, Section I.

[29]*The Wall Street Journal,* October 10, 1978, pp. 1 and 10. For a profile of the management practices of another Japanese firm, Sony, see *U.S. News and World Report,* December 11, 1978, p. 58.

[30]*The New York Times,* May 31, 1977, pp. 39 and 57.

[31]*Forbes,* October 16, 1978, p. 109.

[32]U.S. Department of Commerce, *Foreign Direct Investment,* Vol. 1, pp. 61 and 64.

[33]Ibid., Vol. 3, p. A-5.

[34]*The Wall Street Journal,* July 21, 1978, p. 5.

[35]Ibid., July 3, 1978, p. 1.

Chapter 5

[1]Recounted in Chris Welles, "Bankers, Bankers Everywhere—But How Much Business Are They Getting?" *Institutional Investor,* September 1977, p. 115.

[2]*San Francisco Chronicle,* August 31, 1978, p. 2. Representatives of the Soviet Union have denied that the Moscow bank has had any interest whatsoever in acquiring American banks.

[3]U.S. Department of Commerce, *Foreign Direct Investment,* Vol. 4, p. F-2.

[4]Ibid., Vol. 1, pp. 106–107. The foreign banks reasoned that any legislation passed by Congress would contain a grandfather clause exempting existing banking operations from some of the restrictive conditions.

[5]"Foreign Banking's U.S. Invasion," *Dun's Review,* February 1978, p. 77.

[6]Welles, "Bankers," p. 116.

[7]The name of this bank was later changed to California First Bank.

[8]*Forbes,* July 10, 1978, pp. 32–33.

[9]*Business Week,* August 7, 1978, p. 41, and November 27, 1978, p. 123; and *The Wall Street Journal,* November 10, 1978, p. 10.

[10]U.S. Department of Commerce, *Foreign Direct Investment,* Vol. 4, p. F-23.

[11]*The Wall Street Journal,* July 20, 1978, p. 24. The Pharaon-National Commercial Bank linkage is discussed in *Business Week,* January 23, 1978, p. 86.

[12]The alleged Lance episode is examined in *Esquire,* April 25, 1978, pp. 20–22.

[13]A detailed study of federal and state regulations of foreign banking operations in the United States is presented in the U.S. Department of Commerce, *Foreign Direct Investment,* Vol. 4, pp. F-31–F-41. Much of the information in this section of the chapter was derived from the Commerce study.

[14]The Federal Reserve is permitted to regulate bank holding companies, which are defined as entities which exercise control over the management or policies of U.S. banks. Foreign banks that have U.S. banking subsidiaries have been placed in the category of a holding company (see ibid., pp. F-32–F-33).

To keep things in perspective, almost two-thirds of all U.S. banks, mainly the smaller ones, are not members of the Federal Reserve System.

[15]Ibid., p. F-6–F-7.

[16]In California, foreign-controlled branches actually operate as agencies because California law requires that deposits accepted from domestic sources must be insured. However, Federal Deposit Insurance Corporation (FDIC) coverage has been available only to U.S.-chartered banks, effectively precluding the foreign-chartered institutions from accepting such deposits.

[17]U.S. Department of Commerce, *Foreign Direct Investment,* Vol. 4, p. F-9.

[18]Illinois, for example, explicitly authorizes the entry of alien banks while making no provision for out-of-state U.S. banks to come into the state.

[19]For more about the "unitary" tax system which also applies to foreign corporations outside of the banking sector, see *Business Week,* July 17, 1978, p. 28, and *Economist,* April 15, 1978, p. 124.

[20]*Forbes,* October 30, 1978, p. 142.

[21]U.S. Department of Commerce, *Foreign Direct Investment,* Vol. 4, p. F-33.

[22]Ibid., pp F-40–F-41.

[23]*Federal Reserve Bulletin,* July 1978, p. 538.

[24]Perhaps somewhat surprisingly, many of the largest U.S. banks have supported the continuation of the exemption permitting foreign banks to have operations in more than one state. Some commentators have suggested that the large U.S. institutions hope that at some time in the future they may be granted the same right to cross state borders that is now accorded to the foreign firms. See, for example, *Forbes,* August 21, 1978, p. 35, and David C. Cates, "Foreign Banks Are Cracking the Facade of U.S. Banking," *Fortune,* August 28, 1978, p. 98.

[25]U.S. Department of Commerce, *Foreign Direct Investment,* Vol. 4, p. F-12.

[26]Welles, "Bankers," p. 116.

[27]*Institutional Investor,* September 1977, p. 122.

[28]"U.S. Invasion," *Dun's Review,* p. 78.

[29]Ibid.

[30]Ibid., p. 77. This quote was attributed to the manager of the Chicago branch of the Banque Nationale de Paris.

[31]As James H. Higgens, chairman of the Mellon National Bank, has stated: "The foreign banks can undercut our business-lending rates by 50 basis points (one-half a percentage point) and still make a sufficient profit for their needs," (*Fortune,* August 28, 1978, p. 96).

American corporations seem to appreciate this new banking competition. William Valiant, treasurer of Borg-Warner, has offered this perspective: "The U.S. banks and the foreign banks are battling for our business, and that means lower rates, better service and more diverse sources for us. We will always take the best deal we can get." See "U.S. Invasion," *Dun's Review,* p. 78.

[32]In mid-1978, the Fed's reserve requirements were set at various levels, such as 16¼ percent of demand deposits and 6 percent of large certificates of deposit.

[33]"Standard banking assets" are defined by the Fed as the sum of loans, money market investments, and securities holdings.

[34]*Federal Reserve Bulletin,* July 1978, p. 539.

[35]*Forbes,* August 21, 1978, p. 34. Approximately 315 of the largest U.S. banks report weekly to the Federal Reserve System. These 315 institutions do one-half of the total domestic banking business in the United States.

[36]Ibid. According to *Newsweek,* November 27, 1978, p. 88, the foreign share of business loans made by banks in New York in May 1978 was 43.4 percent.

[37]Ibid.

[38]Nevertheless, further restrictions on foreign banking activity in the United States are being pushed by certain groups. Ironically, in view of New York's liberal banking legislation, that state's banking superintendent has urged the state legislature to pass a bill requiring that any investor wanting to buy more than 10 percent of a bank operating in the state would have to seek prior approval from the superintendent of banking. See *U.S. News & World Report,* September 4, 1978, p. 63.

[39]*Fortune,* June 5, 1978, p. 155.

[40]Ibid., p. 156. In spite of these risks, Zurich-based Crédit Suisse recently asserted that it is putting much more money from its investors' portfolios into American stock because it "can buy shares in profitmaking brick and mortar at a discount." See *Newsweek,* November 27, 1978, p. 78.

[41]*Forbes,* March 20, 1978, p. 64.

[42]*Business Week,* May 22, 1978, p. 152.

[43]*The Wall Street Journal,* March 16, 1977, p. 4, and March 21, 1977, p. 2.

[44]*Business Week,* February 21, 1977, pp. 102–103.

[45]Mark Perlgut, "The Clout of Wall Street's New Foreign Owners," *Institutional Investor,* December 1977, p. 147.

[46]*The New York Times,* April 29, 1978, p. 29.

[47]Ibid., May 8, 1978, IV, pp. 1 and 6. The British actually bought the largest chunk of these securities. For example, during the first eight months of 1977, the British accounted for 6.7 billion of the 13.2 billion dollars of total foreign purchases of U.S. government securities, whereas OPEC countries bought 3.1 billion. In fact, the British wanted such a large share that the Federal Reserve Bank of New York asked them to go elsewhere for investment opportunities (*Economist,* November 26, 1977, p. 121).

[48]*Business Week,* January 23, 1978, p. 86.

[49]*Fortune,* June 5, 1978, p. 156.

[50]Associated Press story reported in the *Idaho Statesman,* November 23, 1978, p. 6-D.

[51]*Business Week,* November 7, 1977, p. 88. American portfolio investment and government securities holdings overseas were estimated at 200 billion dollars at the end of 1976, as compared to 60 billion dollars of similar foreign investment in the United States (*The New York Times,* January 8, 1978, XII, pp. 40 and 52).

[52]*Fortune,* June 5, 1978, p. 155.

[53]In a related sphere, foreigners have also become very active in the American insurance business (see *Forbes,* October 1, 1977, pp. 74–75). The McCarran-Ferguson Act authorizes the state governments to handle most aspects of regulating and supervising the foreign firms. Usually the states require more stringent compliance by alien insurance firms than by out-of-

state companies. Typically, special financial reserve requirements are placed on the alien companies in order to protect the citizens of the state who are insured by these foreign firms.

At times, however, the laws governing the foreign companies differ significantly from state to state. For example, the Florida Insurance Commissioner excluded Caisse Centrale de Réassurance from doing business in that state because it is controlled directly by the French government. On the other hand, the New York authorities permitted Volkswagen Insurance to operate within its jurisdiction even though the Bonn central government and the Lower Saxony Land government have significant holdings in the company. The New York decision was based on the fact that these governments controlled only 36 percent of Volkswagen's overall stock (see U.S. Department of Commerce, *Foreign Direct Investment*, Vol. 7, p. 213).

In addition, efforts are now under way to internationalize the insurance brokerage business which up to this point has been dominated by U.S. companies in the United States and London brokers in the rest of the world. The four largest U.S. insurance brokers have recently entered into discussions with London brokers who are permitted to do business with Lloyd's of London, the British insurance marketplace and trading floor. If mergers do result from these discussions, the British brokers will exert greater influence over the American market; and their U.S. counterparts will expand their brokerage business into other parts of the world. See the *The Wall Street Journal*, November 20, 1978, p. 10.

Moreover, the state of New York has recently established a free trade zone for insurance companies in an effort to facilitate the creation of a Lloyd's of London-style international insurance network in the United States, with New York City serving as the network's headquarters.

Chapter 6

[1]U.S. Department of Commerce, *Foreign Direct Investment*, Vol. 8, p. 184.

[2]*The New York Times*, May 14, 1978, p. 40.

[3]*Economist*, May 14, 1977, p. S20.

[4]*The New York Times*, May 5, 1978, p. 1.

[5]For the Canadian perspective of Florida, see the *Toronto Globe and Mail*, February 15, 1978, p. 4.

[6]See Kenneth Cook, "Foreign Investment in U.S. Farmland," Library of Congress Congressional Research Service, July 11, 1978.

[7]*Newsweek*, May 22, 1978, p. 55.

[8]*Saturday Review*, October 15, 1977, p. 22.

[9]*Newsweek*, May 22, 1978, p. 56.

[10]*The Christian Science Monitor*, May 10, 1978, p. 24.

[11]Ibid.

[12]U.S. Department of Commerce, *Foreign Direct Investment*, Vol. 8, p. 184.

[13]This information was obtained from an August 1978 interview with a Farm and Land Realtor Association official.

[14]*European Community*, May–June 1978, p. 34.

[15]Robert J. Samuelson, "Rising Tide of Foreign Investment," *National Journal*, April 29, 1978, p. 669.

[16]*Barron's*, July 3, 1978, p. 9.

[17]*The New York Times*, April 17, 1977, p. 48. In U.S. Department of Agriculture, Economic Research Service, *Foreign Investment in U.S. Real Estate*, 1976, pp. 5–6, a dozen incentives for overseas investment in U.S. land are identified. These incentives include:

1. *Hedge against inflation.* The United States has traditionally experienced relatively stable prices and costs, compared with other countries. Although the United States has expe-

rienced considerable inflation during the past decade, the rate has been relatively lower than in most other countries. Also, foreign investors expect that the United States has the capability and necessary institutions to manage inflation better than other countries. This opinion appears to be warranted by current trends.

2. *Safety of investment.* Investment in U.S. land provides a refuge from internal reforms and disorders. This incentive is particularly important to foreign investors in light of substantive land reforms in process and in prospect throughout the world. Also, the economic and political power of the United States minimizes the threats of external disturbances.

3. *Capital appreciation.* Expectations of capital appreciation in both urban and rural land appear warranted in the rural and urban land sectors. Recent upward trends in land values are expected to continue, particularly in selected growth centers and industries.

4. *Income flows.* Income generated from U.S. land investments as inherent constituents of the national economy, appear competitive with alternative investments open to foreign investors.

5. *Tax advantages.* U.S. land investments offer tax advantages compared with taxes in other countries, particularly European countries.

6. *U.S. dollar versus other currency.* The relative stability and acceptability of the U.S. dollar throughout the world provides another incentive for foreign investment in the United States.

7. *Access to resources and technology.* Investment in U.S. land provides access to U.S. natural resources, materials and technology. This constitutes another incentive for foreign investment, particularly in land.

8. *Access to internal markets for products and product components.* This incentive may be particularly attractive to specific foreign investors.

9. *Balancing investment portfolios.* In terms of safety, income, capital appreciation, and other factors, U.S. land provides incentives for portfolios in which such incentives are needed.

10. *Capital and personal haven.* Some foreign investors may be interested in establishing a haven in the United States for further investment of flight capital. Such investments may provide personal refuge from internal uprisings, reforms, and disorder within their native countries.

11. *Intangible benefit.* Other foreign investors may be attracted to land investments because of satisfactions, prestige, and psychic values derived from owning land within the United States.

12. *Control factors.* The motive of gaining control of strategic land resources as a basis for economic and political power within the United States remains a possible incentive for foreign investors.

[18]U.S. General Accounting Office, *Foreign Ownership of U.S. Farmland—Much Concern, Little Data,* June 12, 1978, p. 2.

[19]Gene Wunderlich, *Summary of the Report: Foreign Investment in U.S. Real Estate* (Washington, D.C.: U.S. Department of Agriculture, December 1976), p. 1. Quoted originally in S. Livermore, *Early American Land Companies,* 1968, p. 27.

[20]Ibid.

[21]Fred L. Morrison, "Limitations on Alien Investment in American Real Estate," *Minnesota Law Review,* 60 (April 1976): 622.

[22]Ibid., p. 625.

[23]Ibid., p. 626.

[24]U.S. Department of Commerce, *Foreign Direct Investment,* Vol. 8, p. M-11.

[25]Ibid., pp. M-17–M-22. Also consult Michael Abrutyn, "Investment in United States Real Estate by Non-Resident Alien Individuals and Foreign Corporations," *Tax Management International Journal,* September 1977, pp. 22–25.

[26]Morrison, "Limitations," p. 663.

[27]U.S. General Accounting Office, *Foreign Ownership,* pp. 4–5. The ten states considering

further constraints are Alabama, California, Georgia, Illinois, Iowa, Kansas, Nebraska, Ohio, Oklahoma, and Wisconsin.

[28]U.S. Department of Commerce, *Foreign Direct Investment,* Vol. 8, p. M-25.

[29]*Congressional Record,* August 11, 1978, pp. S13140–S13143. Foreign leaseholds of agricultural land lasting more than five years must also be reported.

[30]U.S. Department of Commerce, *Foreign Direct Investment,* Vol. 8, pp. M-24–M-27.

[31]*Nation's Business,* August 1978, p. 67.

[32]Senator Malcolm Wallop and Representative Charles Grassley introduced bills in their respective chambers in the 1978 session of Congress which would eliminate the capital gains bonanza for foreigners.

[33]See U.S. Department of Commerce, *Foreign Direct Investment,* Vol. 8, p. M-38, for a list of some of these treaty provisions. Some experts contend, however, that a prohibition on alien ownership of agricultural land would not violate any existing U.S. treaty. See Joshua M. Morse III, "Legal Structures Affecting International Real Estate Transactions," *American University Law Review,* 26 (Fall 1976): 65.

[34]*The New York Times,* May 14,1978, p. 1.

[35]Ibid.

[36]*The Wall Street Journal,* July 20, 1978, p. 24.

[37]*Newsweek,* May 22, 1978, p 55, and *U.S. News & World Report,* July 24, 1978, p. 53.

[38]U.S. Department of Commerce, *Foreign Direct Investment,* Vol. 5, p. G-14, and Vol. 3, p. A-104.

[39]U.S. Department of Agriculture, Economic Research Service, *Foreign Investment in U.S. Real Estate,* 1976, pp. 164–178.

[40]Gene L. Wunderlich, *Foreign Ownership of U.S. Real Estate in Perspective* (Washington, D.C.: U.S. Department of Agriculture, June 1978), p. 1. Wunderlich concludes that even if the 4.9 million acres which the Commerce Department reported were controlled by foreign owners in 1975 were doubled, this "would still have been less than 1 percent of the 1.3 billion acres of private land." Wunderlich also points out that even if "all the foreign owned land had been farmland (and it was not), it would have represented only slightly more than 1 percent of the farmland in the Untied States, since most of the privately held land is in farms."

[41]U.S. General Accounting Office, *Foreign Ownership,* p. 26.

[42]Cook, "Foreign Investment."

[43]*U.S. News & World Report,* July 24, 1978, p. 53.

[44]The investment process can indeed be quite complicated. For example, a foreign investor in timberland must take into account such things as federal income taxes, federal estate and gift taxes, U.S. state income, death, and gift taxes, home country laws, and third country laws if using offshore holding companies as an investment intermediary.

[45]*Saturday Review,* October 15, 1977, p. 19.

[46]This information was derived from the author's interview with the president of this firm.

[47]*Newsweek,* May 22, 1978, p. 56, and personal interviews conducted by the author with selected Western real estate brokers. For example, one Northwest broker admitted that he had received inquiries from Belgian, Swedish, and French investors in a five-day period just prior to the interview.

[48]*Business Week,* December 26, 1977, p. 115.

[49]Even the government has prognosticated, for example, that foreign activity in the commercial timberland sector will increase substantially. See U.S. Department of Commerce, *Foreign Direct Investment,* Vol. 4, p. C-18.

[50]See, for example, ibid., Vol. 8, p. 189.

[51]*The New York Times,* May 14, 1978, p. 40.

[52]Ibid., May 5, 1978, p. 1.

[53]*Business Week,* September 25, 1978, p. 55.

[54]Based on an Associated Press story appearing in the *Idaho Statesman,* June 15, 1978, p. 6C.

[55]*Business Week,* June 5, 1978, pp. 146–147.

[56]Ibid.

[57]Ibid., August 1, 1977, p. 55.

[58]Ibid.

[59]Ibid., August 7, 1978, p. 41, and *Newsweek,* November 27, 1978, p. 78.

[60]*The Wall Street Journal,* October 30, 1978, p. 6.

[61]*U.S. News & World Report,* July 24, 1978, p. 54.

[62]*Economist,* May 14, 1977, p. S20.

[63]*U.S. News & World Report,* July 24, 1978, p. 54, and *Newsweek,* November 27, 1978, p. 78.

[64]*Barron's,* July 3, 1978, p. 9.

[65]*National Real Estate Investor,* January 1978, p. 39.

[66]Overseas pension funds have been particularly interested in commercial development projects in the United States. For example, the British Post Office pension plan has already earmarked 100 million dollars for commercial property purchases in the United States. (*Economist,* September 24, 1977, p. 129).

[67]*National Real Estate Investor,* January 1978, p. 73.

Chapter 7

[1]As the Department of Commerce study on foreign direct investment concludes: "The many types of foreign direct investment, as well as their differing motivations, make it difficult to generalize about the economic effects of such investment. Moreover, the relatively small share of foreign-owned companies in U.S. aggregate employment, sales, and investment indicates that the associated economic impact is principally of a micro-economic nature affecting localities, regions, or industries rather than macro-economic affecting the national economy." See Vol. 1, p. 211.

[2]Conference Board, *Foreign Investment in the United States: Policy, Problems and Obstacles* (New York: Conference Board, 1974), p. 9.

[3]U.S. Department of Commerce, Domestic and International Business Administration, *State Government Conducted International Trade and Business Development Programs,* June 1977, p. 27.

[4]Ibid., pp. 65–66.

[5]Bank of America, *Direct Investment,* p. 3. Also see Jacobus T. Severiens and James C. Baker, "Assessing U.S. Controls over Foreign Investment Firms," *Borroughs Clearing House,* May 1978, pp. 20, 46–50.

[6]Daniels, *Recent Manufacturing Investment,* p. 69. A survey of 25 foreign firms which had purchased existing companies in the United States revealed that 16 were primarily interested in acquiring the company itself and not in the location of the company. The other nine selected regions for operations first of all and then sought to find companies within the region. Approximately two-fifths of the 25 surveyed firms had worked extensively with state development agencies.

[7]*Dun's Review,* January 1978, pp. 33–38.

[8]After reviewing several state operations overseas, the U.S. Department of Commerce listed the following factors as contributing to the success of state programs in attracting foreign investment:

1. *Commitment*—The commitment of state officials (executive and legislative branches) reinforced by enabling legislation. The degree and extent of success, domestically and

internationally, is strongly influenced by the personal support of the governor and other leading and influential public and private sector personalities.

2. *Money*—The degree of success of a state's international trade programs is, as a general observation, consistent with funds allocated in support of the program. Appropriated funds specifically designated for international trade programs ensure stability, continuity, and quality of programs.

3. *Persuasion*—Convincing responsible individuals within the state that establishing an overseas office will enhance local economic development, that the office will be a paying proposition and that the proposed office will not be a "frill."

4. *Staffing*—Selection of professionally qualified and technically experienced personnel, individuals who have had several years of industrial development (private or public sector) or business development (private sector) experience, with international exposure and preferably having worked and lived abroad, knowledge of their own state government and local industry and commerce and an understanding of host country government.

5. *Communication*—Providing rapid, reliable and efficient verbal, written, and electronic communications between overseas office and state office is imperative and critical. Telex communications are considered vital and critical to a successful export promotion program.

6. *Functional Organization*—Lines of responsibility and authority should be clearly defined, and the overseas office should know exactly to whom it reports, the frequency of reporting, and in what form the reporting procedures should be. Reporting requirements as to performance should be clearly defined and rigidly followed.

7. *Initial Objective*—States' overseas offices are believed to operate best if they start out strongly emphasizing the promotion of export sales. The heavy export sales emphasis accomplishes several important results in a relatively short period of time, including: (a) state becoming an interested and responsible partner in international commerce; (b) state presence becoming established in the host country, and European business community having readily available a local source to answer trade and investment inquiries below the national level; (c) establishing a connecting link between the small and medium-sized state manufacturers and foreign buyers, often resulting in new markets in which to sell their goods; (d) a foreign direct investment clientele usually results from the export sales and natural follow-up to export sales promotion programs; and (e) establishing the credibility and viability of the overseas office back home with immediate and tangible results thereby allowing the office and responsible staff personnel sufficient lead time to develop and execute the appropriate long-term strategy and tactics for foreign direct investments.

See the U.S. Department of Commerce, *State Government International Programs,* pp. 67–69.

[9]*The Wall Street Journal,* July 19, 1978, p. 1.

[10]Ibid., June 30, 1978, p. 1.

[11]Derived from an Associated Press survey published in the *Idaho Statesman,* November 5, 1978, p. 14B.

[12]See *The New York Times,* December 31, 1978, pp. 1 and 18. After surveying state development programs in Pennsylvania, Virginia, Georgia, Texas, Washington, and Illinois, the U.S. Commerce Department came up with the following "major findings" concerning the international trade and reverse investment programs at the state government level:

1. An individual state's direct trade and investment stimulation activities in overseas markets are significant to the state's economy, particularly in attracting small to medium-sized domestic manufacturers to international commerce. While the composite of all such state activity has yet to be statistically evaluated relative to the overall economy, the net effect has been the creation of a positive, economic growth oriented environment at the local level for both domestic manufacturers and potential foreign investors.

2. The process of state and regional representation in foreign market exploitation and attracting foreign direct investments bringing together, on a periodic basis, federal

and state government officials responsible for promoting and developing foreign trade and investment. A federal-state advisory body would significantly enhance communications, cooperation, and coordination, and provide added credibility and viability to state international trade programs.

3. There exists at the federal and state levels a very visible and high degree of proven professionalism and competence relative to the administration, conduct, and effectiveness of international trade programs. Efforts should be made, or administrative mechanisms should be created to bring federal and state personnel together as an integral part of continuing federal and state activities.

4. The efforts of federal and state officials to stimulate exports and attract foreign investments are both cooperative and collaborative in nature and noncompetitive. New methods should be found to assist state officials in the gathering of pertinent data to reflect the very positive and significant efforts states are making to stimulate exports and attract foreign investments, and that the dollar amounts channeled to promote exports should be increased.

5. The data collected here suggest a predictable relationship between foreign investment and job creation which, for industrial plants, calls for a $30,000–$40,000 off-shore investment for each job created. There is also suggested a predictable relationship between the amount invested by a state and the attraction of direct foreign investment which for industrial plants, calls for an investment of $1 of state funds to attract $667 of direct foreign investment; thus this preliminary arithmetic comes out that for $60 in state funds spent in attracting $40,000 in foreign investment, one new industrial job will be created within the state. If this preliminary arithmetic holds up, it is a bargain for states to get directly involved in seeking foreign investments.

6. Twenty-three states, one commonwealth and eleven port authorities have already established offices in Western Europe. One regional office represents six states, and two states and two port authorities have more than one office each. Seven states have offices in Tokyo, two in Hong Kong, and one state has established an office in São Paulo, Brazil. Iowa, Louisiana, Missouri, Oklahoma, and possibly Tennessee anticipate establishing offices in Western Europe in FY76/77.

7. Although some states have combined their resources—International Trade Office/Port Authority/Department of Agriculture—most overseas offices operate as single units, reporting directly to the state economic development office within their respective state capitols. Program emphasis, within the sum total of overseas offices, is equally divided between export sales and foreign direct investment. Tourism received little or, at most, only marginal attention.

8. Foreign direct investments are expected to grow and continue to enhance significantly the future growth within individual states. During the three-year period 1973–75, announcements of the number of foreign investments in the United States manufacturing sector—one measure of the overall phenomenon—totalled about 580; during the previous five years, 1968–72, less than 400 such investments were announced. Approximately 337, or roughly 58 percent of the 580, originated in Western Europe. In 1959, the total dollar amount of foreign direct investments in the United States was $6.6 billion. In 1966, the annual foreign direct investment rate was $90 million. In 1975, it was $4 billion—45 times greater in just ten years. In 1980, projected total estimate is $50 billion. It is a prize worth state pursuit.

9. States representation on-site in foreign markets is currently concentrated in three areas—Western Europe, Japan, and Hong Kong, with Western Europe being the leader in number by far. The development of markets and emerging investor interest in Eastern Europe, Southeast Asia, Latin America, Australia, China, Korea, Taiwan, and the Persian Gulf nations can be expected to generate a movement of states' offices into these areas. It is observed that the Canadian provinces are currently far advanced of the American states in self-representation in such foreign markets.

10. There is evidence that the efforts to attract both foreign commerce and investment is being more actively pursued by Sunbelt states of the South and West. This energy reflects the national growth activities of the past two decades, including:

   a. Population of the South and West having grown by some 60 percent since 1950, compared with a growth of about 32 percent nationally.

   b. The number of companies in *Fortune's* list of 500 that are based in the South and West having risen from 75 to 112 during the past decade.

   c. An expanded and responsive economic development servicing network including transportation, financial and industrial infrastructures, and reinforced with aggressive and coordinated government-business working relationships.

See the U.S. Department of Commerce, *State Government International Programs,* pp. 61–64.

[13]*The Wall Street Journal,* September 15, 1978, p. 33. These comments were made by Assistant Treasury Secretary Fred Bergsten to the Advisory Commission on Intergovernmental Relations.

[14]U.S. Department of Commerce, *Foreign Direct Investment,* Vol. 3, pp. A-128–A-130.

[15]*The Wall Street Journal,* July 25, 1978, p. 5. In 1976, 198 completed foreign investment transactions were recorded by the Commerce Department, involving 467 sites in 41 states. Of these sites, 77 were in California, 61 in New York, 32 in Texas, 30 in Illinois, and 29 in Pennsylvania. In all, these five states accounted for 49 percent of the total sites. See U.S. Department of Commerce, *Foreign Direct Investment,* December 1977, p. 8.

[16]U.S. Department of Commerce, *Foreign Direct Investment,* Vol. 8, p. 184.

[17]*Economist,* June 4, 1977, p. 101.

[18]Ibid.

[19]Louis W. Truman, "Georgia Reaches across the Globe," *State Government,* Winter 1975, p. 10.

[20]Louviere, "Tiny Federal Office," p. 67.

[21]*Economist,* June 4, 1977, p. 101.

[22]Ibid., May 14, 1977. p. S3.

[23]*The New York Times,* May 7, 1978, III, p. 5.

[24]Stern, "Invasion of the Heartland," p. 19.

[25]U.S. Department of Commerce, *Foreign Direct Investment,* Vol. 4, p. E-25.

[26]Ibid.

[27]*New Times,* August 21, 1978, p. 16.

[28]U.S. Department of Commerce, *Foreign Direct Investment,* Vol. 3, pp. A-100–A-108.

[29]Ibid., pp. A-109–A-119.

[30]Ibid., p. A-111. In addition, an interview which the author had with a Commerce Department official revealed that a new study on the impact of foreign investment activity in Hawaii was being conducted during the summer of 1978. It was a distinct possibility, according to the official, that the Hawaiian study would serve as a prototype for future studies in other states.

[31]U.S. Department of Commerce, *State Government International Programs,* pp. 72–73.

Chapter 8

[1]*The New York Times,* July 28, 1976, p. 63.

[2]Ibid., May 28, 1976, III, p. 4.

[3]Ibid., July 8, 1976, p. 53.

[4]Ibid.

[5]Ibid., September 16, 1976, p. 63.

[6]The "unlovely little town" label was coined by a reporter for *The New York Times.* See ibid., October 9, 1977, III, p. 5.

[7]Ibid.

[8]Ibid., October 26, 1978, IV, p. 15.

[9]*Business Week,* February 6, 1978, p. 106.

[10]*The New York Times,* October 9, 1977, III, p. 84. Detroit's Big Three, of course, retained U.S. management teams when they first penetrated the European market.

[11]*Forbes,* November 13, 1978, pp. 46–47.

[12]*Time,* April 10, 1978, p. 84.

[13]*U.S. News & World Report,* October 31, 1977, p. 41.

[14]*The New York Times,* June 15, 1977, IV, p. 1. Toni Schmücker, VW's chairman, contends that the Wolfsburg-based company has learned the lesson well that "you can't supply a mass market product like a popular car to the United States from abroad."

Moreover, VW's metal workers union in Germany, one of that country's most militant labor organizations, went along with the decision to set up a facility in the United States because it feared that a further erosion in VW's share of the American market might eventually lower German production figures and precipitate the loss of jobs. One should remember, of course, that VW itself lost 336 million dollars in 1974 and was on the verge of bankruptcy. See ibid., May 19, 1976, p. 64, and *European Community,* July 1978, pp. 10–12.

[15]Volvo announced in 1973 that it would operate an assembly plant in the United States, but indefinitely shelved the opening of a Virginia plant in 1976 because of "uncertain economic conditions." Prior to the postponement of the project, Volvo had already spent 25 million dollars on its U.S. venture.

[16]Joseph S. Coyle, "Job Meccas for the 80's," *Money* magazine, May 1978, p. 40.

[17]*The New York Times,* August 1, 1976, III, p. 2.

[18]*Time,* July 25, 1977, p. 50.

[19]*Vision,* January 1977, p. 36.

[20]Louviere, "Tiny Federal Office," p. 67.

[21]*Vision,* January 1977, p. 37.

[22]The "Euroville" designation was used in ibid., p. 36. *Vision,* by the way, is a European business magazine which publishes editions in English, French, German, and Italian.

[23]Other pertinent information on Spartanburg is found in *Reader's Digest,* January 1974.

[24]Much of the information for this section was derived from the author's interview with Mr. Jackson on August 31, 1978.

[25]Many people have expressed an interest in Jackson's project and his particularly close ties to foreign investors. For example, a one-liner in the Kiplinger Washington letter of July 8, 1977, stated "lots of interest by Europeans in U.S. real estate," and recommended that those wanting further information should contact Amrex, Jackson's organization received 1,100 inquiries. Another short message in Kiplinger's August 4, 1978, letter brought 1,500 inquiries to Amrex.

[26]*New York Daily News,* June 29, 1977.

[27]Some officials in national real estate associations expressed the opinion to the author that Jackson's scheme consists more of bravado than of substance, and that his statements about foreign money flooding into the United States for the purchase of agricultural land and other properties are highly exaggerated.

Chapter 9

[1]*Institutional Investor,* December 1978, p. 138. In addition, the 1978 Tax Reform Act, which reduced the capital gains tax, has now made cash offers from foreign firms more acceptable to stockholders of U.S. corporations.

[2]*Los Angeles Times,* October 24, 1978, p. 18. Some critics claim that this is a grossly unfair loophole in immigration laws which unduly favors the rich. On the other hand, some seem to echo the sentiments expressed by a Southern California businessman: "My hat is off to

them. They aren't begging or going on relief; they are willing to try most anything and work very hard. They really believe in the American dream we all have talked about."

[3]*Forbes,* May 29, 1978, p. 118. The Dutch official was Karel H. Beyen, State Secretary for Economic Affairs.

[4]*The New York Times,* May 19, 1976, p. 64.

[5]*Business Week,* January 23, 1978, pp. 85–86.

[6]The Carter administration's policy toward OPEC investment was expressed by a U.S. Treasury official before a House subcommittee. See *The Wall Street Journal,* September 8, 1978, p. 7.

[7]John Sparkman, "The Multinational Corporation and Foreign Investment," *Mercer Law Review,* 27 (Winter 1976): 381–389. Senator Sparkman points out that foreign firms operating in the United States are subject to U.S. laws, antitrust regulations, and tax provisions. Moreover, if the situation were to become very serious, the United States could freeze or even nationalize the assets of foreign nationals.

[8]As Thomas Enders, former Assistant Secretary of State, has asserted, "the danger is that uncoordinated or excessive national and international regulation—particularly if aimed at potential rather than actual abuses—runs the risk of killing the goose which lays the golden eggs." See ibid., p. 385.

An example of overblown rhetoric divorced from empirical reality is found in the statement made by Congressman Tom Harkin that the oil-producing nations "could buy the whole state of Iowa, every acre of farm producing land, with just 394 days of oil production." In actuality, official Iowa state studies have indicated that there has been little interest thus far in Iowa farmland from residents of oil-producing nations or any other nation in the world. See *Time,* January 8, 1979, p. 40.

[9]The Northeast-Midwest Congressional Coalition has bitterly criticized Canada's success in enticing Ford to Canadian soil. In particular, Congressman Robert W. Edgar of Pennsylvania complained that "recent Canadian efforts to attract American automobile plants threaten to accelerate the drain of jobs and tax revenues from industrial states in the region." See *Nation's Business,* December 1978, p. 17.

[10]One should remember that many of the major foreign enterprises must have access to the U.S. market in order to survive. As François Michelin, chairman of the famous French tire firm, has candidly admitted, "without Michelin's foreign operations, Michelin would be bankrupt," (see *Newsweek,* November 27, 1978, p. 78). VW was also on the verge of bankruptcy in 1974 and its new Pennsylvania plant is viewed as a partial panacea for some of the company's past financial woes.

Index